SHTETL

Key Words in Jewish Studies

Series Editors
Deborah Dash Moore, University of Michigan
MacDonald Moore, Vassar College
Andrew Bush, Vassar College

I. Andrew Bush, *Jewish Studies*
II. Barbara E. Mann, *Space and Place in Jewish Studies*
III. Olga Litvak, *Haskalah: The Romantic Movement in Judaism*
IV. Jonathan Boyarin, *Jewish Families*
V. Jeffrey Shandler, *Shtetl: A Vernacular Intellectual History*

SHTETL

A Vernacular Intellectual History

JEFFREY SHANDLER

RUTGERS UNIVERSITY PRESS
New Brunswick, New Jersey, and London

Library of Congress Cataloging-in-Publication Data

Shandler, Jeffrey, author.
Shtetl : a vernacular intellectual history / Jeffrey Shandler.
pages cm. — (Key words in Jewish studies ; 5)
Includes bibliographical references and index.
ISBN 978–0–8135–6273–5 (hardcover : alk. paper) — ISBN 978–0–8135–6272–8 (pbk. : alk. paper) — ISBN 978–0–8135–6274–2 (e-book)
1. Shtetls in literature. 2. Jews in literature. 3. Europe, Eastern—In literature. 4. Shtetls. I. Title.
PN56.S545S53 2014
809′.93352992404—dc23

2013013410

A British Cataloging-in-Publication record for this book is available from the British Library.

Visit our website: http://rutgerspress.rutgers.edu

Manufactured in the United States of America

Contents

Foreword

The Rutgers book series Key Words in Jewish Studies seeks to introduce students and scholars alike to vigorous developments in the field by exploring its terms. These words and phrases reference important concepts, issues, practices, events, and circumstances. But terms also refer to standards, even to preconditions; they patrol the boundaries of the field of Jewish studies. This series aims to transform outsiders into insiders and let insiders gain new perspectives on usages, some of which shift even as we apply them.

Key words mutate through repetition, suppression, amplification, and competitive sharing. Jewish studies finds itself attending to such processes in the context of an academic milieu where terms are frequently repurposed. Diaspora offers an example of an ancient word, one with a specific Jewish resonance, which has traveled into new regions and usage. Such terms migrate from the religious milieu of Jewish learning to the secular environment of universities, from Jewish community discussion to arenas of academic discourse, from political debates to intellectual arguments and back again. As these key words travel, they acquire additional meanings even as they occasionally shed long-established connotations. On occasion, key words can become so politicized that they serve as accusations. The sociopolitical concept of assimilation, for example, when turned into a term—assimilationist—describing an advocate of the process among Jews, became an epithet hurled by political opponents struggling for the mantle of authority in Jewish communities.

When approached dispassionately, key words provide analytical leverage to expand debate in Jewish studies. Some key words will be familiar from long use, and yet they may have gained new valences, attracting or repelling other terms in contemporary discussion. But there are prominent terms in Jewish culture whose key lies in a particular understanding of prior usage. Terms of the past may bolster claims to continuity in the present, while newly minted language sometimes disguises deep connections reaching back into history. Attention must be paid as well to the transmigration of key words among Jewish languages—especially Hebrew, Yiddish, and Ladino—and among languages used by Jews, knitting connections even while highlighting distinctions.

An exploration of the current state of Jewish studies through its key words highlights some interconnections often only glimpsed and holds out the prospect of a reorganization of Jewish knowledge. Key words act as magnets and attract a nexus of ideas and arguments as well as related terms into their orbits. This series plunges into several of these intersecting constellations, providing a path from past to present.

The volumes in the series share a common organization. They open with a first section, Terms of Debate, which defines the key word as it developed over the course of Jewish history. Allied concepts and traditional terms appear here as well. The second section, State of the Question, analyzes contemporary debates in scholarship and popular venues, especially for those key words that have crossed over into popular culture. The final section, In a New Key, explicitly addresses contemporary culture and future possibilities for understanding the key word. In the present volume, the author has taken this structure as a point of departure and provided his own headings for the sections.

To decipher key words is to learn the varied languages of Jewish studies at points of intersection between academic disciplines and wider spheres of culture. The series, then, does not seek to consolidate and narrow a particular critical lexicon. Its purpose is to question, not to canonize, and to invite readers to sample the debate and ferment of an exciting field of study.

Andrew Bush
Deborah Dash Moore
MacDonald Moore
Series Co-Editors

Acknowledgments

This book is inspired by the intellectual nurture of many mentors—including Dina Abramowicz, Zachary Baker, Adrienne Cooper, Lucjan Dobroszycki, Benjamin Harshav, Marvin Herzog, Barbara Kirshenblatt-Gimblett, Jack Kugelmass, Dan Miron, Abraham Nowersztern, Beatrice Weinreich—and by scholars and writers whose work has enriched my understanding of the topic at hand: Israel Bartal, Jim Hoberman, Gershon Hundert, Samuel Kassow, Anita Norich, David Roskies, Naomi Seidman, Adam Teller, and Steven Zipperstein, among others. For their kind assistance in preparing this book, I am also indebted to Shlomo Berger, Jesse Cohen, Olga Gershenson, Arlene Goldstein, Anna Manchin, Barbara Mann, Roberta Newman, Edward Portnoy, Robert Rothstein, Nancy Sinkoff, Mark Slobin, Alisa Solomon, Daniel Soyer, Barry Trachtenberg, Kalman Weiser, and Hana Wirth-Nesher.

I thank the editors of this series for inviting me to write this book, and I am especially grateful to Olga Litvak for her thoughtful reading of the manuscript. As always, my partner, Stuart Schear, has enriched this work immeasurably with his intelligence, patience, and enthusiasm.

SHTETL

Introduction

In Yiddish, *shtetl* (plural: *shtetlekh*) simply means "town." How does such an unassuming word come to loom so large in modern Jewish culture, with a proliferation of uses and connotations? And how has *shtetl* come to be a key word in Jewish studies? Unlike other key words in this field, *shtetl* can refer to something that seems very ordinary. As used in Yiddish, a *shtetl* is not a specifically Jewish locus, not inherently tied to a particular geography inhabited at one time or another by Yiddish speakers, and not readily evident as a phenomenon of Jewish religious, social, cultural, or political life. Indeed, *shtetl* is a decidedly vernacular key word for Jewish studies. Besides being a word in Yiddish, the traditional language of daily life of East European Jews, *shtetl* has become a key word in Jewish life and Jewish studies by dint of the trajectory of Jewish vernacular culture in Eastern Europe, as the region became home to the world's largest Jewish population by the eighteenth century, and as this culture subsequently extended its reach to most major centers of Jewish life around the world.

Though long centered on Yiddish as its vernacular, this culture has increasingly been realized in other languages. The intellectual history of *shtetl* as a key word is therefore a case study in the changing nature of vernacularity in Jewish life and of the place of vernacular culture in Jewish studies. Examining the many ways that people have engaged *shtetl* reveals larger insights into the dynamics of how Jewish vernacular culture is understood—by Jews and others, by practitioners of Jewish culture and by those who observe it. Changes in the way that many "ordinary" Jews live—and, moreover, in how this way of life is conceptualized, scrutinized, and evaluated—are central to the significance of *shtetl* as a key word in Jewish studies.

In this case study, language use is as important as meaning. *Shtetl* is a key word in Jewish studies, but "town" is not. Moreover, though in Yiddish *shtetl* can refer to any town, anywhere, inhabited by anyone, at any time, when this word enters other languages it acquires added meanings that restrict its scope as they expand its semantic value. Consider these definitions of *shtetl*, culled from sources for the general reader in English, French, Hungarian, Italian, Polish, and Russian:

> Little city, small town, village—in particular, the Jewish communities of eastern Europe, where the culture of the Ashkenazim flourished (before World War II).[1]

Term for a small town or a large "village," even a Jewish neighborhood, in Central Europe before the Second World War, inhabited by between 1,000 and 20,000 people. These shtetls were located in Poland, Ukraine, Belorussia, and Lithuania. The principal language spoken was Yiddish. During the Shoah, most of the Jews living in these villages were deported or killed on the spot, and these shtetls were destroyed.[2]

The Yiddish word *shtetl* . . . means an East European small town that was formerly inhabited largely by Jews. It gives a good sense of the unusually intimate feeling that our ancestors living here felt toward their environment. East European Jews grew to love the world around them deeply, even though at times it was hostile toward them.[3]

In Yiddish, a village in which the population, until the Holocaust, was predominantly Jewish.[4]

Small urban center that retained traditional Jewish customs.[5]

As a rule, a small, semi-urban type of settlement, with a predominantly Jewish population in Eastern Europe in the historical period before the Holocaust.[6]

These elaborated definitions of *shtetl* exemplify what I have termed elsewhere *postvernacular* Yiddish—a mode of engaging the language in which its secondary, symbolic value is privileged over its primary value as a means of communicating information, opinions, or ideas. In postvernacular Yiddish, "the very fact that something is said (or written or sung) in Yiddish is at least as meaningful as the meaning of the words being uttered—if not more so." As a consequence of this notion that the language itself has an intrinsic significance, "Yiddish terms in isolation can take on additional meaning."[7] As a postvernacular Yiddish word, *shtetl* has acquired connotations of Jewishness, East Europeanness, and, since the end of World War II, of life before the Holocaust. With this restriction of meaning to a particular place, demographic, and time comes an expanded understanding of what values—religious, ethnic, ideological, affective—*shtetl* symbolizes.

Even as *shtetl* acquires added significance in the postvernacular mode, its new value rests on the word's meaning in vernacular Yiddish. *Shtetl* is a diminutive noun, and this very productive linguistic feature in Yiddish informs the word's possible meanings. In Yiddish, diminutives can have one or more of four different semantic values:

- A diminutive of a noun can have a meaning separate from its base form: e.g., *finger* (finger) ~ *fingerl* (ring [jewelry]); *hoyz* (house) ~ *hayzl* (brothel).

- A diminutive can modify the meaning of the base noun by signifying smallness or youngness: *shteyn* (stone, rock) ~ *shteyndl* (small stone, pebble); *kats* (cat) ~ *ketsl* (kitten).
- A diminutive can modify the meaning of the base noun by signifying endearment: *zun* (son) ~ *zindl* (sonny); *bakn* (cheeks) ~ *bekelekh* (cute, adorable cheeks).
- A diminutive can modify the meaning of the base noun (usually animate) by signifying low regard: *shrayber* (writer) ~ *shrayberl* (minor writer, not much of a writer); *mentsh* (person) ~ *mentshl* (sorry excuse for a human being).

In its various uses, all four of these values can inform the meaning of *shtetl*; context is key. The first two categories pertain to the challenge of distinguishing *shtetl* from other social geographies, especially with regard to size or scope: *shtot* (city) ~ *shtetl* (small city; town). (Note that *shtetl*, in turn, has its own diminutive: *shtetele* [small town].) The last two categories pertain to the spectrum of affective values, from devotion to disparagement, that might be attached to this term.

Given this range of possible meanings in vernacular Yiddish, it is telling when *shtetl* begins to be used in other languages, rather than being translated. (In English the word is variously rendered as town, small town, little-town, townlet, township, Jewish town, market town, commercial town, little city, village, hamlet.) *Shtetl* appears seldom, if at all, in major European languages before World War II. Use of the word becomes more frequent in texts in English immediately after the war, in German and French in the 1970s, in Spanish in the 1980s, and in Russian in the 1990s. In Hebrew texts, *shtetl* appears with increasing frequency beginning during World War II and peaking around 1970; the use of *'ayarah*, the Hebrew equivalent of *shtetl*, peaks around 1920 and then declines, especially after the war, though *'ayarah* is used much more frequently than *shtetl*.[8]

There is prior discussion of Jewish life in provincial East European towns in books and articles published in these languages, but these works rarely use the word *shtetl*. Proliferating use of the term after World War II betokens a shift in how East European Jewish life is understood, as well as how it is discussed. Linguist Hans Peter Althaus notes that by the turn of the millennium *shtetl* had become "the central word for indicating Yiddish-speaking East European Jewry and its endangered culture. As a word, *shtetl* has the desired pithiness, it is easily understood and clearly identifiable." At the same time, he cautions: "A word that is in everyone's mouth can, of necessity, also be used in cases in which it appears to be less appropriate."[9]

The sprawling use of *shtetl* in various languages, including uses that may well seem "inappropriate" vis-à-vis its base meaning in Yiddish, is nonetheless revealing, reflecting a range of motives. The word might simply serve as shorthand for "Jewish Eastern Europe," or *shtetl* might be employed as emblematic of a certain kind of Jewish place, community, or sensibility. Thus, the online magazine *Shtetl*, produced in Montreal, explains: "*Shtetl* aspires to a highly inclusive vision of Judaism. Never nasty in tone, Shtetl is an open place to dialogue and share. Ours is a shtetl with pourous boundaries, open and accepting of guests and contributors from all communities."[10] Writers may thus refer to a locus (including a virtual one) as a *shtetl* to distinguish its Jewish character or emphasize its special importance to Jews, similar to how the term *pogrom* is widely used in English, among other languages, to mean a violent attack on Jews, as opposed to a massacre of any kind, per its meaning in Yiddish and in Slavic languages.

Shtetl is also used more paradigmatically as a byword for communality. When sociologist Egon Mayer titled his study of hasidim in the Brooklyn neighborhood of Boro Park *From Suburb to Shtetl*, he explained that this was not "meant to suggest that the Orthodox Jews of Boro Park have recreated the Eastern European *shtetl*. . . . Rather, I would like to offer the *shtetl* as an evocative metaphor of Jewish cultural and social autonomy, which the Jews of Boro Park seem to have created along uniquely American lines."[11] The paradigmatic use of *shtetl* can have either positive or negative associations and may not refer to Jews per se. For example, *New York Times* columnist Maureen Dowd quotes a "top Democrat" on the party's 2008 national convention in Denver: "It's something about our party, the shtetl mentality."[12]

As *shtetl* moves from Yiddish into other languages, the term is employed less in routine conversation and more in acts of abstract thinking and cultural creativity, including works of literature, scholarship, and performance. Sometimes as writers use *shtetl* they contest the term's assumed meaning. Thus, author Heszel Klepfisz writes: "Detractors of the Eastern European period claim that all that was produced was a shtetl culture, with all the innuendo with which this appellation is loaded. If such a view prevails, future generations will have a distorted picture of that history and culture."[13] The intellectual history of the term *shtetl* therefore exemplifies the dynamics of East European Jewish vernacularity, tracking how this culture of everyday life became a major force in shaping modern Jewish life beyond Eastern Europe, beyond Yiddish speakers, and beyond the demotic, including the entry of *shtetl* into the academy.

Given the central goal of approaching the *shtetl* as an exemplar of vernacularity and its changing place in modern Jewish life and scholarship, a tension runs throughout this volume—which is itself a scholarly work, of course—between the academic and the popular. Chapter 1, "Talk of the Town," addresses this tension by considering two different dynamics in the study of the *shtetl*: the changing phenomenon of Jewish life in East European provincial towns, and the changing conceptualization of the *shtetl* as a subject of discourse and cultural creativity. Recent scholarship often juxtaposes these two dynamics as the "history versus memory" or "reality versus myth" of the *shtetl*. Historians working within this rubric often seek to correct ostensibly wrongheaded representations of *shtetl*, whether misguided by the vagaries of memory or distorted by willful fabrication, with facts about the actuality of East European Jewish experience. Scholars of literature and culture, by contrast, sometimes work within the same rubric to make the case for creative engagement with *shtetl* as its true essence, arguing that *shtetl* is an inherently discursive practice or artistic invention. Bearing in mind that these dynamics and their opposition to one another are constructs of modern scholarship, I argue for a different approach, centered on studying vernacular engagement with *shtetl* on its own terms. This approach displaces certain questions that other scholars foreground, such as how to define what a *shtetl* is, and focuses instead on an integrated, cross-disciplinary analysis of the experiences people have had—as residents, visitors, scholarly observers, or creative artists—with this social geography, reflected in a wide range of cultural practices. Rather than characterizing as problematic the shifting range of these engagements or the disparities among different understandings of *shtetl*, the approach taken here regards this unstable complex as defining of this subject's enduring interest.

Writing about *shtetl* life is a longstanding fixture of East European Jewish vernacular culture. Scholarly work comes relatively late in the chronology of *shtetl* writing—well after the advent of community chronicles, memoirs, prose fiction, or satirical plays that address the topic—and entails a complex reciprocity with these other works, often drawing on earlier writings as resources and, in turn, informing subsequent work of a wide variety. Rather than treating scholarship as either central or adventitious in the intellectual history of *shtetl* writing, this volume situates scholarly work within the larger chronology. Chapter 2, "*Forsht ayer shtetl!*" ("Research Your Town!") examines the advent of various scholarly approaches to the *shtetl* in relation to changing valuations of its vernacular culture.

Throughout the intellectual history of *shtetl*, its scrutiny exists in tension with the often elusive actuality of life in the communities in question. Even as novelists, scholars, journalists, and artists negotiated their relationship with this subject through the respective protocols of the kind of work each pursued, Jewish life in provincial towns of Eastern Europe became imbricated with these undertakings. Reading fiction about *shtetlekh*, participating in the fieldwork of social scientists, or encountering tourist visitors became part of living in these communities, especially in the years between the two world wars. This give-and-take appeared to come to an abrupt end with the devastations of the Holocaust. Yet in its wake, the *shtetl* received unprecedented scholarly attention. Creative engagements with the *shtetl*—in visual art, fiction, film, tourism, and museums, among other practices—have also flourished in the postwar era. In addition to responding to unprecedented destruction, these efforts address a particularly daunting challenge as they confront the limits of engaging an ostensibly lost vernacular culture. This challenge and the opportunities that it affords postwar creative engagement with the *shtetl* are examined in chapter 3, "*Shtetl* Fabulous."

Although it offers a wide range of examples of engaging with the *shtetl*, this study is not comprehensive. Given the target readership of the Key Words series, this volume pays particular attention to primary and secondary sources available in English, with more selected attention to works in other languages. All translated passages cited are the author's unless otherwise noted. Except for terms that have accepted spellings in English (e.g., yeshiva) or have standard scholarly spellings (e.g., Haskalah), Hebrew and Aramaic terms that are also used in Yiddish are romanized according to the Ashkenazi pronunciation (e.g., *kohol* rather than *kahal*), generally following the YIVO system.

1 Talk of the Town

The intellectual history of the term *shtetl* entails two interrelated dynamics: that of Jewish settlement in Eastern Europe and that of *shtetl*, understood as a Jewish phenomenon, as a subject of discourse among both Jews and others. The first dynamic has its origins in the expansion of Jewish settlement in the Polish-Lithuanian Commonwealth during the sixteenth century, after the initial migration of Jews from German lands to the Kingdom of Poland in the late Middle Ages. The second dynamic is usually understood as beginning later, during the partitions of Poland in the late eighteenth century and the concomitant advent of the Haskalah, which historian Todd Endelman characterizes as a Jewish "intellectual response to the challenge of modernity."[1] Both dynamics extend into the present, though they are widely thought of as either ending with or profoundly transformed by the Holocaust. Though the interrelation of these two dynamics is sometimes termed the "history versus memory" or "reality versus myth" of the *shtetl*, it is more fitting to characterize them as the *phenomenon* of this kind of settlement, within the actuality of East European Jewish life, and the *shtetl* as *concept*—that is, as an idea about this actuality. On one hand, examining these two dynamics separately provides the opportunity to consider what distinguishes each from the other. For example, these settlements not only constitute but a part of East European Jewish history, they also are not a fixed part and change over time in their number, location, size, and status. And though it is possible (at least in languages other than Yiddish) to trace the first dynamic without using the word *shtetl*—as will be done here—it eventually becomes central to the conceptualization of East European Jewish life. On the other hand, rather than maintaining this rubric of two distinct, competing modes of engaging this subject, they are ultimately best understood as interdependent aspects of an ongoing cultural engagement with a vernacular Jewish culture of unrivaled scope.

Phenomenon

In the late twelfth and early thirteenth centuries, Jews and Christians immigrated from German lands to the westernmost regions of the Kingdom of Poland, invited by the Polish monarchy to help establish a new monetary economy and urban culture in Poland's feudal society.

Jews arrived somewhat later, and by different routes, in the Grand Duchy of Lithuania. Like the Polish kings, Lithuanian dukes encouraged Jewish settlement to support urban and economic development.

The monarchs of Poland and Lithuania recognized Jews as a separate estate. As such, Jews were assigned a distinct set of obligations, entitlements, and restrictions, as were peasants, Christian clerics, burghers (city dwellers), and members of the aristocracy. Polish and Lithuanian monarchs granted Jews, like other immigrants settling in these lands, rights of residency in a series of formal charters in the thirteenth and fourteenth centuries. These documents offered Jews particular rights—including royal protection, religious toleration, and freedom to engage in commerce—and imposed on them certain obligations and limitations: taxes, restrictions on means of earning a living and sometimes even on dress. This formalization of Jewish life in Poland and Lithuania took place as these two realms initiated their eventual merger as the Polish-Lithuanian Commonwealth (also known as the Federation of Poland and Lithuania). This attenuated process began with a royal marriage in 1386 and culminated with the Union of Lublin in 1569.[2]

The number of Jews in the Commonwealth remained small—perhaps 10,000—through the end of the fifteenth century.[3] Nevertheless, following the expulsions of Jews from Iberia at that time, the Jewish population of the Polish-Lithuanian Commonwealth was the largest in Europe at the start of the sixteenth century. The Commonwealth was then Europe's second largest state in area and sixth largest in population. This population was diverse in language, religion, and nationality. Besides Poles, Lithuanians, Ukrainians, and Belorussians, the Commonwealth was also home to Armenians, Germans, Italians, Jews, Roma, Scots, Tatars, and Turks. In addition to large numbers of Roman Catholics and followers of Uniate and Eastern Orthodox churches, there were Arians, Armenian Orthodox Christians, Jews, Karaites, Muslims, and Protestants.[4]

Beginning in the sixteenth century, Jewish life in Eastern Europe expanded considerably, with regard to population numbers, geographic distribution, and economic activity, as part of a larger growth in the Polish-Lithuanian Commonwealth and a related shift in its power structure. This period witnessed an extensive territorial expansion of settlement to the south and east, especially in present-day Ukraine, following the Union of Lublin. There, Polish magnates, the upper stratum of the aristocracy, gained control of large stretches of land. With this territorial expansion, the magnates acquired new political and economic power, while the Commonwealth's monarchy weakened.

Polish expansion into these new territories fostered a new socioeconomic order, defined by the development of a manorial economy on the magnates' vast latifundia (estates), where they established farms, orchards, forests, fisheries, and mines. Their produce—lumber, livestock, minerals, and agricultural products, especially grain—was sold to generate income for the magnates, who maintained lavish lifestyles both on their estates and while traveling. This geographic and economic expansion also placed local governance in the hands of the magnates, who ruled their individual latifundia with near absolute authority. Central to this new socioeconomic order was the colonization of the peasantry, the region's majority population, whose land and livelihood came under the magnates' control. They also hired an elaborate network of employees to oversee the peasants' work, manage the sale and shipping of produce, and maintain the magnates' manor houses and estates. In order to maximize profit from their latifundia, magnates leased much of their holdings, together with the service of the peasants who resided there, to others to oversee; this practice was known in Polish as *arenda*.[5]

This economic expansion prompted the founding of numerous small towns that served as administrative and commercial centers, linking the produce of rural estates with cities and export markets. Typically, these towns were private entities, as were the surrounding rural villages, which were inhabited mostly by peasants. The land on which these towns and villages were built belonged to the local magnate, who granted the inhabitants rights of residence and leased property for businesses under their purview, such as mills and distilleries. Magnates also provided land for building both private homes and public institutions, including schools, houses of worship, and cemeteries.

The colonization of these territories and their new socioeconomic order constituted threshold developments for Jews in the Commonwealth. Magnates leased to Jews the rights to an array of income-producing functions, ranging from managing fields, orchards, forests, or lakes (for fishing rights), to operating mills, distilleries, and taverns, or collecting taxes and tolls. Other Jews worked as merchants, running shops that catered to both peasants and the aristocracy, as artisans serving a variety of local needs for craftsmanship, or as brokers, clerks, wholesalers, and transporters, who oversaw the sale and shipping of raw materials and agricultural products. These activities entailed a close interrelation among Jews and their neighbors, bound together in a complex and sometimes competitive economic network.[6]

As a consequence of participating in this economy, Jews established many new communities throughout this expanded territory. These settlements constituted a frontier for Jews, not only geographically but also culturally and politically. In addition to offering Jews unprecedented economic opportunities, these settlements enabled the Commonwealth's

Jewish population to establish a new critical mass. Over time, Jews became a pervasive presence throughout the region and in numerous individual towns eventually constituted a majority population. Though centered in Ukraine, this pattern of settlement extended to other parts of the Commonwealth.

This expansive frontier provided Jews with an exceptional degree of autonomy, both external and internal. Jewish communities in these new towns were at further remove from ruling authorities, whether the Commonwealth, which was a remote and declining power, or the local aristocracy, which was inconsistent and often absent. During the initial period of expansion, Jews in this region were also relatively less subject to traditional rabbinic authority, which was not as established a presence in these new settlements as in older Jewish communities. Members of the Jewish community appointed local rabbis for limited terms, and they depended on lay leaders for support of their rulings as well as the terms of their employment. Rabbis in the region frequently bemoaned a lack of respect for their authority by a lay community with its own strong convictions about religious matters.[7]

Thus, in several key respects, Jewish life in and around these towns was unlike that of earlier urban communities in the Commonwealth, starting with a different geography tied to a different economy. Earlier communities had been established in medieval cities (sometimes walled) and towns, in which small numbers of Jews typically lived together on the same few streets in one neighborhood and engaged primarily in an urban-based economy, often within restrictions imposed by the monarchy. By contrast, these newer communities flourished in small towns, estates, and villages scattered throughout a vast rural environment, where Jewish residence was more sizable and, in towns, geographically central. Jews were primarily engaged in the management, distribution, and support of an agrarian economy in a wide range of roles. In order to encourage this participation, magnates granted Jews privileges that fostered their economic activity and accommodated their needs to establish Jewish communal infrastructures. In return, Jews were expected to contribute to the economic flourishing of the magnates' latifundia. As generating income through export of raw materials and agricultural produce was the driving force behind these settlements, the marketplace was the central geographic feature of the region's new private towns, where most Jews lived. The marketplace defined much of Jews' community life and their relationship with their neighbors.

The establishment of these towns proved both liberating and destabilizing for Jews. For them, these towns' main virtue was providing a critical mass of Jews with greater economic opportunities in a relatively unregulated political environment. Local rule by magnates was highly contingent and often a matter more of personal influence than established law. The loose governance of this vast region's widely scattered complex of aristocrats, clerics, burghers, Jews, peasants, and others was riven with ethnic and religious tensions exacerbated by colonization, especially between the Polish Roman Catholic aristocracy and townsfolk and the largely Ukrainian Uniate peasantry. In environments with unstable or conflicting ruling authorities, these tensions sometimes led to violence. Not only were Jews subject to attacks—most infamously, Polish nobles beating Jews (along with others) who worked for them and Jews assaulted (along with Poles) during Ukrainian peasant uprisings. Jews also resorted to violence themselves; internal Jewish conflicts sometimes led to physical fighting. Given the relative weakness of rabbinic authority or of an established Jewish elite class, as would be found in the Commonwealth's older cities and towns, wealthy members of the lay community in these settlements wielded greater influence over local Jewish life and over Jewish relations with their Christian neighbors.[8] The power of the marketplace was key.

Jews evolved a diverse array of occupations in these new settlements, ranging in income and prestige. Although town life was central to Jews' economic activity in the region, they also resided in the countryside. Jews were most prominent a presence there as managers of magnate properties, mediating between the aristocracy and the peasantry—so much so that in Polish the term *arendarz* (lease holder) was sometimes considered a synonym for "Jew."[9] Some Jews also lived in the countryside and worked the land; relatively few in number, they tended to live apart from peasant villages. Jews who resided in these villages mostly worked in non-agricultural occupations—as innkeepers, millers, distillers, and blacksmiths—that served the needs of peasants, rural gentry, and travelers. Jews were also an itinerant presence in villages as peddlers and artisans. Rural Jews were further distinguished by living among a peasant majority in relative isolation from their coreligionists and, consequently, lacked regular, direct contact with Jewish communal institutions, which were based in nearby towns.[10]

These towns were home to more substantial Jewish populations, who pursued a variety of livelihoods that were strategic to the manorial economy. Some Jews worked as wholesale brokers, buying produce and other raw goods from peasants and transporting it to urban centers or for export, and as proprietors of retail shops and stalls located on or near the marketplace. Other Jews became artisans; in addition to tailoring, which eventually became the most common artisanal trade that Jews pursued, they were also bakers, brewers, carpenters, cobblers, glaziers, masons, and tinsmiths. Poorer Jews in these towns typically worked as porters, drivers, water carriers, and other unskilled manual laborers. These towns also supported an array of Jewish religious professionals, including rabbis, cantors, teachers, synagogue caretakers, scribes, kosher slaughterers, and makers of ritual objects, such as prayer shawls and tombstones. Jews in the Commonwealth often pursued shifting, multiple ways of making a living rather than "engag[ing] consistently and permanently in one precise category of livelihood."[11]

As this occupational diversity indicates, Jews within an individual community, let alone throughout the region, ranged from extremes of poverty to wealth and were found at all points in between. Their economic status could change with the vagaries of circumstances, personal as well as regional. Economic difference was an ongoing concern for these Jewish communities, which had established institutions to provide for their own who were in need; at the same time, these differences were also frequent sources of internal tension.

Jews' political recognition centered on individual communities, based in towns, and their lay leaders. These leaders were responsible collectively for paying taxes and fulfilling other obligations to the crown, regional governments, and local nobility, as well as supervising Jewish communal affairs. The leadership of each Jewish community, as per those in older towns and cities throughout the Commonwealth, was incorporated in the form of the *kohol* (Jewish community council), whose members were elected by the local Jewish community.[12] Though political recognition of the Commonwealth's Jews was localized, the great extent of their communities, ranging across hundreds of towns and other settlements scattered throughout a vast territory, prompted Jews to form their own institutions of regional governance. Beginning in the early sixteenth century, Jewish communal leaders established a series of regional Jewish councils, culminating with the founding in 1580 of the Vaad Arbe Arotses (Council of Four Lands), which endeavored to represent Jewish communities throughout the Commonwealth. These councils were inaugurated in order to regulate Jews' payment of taxes levied by regional governments (or, in the case of the Vaad Arbe Arotses, by the Sejm, the parliament of the Commonwealth). Over time, these councils addressed a variety of concerns regarding both internal Jewish life and Jews' relations with royal, regional, and ecclesiastical powers.[13] Although these regional councils lasted, in some cases, for more than two centuries, they were inherently contingent institutions. None were ever officially recognized by a state or royal body, even though these authorities acknowledged and engaged with the councils' representatives. Consequently, the regional Jewish councils' rulings had no force of their own but depended on local Jewish communities to accept and enforce them.

The Commonwealth's expansion of settlement lasted some two centuries, reshaping the social geography of East European Jewish life. What had been a cultural and demographic frontier in the sixteenth century was a major center by the start of the eighteenth century. During this period, the Jewish population of the Commonwealth burgeoned, coming close to 750,000 by the middle of the eighteenth century, with about half living in private towns or on lands owned by magnates.[14] As the scope of Jewish life grew during this period, it experienced upheavals in social, political, economic, and religious life, reflecting the region's instability. While the Commonwealth's territory and population expanded, it grew gradually weaker as a polity, in the wake of foreign wars, internal rebellions, and the shift of political power away from the monarchy and toward the aristocracy. Most consequential for the region's Jews were Ukrainian uprisings against Polish rule in 1648–1649, the largest of several such revolts. Many dozens of Jewish communities throughout the region were affected, some of them completely destroyed. An unprecedented number of Jews died in the course of this violent wave of rebellion (the estimated number of victims being at least 13,000), and many more Jews in the region suffered extensive destruction of property and displacement. Nevertheless, within several decades, Jewish communities were reestablished as a major presence in the region. However, the legacy of this destruction and the roiling of relations with Polish and Ukrainian neighbors endured in Jews' public memory for centuries.[15]

Similarly, East European Jews' religious life witnessed the expansion of publishing and rabbinic training, on one hand, and controversial new religious movements, on the other hand. The spread of print culture engendered greater literacy generally—including among women, for whom a popular religious literature in Yiddish flourished in the seventeenth century—and disseminated rabbinic rulings and teachings to a learned readership of unprecedented scope. In contrast to earlier Jewish practice in German lands, where yeshivas were established and administered privately, these rabbinical academies were founded, supported, and maintained by local communities throughout Eastern Europe.

In the wake of the violence and political upheavals of the seventeenth and eighteenth centuries, desires for salvation prompted some Jews to embrace radically new religious movements. Sabbateanism—the movement claiming Shabetai Zevi, a Jew born in Turkey in 1626, as the long-awaited messiah—attracted a considerable following among East European Jews in the 1660s, before Jewish authorities throughout the Commonwealth denounced this movement as heresy. Nevertheless, a new form of Sabbateanism, inspired by the charismatic leader Jacob Frank, briefly flourished in Poland in the following century.[16] Simultaneously, hasidism proved to be a divisive innovation in Jewish religious life with more enduring consequences. After emerging in towns in western Ukraine in the late eighteenth century, hasidism spread to communities throughout much of Poland. This movement, originating in the teachings of Israel ben Eliezer (known as the Baal Shem Tov, i.e., miracle worker), was committed to a spiritual revitalization of Jewry through the popularization of esoteric mystical teachings and, subsequently, the empowerment of charismatic leaders, known as *rebeyim* (masters).

Hasidism offered a radically new approach to Jewish religiosity that might well have had a much more limited impact had it emerged in an environment where rabbinic authority was stronger. Hasidism fostered a new, entrepreneurial form of spirituality. Its leaders cultivated both a populist appeal, promoting the ability of *rebeyim* to perform miracles, and the support of mercantile elites. On one hand, this new approach to Jewish religiosity was liberating; hasidism democratized Jewish engagement with mysticism and thereby challenged established religious and lay authorities. On the other hand, hasidism established a new authoritative structure of its own, centered on *rebeyim* and their courts, which were modeled on the magnates' courts. Hasidim proved adroit at adapting the social order of Jewish communities based in provincial towns, both individually and as a network, to build constituencies and establish institutional support. This social network was key to hasidism's spread beyond its small-scale origins among the Baal Shem Tov and his circle.[17]

In the final decades of the eighteenth century, the Commonwealth came to an end through a series of partitions (in 1772, 1792, and 1795) by more powerful polities to the west, south, and east. The Commonwealth's dissolution was a threshold event for the Jews who had lived under its rule in communities that were, in some instances, several centuries old. Now, along with their neighbors, these Jews found themselves in one of three new political contexts: as subjects of Prussia, which annexed the Commonwealth's westernmost provinces, home to a relatively small Jewish population; as subjects of the Austro-Hungarian (Habsburg) Empire, where the annexed portion of the Commonwealth was named Galicia; or as subjects of the Russian (Romanov) Empire, which acquired both the largest share of territory and, with it, the largest number of Jews (including those living in Congress Poland, which, though nominally independent, was subject to Russian control).[18] Shortly after these partitions, most Jews under Russian rule were restricted to permanent residence in the former Commonwealth territories and other western provinces of the Romanov Empire; this region is referred to in English as the Pale of Settlement.

This sweeping political change had wide-reaching social and economic consequences. Along with their neighbors in the partitioned lands, Jews were now the subjects of absolutist states, encountering new levels of regulation by imperial authorities. In each of these new political contexts Jews were accorded different privileges and restrictions, which varied considerably during the "long nineteenth century" that ended with World War I. But the overarching circumstances of East European Jewry were set by these empires' agendas of undoing the Commonwealth's loosely confederated complex of different estates and integrating all subjects into the hierarchy of evolving and increasingly centralized state bureaucracies, subject to an ultimate imperial authority. Rather than Jews having a fixed set of rights and obligations, they were granted and revised or revoked by successive emperors. This new system of governance sometimes provided Jews with new opportunities—for example, to participate in municipal government in Austria, or to operate schools offering Jewish youth a modern education with state support under the Romanovs. Jews were also subject to new rubrics of oversight and restriction, be it state committees on Jewish affairs, which replaced the *kohol* in Galicia, or unprecedented constraints on Jewish publishing in Russia. Some aspects of imperial governance treated Jews like other subjects. Jews were required to participate in such integrative practices as taking surnames, so that they could be accounted for in censuses and tax rolls as individuals, or compulsory military service. At the same time, the Jewish presence in the Habsburg and Romanov Empires remained marginal, given the extent to which they remained a culturally distinct people, whose settlements in the former Commonwealth territories were now situated at these empires' peripheries.[19]

Signal shifts in East European Jewish religious life that took place in the wake of the partitions of the Commonwealth also had enduring consequences. During the nineteenth century, hasidism became increasingly popular throughout Russia's Ukrainian provinces, Congress Poland, Galicia, and Hungary. The spread of hasidism proved controversial and inspired a countermovement of *misnagdim* (opponents), who repudiated hasidic innovations and asserted the authority of rabbinic law, especially through the enhanced importance of yeshiva training. At the same time, the Haskalah began to make inroads among a nascent East European Jewish intelligentsia. Even when it inspired the censure of both hasidim and *misnagdim*, the Haskalah compelled East European Jews to grapple with the implications of modernity for Jewish life.[20]

Maskilim (proponents of the Haskalah) raised provocative new intellectual possibilities for East European Jews through new reading practices. With a small number of advocates scattered among communities large and small across the region's wide expanse, the Haskalah was realized primarily in the pamphlets, missives, periodicals, and books that circulated among the movement's following. In addition to fostering this new "literary ingathering," the Haskalah promoted such modern, bourgeois activities as attending the theater and pursuing secular studies.[21]

These new political and religious developments took place in tandem with significant economic change. During the nineteenth century, enhanced control of new borders, Russia's liberation of serfs in 1861, industrialization, and the expansion of railroads helped transform much of Eastern Europe's economy, thereby weakening the longstanding economic role played by the region's vast network of market towns.[22] The manorial system of the Commonwealth era gradually yielded to a variety of new economies. Some towns became centers of industry, their economies dominated by manufacture in factories or in artisanal workshops. Jews participated in these industries both as laborers and as owners or managers of factories and workshops. The economic fortunes of some localities rose or fell as a consequence of geopolitical changes. Some towns located near new borders were designated garrisons and evolved an economy centered on provisioning the military; other such towns became way stations for immigrants, whose temporary presence became a major source of income during the last decades of the nineteenth century. Border towns were also important sites of trade, at times including smuggling, which flourished during periods of political instability. Similarly, being located near the rail system could transform a small town into a sizeable, prosperous urban center; conversely, a town bypassed by the railroad could see the local economy dwindle. The size of local Jewish populations typically grew or shrank with these shifting fortunes.

Compared to most of their East European neighbors, Jews had long been more mobile, due to the ways many earned their livelihoods (as brokers, peddlers, etc.), their pursuit of religious life (traveling to yeshivas or the courts of *rebeyim*), and extensive intercommunal relations, ranging from the arranging of marriages to the meetings of regional councils. Even so, East European Jews become ever more mobile during the nineteenth century. Increasingly Jews abandoned provincial towns where they had established communities to pursue other economic prospects in Eastern Europe—for example, in the late 1800s, in agricultural colonies in Bessarabia or industrial settlements in Donetsk province. Moreover, Jews moved from small towns and villages to major cities in growing numbers over the course of the century. Warsaw's Jewish population expanded from under 8,000 at the end of the eighteenth century (less than one-tenth of the total population) to over 210,000 (over one-third of the total population) by the end of the nineteenth century, an unprecedented and unrivaled concentration of Jews in Europe's history (their number eventually reaching 375,000 on the eve of World War II). At the same time, Jewish populations swelled in other major cities in the Austro-Hungarian Empire and in Russia's western provinces: Budapest (in 1900 approximately 186,000 Jews, about one-fourth of the total population), Odessa (139,000), Łódź (98,000), Vilna (64,000, over 40 percent of the total population), Kishinev (50,000), Lvov (44,000), Białystok (42,000), Bucharest (over 40,000), Kovno (over 35,000, more than one-third of the total population), Kiev (31,800), Cracow (25,000), Lublin (over 23,000, slightly more than half of the total population), and Riga (22,000). Cities were a prime attraction for Jews seeking to live in Russia east of the Pale of Settlement. In St. Petersburg, which restricted the number of Jewish residents, over 17,000 Jews lived legally (and more lived illegally) at the start of the twentieth century. By this point, the majority of Jews in the Russian Empire resided in cities.[23]

In the final decades of the nineteenth century, Jews' internal migration from smaller settlements to cities was compounded by another major population shift in the form of transnational immigration. From the early 1880s until the start of World War I, some two million Jews emigrated from Eastern Europe, most settling in the United States. Thus, over the course of a generation, about one-third of Eastern Europe's Jewish population left the region, the great majority never returning (unlike some other European immigrant groups heading to America at the same time, for whom rates of return migration were much higher). Although immigrants were more likely to be younger rather than older and poorer rather than wealthier, they came from all segments of East European Jewish society. Even small communities felt the impact of mass immigration; during this period few Jewish families were without some relation who had left, and immigration was an ongoing subject of public discussion.[24]

These social and economic changes had political consequences for Eastern Europe generally and its Jews in particular. Nationalist movements inspired many different peoples living in the Habsburg and Romanov Empires to advocate for cultural autonomy or political independence. Among East European Jews a spectrum of Jewish nationalist ideologies flourished at the end of the nineteenth century, including not only Zionism and Territorialism but also the diaspora nationalism of the Jewish Labor Bund and Folkspartey. The advent of organized labor movements and radical political parties in Eastern Europe also attracted many of the region's Jews, especially in Russia, some of whom formed Jewish political parties or labor unions, while others joined general political organizations. Just as urbanization and immigration atomized many East European Jewish communities, these new political movements disrupted and reconfigured these Jews' longstanding notions of social order, both locally and globally.[25]

Increasingly, the organizations and institutions that shaped East European Jewish life were centered in cities. As a consequence, the many Jewish communities in provincial towns that had been established during the centuries of the Commonwealth's colonizing expansion—towns that once constituted a frontier and then emerged as a cultural center—came to be regarded as a backwater. At the same time, these towns were themselves undergoing transformations. Some grew over the course of the nineteenth century to the size of small cities, often largely due to burgeoning Jewish populations, which sometimes comprised over three-fourths of a town's residents. Exemplary of this phenomenon is Berdichev, which did not have a substantial Jewish community before the eighteenth century. Local magnates, the Radziwiłłs, invited Jews to settle in the town in the early 1700s. During the mid-eighteenth century, both the town's economy and its Jewish population expanded. By the end of the century there were some 2,500 Jews in Berdichev and its neighboring villages. Both economic growth and the town's emergence as an important early center of hasidism stimulated the rapid expansion of Berdichev's Jewish community, which became the town's majority population and transformed it into a small city. By 1861, over 45,000 Jews lived in Berdichev, making it one of Russia's largest Jewish communities. By the end of the nineteenth century, Jews constituted 80 percent of the population. On the eve of World War I, Berdichev's Jewish population peaked at over 55,000.[26]

Other towns boomed and then declined, according to the vagaries of a changing economy and political geography. A case in point is Shklov, where Jews first settled in 1668, and which became an important regional commercial hub during the seventeenth and eighteenth centuries. The town also enjoyed a brief heyday as a major locus of Jewish intellectual life, starting after the first of the partitions of Poland and continuing until the Napoleonic war of 1812. During this period, Shklov was an early center of the Haskalah in Russia and an important site for Hebrew publishing. But during the second half of the nineteenth century, Shklov's economy weakened after Russia's rail system bypassed the town, and as a consequence its Jewish population declined.[27]

These modernizing trends continued to characterize much of East European Jewish life during the first years of the twentieth century, until they were disrupted—and then transformed—by World War I, the Bolshevik Revolution, and the Russian Civil War. During these wars, Jews experienced multiple hardships, including the German occupation of much of the northern part of Eastern Europe, violent border disputes among Poland, Lithuania, and Soviet Russia at the wars' end, and massacres in Ukraine as the region was torn apart by civil war. Some towns' entire populations were forced to relocate during wartime, at times fleeing to large cities; conversely, some city dwellers evacuated to small towns and villages as temporary havens.

After this near decade of violent turmoil, East European Jews recovered from the devastating toll of warfare under new political and social circumstances. Dislocation continued in the wake of these wars, as many Jews resettled in major cities, immigrated to Western Europe, the Americas, Palestine, and South Africa, or found themselves living in new countries even as they remained in their prewar hometowns. After the Versailles Treaty, the map of Eastern Europe was redrawn, and the region's millions of Jews were, along with their neighbors, no longer subjects of empires but now citizens of newly independent countries: Poland, Lithuania, Latvia, Estonia, Czechoslovakia, Hungary, Romania, and Soviet Russia.[28]

Eastern Europe's Jews were now afforded new rights, including participation in local and national governments and opportunities to establish Jewish educational, cultural, and political institutions. This rapidly expanding Jewish institutional life was headquartered in major cities, with satellites—individual schools, political clubs, branches of youth organizations, and the like—in smaller towns. Established networks of economic and religious life, which had long linked Jews living in these towns with one another and with urban centers, now served new political and cultural activities. Another novelty for East European Jewry was return travel by former neighbors who had emigrated in the decades preceding World War I. During the interwar years, Jewish visitors from America, the largest and most prosperous center of immigration, were an occasional presence in both cities and towns, whether on personal trips to see family or as delegates from agencies bringing relief to communities suffering from the economic hardships of war and its aftermath. For these immigrants, Eastern Europe had become the Old World, embodying a personal as well as collective past.[29]

Among East European Jews, those in the USSR found themselves in a unique situation, as participants in the Bolshevik transformation of the former tsarist empire into a socialist state. Many Jews moved to major cities in Russia that had hitherto restricted Jews' residence, and some settled in state-run Jewish agricultural colonies in the Ukrainian SSR and in Birobidzhan, the Jewish Autonomous Region, located in far eastern Russia on its border with Manchuria. Nevertheless, a considerable number of Jews remained in small towns, which became proving grounds for the new social and economic order. Traditional Jewish mercantile professions were targeted for replacement; indeed, the provincial Jewish petit bourgeois became, along with the *kulak* (the wealthy Russian peasant), a repudiated archetype of the old economic order. Similarly, Jewish religious life suffered under Bolshevik suppression, as did Christian denominations. At the same time, the USSR recognized Jews as citizens, condemned antisemitism, supported Yiddish as the official language of the Jewish national minority, and underwrote an array of Jewish educational, cultural, and political institutions, albeit within a Marxist rubric. As in other new nations to the west, Soviet Jewish cultural activities—publishing, scholarship, theater—were centered in major cities and reached smaller locations in the form of schools, libraries, periodicals, and traveling performances and exhibitions.[30]

Germany's invasion of Poland in September 1939 initiated the greatest watershed in the long history of East European Jewry. During World War II, cities and towns throughout the region were variously sites of Jews' ghettoization, mass execution, or deportation to labor camps or death camps. Jewish life was destroyed on an unprecedented scale; in some smaller communities, not a single Jew who had lived there when the war began was known to be alive at its end. Few East European Jewish survivors of the Holocaust returned to their hometowns after the war. Many immigrated to Western Europe, the Americas, Australia, New Zealand, and Palestine/Israel. While some Jews who remained in Eastern Europe sought to reestablish small communities, notably in the postwar settlement of thousands of Jews in Dzierżoniów, a town in Lower Silesia, most tended to resettle in large cities, seeking either solidarity with a more substantial Jewish community or, in many cases, anonymity as Jews.[31]

Although the Holocaust brought a violent and tragic conclusion to widespread Jewish communal life in towns across Eastern Europe, it did not end Jews' presence in these locales. Most Jews in the region reside in major cities, but a limited number continue to live in small towns where prewar Jewish communities had thrived in Belarus, Hungary, Moldova, Romania, and especially Ukraine, home to the largest number of Jewish Holocaust survivors to remain in situ. While the Jewish populations of these towns have dwindled, the number of visitors to them in search of the Jewish past has increased. Even in the face of restrictions placed on Western visitors before the fall of communism, Jews living outside of Eastern Europe have made "return" visits (increasingly, these travels are to ancestors' former homes, not those of the travelers themselves) throughout the postwar period. Since the end of communist rule in Eastern Europe, Jewish tourism in the region has burgeoned, attracting visitors (not all of whom are Jews) pursuing an array of interests, including family genealogy, academic research, or Holocaust remembrance.

At the same time, local history enthusiasts and scholars, both Jews and non-Jews, have undertaken research on the Jewish past of Eastern Europe's communities large and small.[32]

East European Jewry is distinguished by both unprecedented expansion and unrivaled destruction. The scope of Jewish life in the region extends beyond its borders as the locus of origin for the largest number of Jewish immigrants in the modern era, who formed both the majority of the United States' Jewish population and the largest ethnic base of Israeli Jews. Beyond its quantitative importance, Eastern Europe served as a proving ground for Jewish encounters with modernity on a mass scale. These encounters followed a distinctive dynamic, defined by the region's emergence as an economic, social, and cultural frontier for Jews in the early modern period. Subsequently, the region's nurturing of an extensive Jewish culture, distinct in many ways from its counterpart to the west, transformed this frontier into a heartland. Over time, the innovative way of life East European Jews had forged in the early modern period confronted new modernizing practices. Political emancipation, immigration, intellectual and cultural secularism, Jewish nationalism, radical political activism, industrialization, and urbanization increasingly led many of these Jews elsewhere, both geographically and ideologically. As a consequence, provincial Eastern Europe came to be regarded as the locus of a Jewish way of life left behind. For immigrants, the erstwhile heartland became the Old World; for European cosmopolitanites, a backwater; for traditionalists, a redoubt. In the first half of the twentieth century, Jewish Eastern Europe was roiled by one world war and vanquished by another, with much of its remnants swept behind the opaque folds of the Iron Curtain. After the Holocaust, Jews in the West envisioned the region as a haunted killing field and, following the end of communism, have explored Eastern Europe as a heritage site.

These large numbers, distinctive subcultures, and singular political, geographic, and demographic shifts have also engendered an exceptional Jewish reflection on Eastern Europe. It is valued not only as a place where many Jews have lived, worked, visited, or died, but also as a locus having definitional significance for Jews. The meanings Jews have invested in Eastern Europe are anything but monolithic; they vary across Jewish cultures and change over time, and they have a complex interrelation with non-Jews' understandings of the region and of Jewishness. And although religious, political, or intellectual elites often articulate these values, they are put forth most extensively and passionately by other, "ordinary" Jews.

As both a colloquial practice and a scholarly endeavor, this discourse on the meaning of Eastern Europe for Jewish life eventually centered on the term *shtetl.* In vernacular Yiddish this term does not reference a distinctly Jewish or East European social geography, nor did all East European Jews live in communities that might be termed *shtetlekh.* Nevertheless, the meaning of *shtetl*, especially as the word is used in other languages, has acquired these specific connotations of geography, demography, culture, and often of epoch and sensibility as well. To speak of the *shtetl*—whether as a scholar, creative artist, visitor, or even as a resident—with this added value is to engage this subject not as a phenomenon, but as a concept.

Concept

Jewish conceptualizations of a particular *shtetl*, of *shtetlekh* as a collective, or of "the *shtetl*" as a paradigm are part of a larger cultural attention to the significance of place in Jewish life, ranging from an individual Jew's immediate concerns (such as the traditional need to live within walking distance of a synagogue) to the mythic stature of ancient sites (Mount Ararat, Ur, the Red Sea). Notions of the symbolic value of the *shtetl* resonate with other symbolic sites in Jewish geography, sometimes explicitly—for example, when characterizing the *shtetl* as a *Yerushelayim shel matah*, a "tiny, exiled Jerusalem."[33] As these are Jewish conceptualizations of the *shtetl*'s significance, they are often not shared by non-Jews living in or visiting these same towns.

Indeed, the term *shtetl* does not readily correspond to an official geographic category in the regions of Eastern Europe with which it has come to be identified. On the latifundia of Polish magnates, where so many of these towns were established, the defining unit of local geography was the *klucze* (literally, "key"), a complex consisting of several villages, aristocrats' residences, as well as one or more towns that served as the commercial and administrative center for the surrounding villages and nobles' estates.[34] Nor did the term *shtetl* correspond directly with any official geographic designation in the Russian or Austro-Hungarian Empires. The Russian government established something of an equivalent legal designation—*mestechko* (small town)—only in 1875 and applied the classification to communities of different sizes inconsistently.[35]

Yiddish speakers in provincial Eastern Europe also conceptualized and referred to this social geography differently. To designate a local Jewish community, which might include Jews living in a town as well as in surrounding villages and on nearby estates, Yiddish speakers would more likely use the term *kehile* and often referred in writing to a Jewish community as a *kehile kedoyshe*—"a sacred [Jewish] community." The Modern

Hebrew calque of *shtetl*—*'ayarah*, a diminutive of Biblical Hebrew *'ir* (city)—"stems from the modern press and literature."[36]

Given the general nature of the term *shtetl* in Yiddish (any town, anywhere) and the idiomatically connotative use of the term in other languages, recent scholarship has struggled to create criteria for defining what constitutes a *shtetl*, understood as a unit of (pre-Holocaust) East European Jewish social geography, both to differentiate it from other kinds of communities and to characterize what the many locations referred to as *shtetlekh* have in common. While these hundreds of towns typically shared certain important features—Yiddish as the Jews' internal vernacular, the marketplace as the original center of their economy, the *kohol* as the traditional organizing structure of Jewish community institutions—these locales were far from uniform culturally. In addition to a rich, longstanding diversity of local Jewish customs for religious observance, language use, architecture, foodways, dress, music, play, and other aspects of daily life, these towns were home to competing Jewish religious and, later, political movements. Nor, of course, were the cultures of these towns exclusively Jewish, even when Jews constituted a town's majority population and dominated its geographic center. Indeed, these towns' Christian populations figured prominently in their Jewish neighbors' lives, however much these groups differed from one another. Even features that epitomized Jewish life in *shtetlekh*—Yiddish inflected by a sizeable Slavic component; Jews' economic interdependence on both gentry and peasantry; Jewish self-government enabled, and eventually disabled, by changing polities—evince the extensive interrelation of Jews with their neighbors as a defining feature of *shtetl* life.

Historians' efforts to set criteria for what constitutes a *shtetl* are complicated by the dynamics of individual towns, changing in size and legal status over the centuries, their complicated, shifting connections with other nearby settlements, as well as by the tendency, over time, to refer to "any small town in Eastern Europe with a large Jewish population" as a *shtetl*.[37] Antony Polonsky notes that the term *shtetl* is often applied, rather indiscriminately, to identify cities, suburbs, summer colonies, and rural villages alike.[38] John Klier observes that the significance of defining the *shtetl* itself changes with time, in particular having vital consequences for Jews under Russian rule in 1882, when the legal taxonomy of communities in the Pale of Settlement determined whether or not Jews could reside in these places. Abandoning efforts to establish criteria of scope for what constitutes a *shtetl*, Klier suggests that it "might better be envisioned as the centre of an economic-cultural zone, linking Jews to Christians and Jews to Jews."[39] Samuel Kassow argues that a *shtetl*, as a Jewish geographical phenomenon, had to have a certain social infrastructure sufficient to support Jews both economically—primarily (at least at first) through *arenda*, trade, and artisanry—and religiously, in the form of institutions (including the synagogue, *besmedresh* [house of religious study and worship for adult males], *kheyder* [school for children's introductory religious education], *mikve* [communal bath for ritual immersions]) and personnel (including rabbi, cantor, kosher slaughterer, *melamed* [*kheyder* teacher], *badkhn* [wedding entertainer], *kohol, khevre kdishe* [group that prepares corpses for burial], etc.). At the same time, the community could not be so large that it was impossible for all Jews to have some familiarity with one another. Kassow thus characterizes the *shtetl* as a Jewish social space both substantial and intimate.[40]

The notion of all Jews in a *shtetl* being on familiar terms with one another implies that the *shtetl* might not qualify as an "imagined community," which, as defined by Benedict Anderson, is any social geography "larger than [a] primordial village of face-to-face contact."[41] Rather, the *shtetl* is envisioned as having a premodern, organic closeness, familiarity, and completeness. And yet, the construct of the *shtetl* as a significantly Jewish, culturally autonomous, small-scale, communitarian social module that was replicated, albeit with variations, by the hundreds across Eastern Europe is in itself a powerful imaginary projection.

Indeed, while some historians formulate definitions of *shtetl* that center on the actuality of Jewish life in Eastern Europe, other scholars classify the *shtetl* as a cultural invention. Historian Ben-Cion Pinchuk, for example, asserts that the *shtetl* "was introduced to Jewish discourse in the nineteenth century by its literature [and] . . . became in the narrative of the Jewish people one of the more lasting symbols of life in the Diaspora."[42] Similarly, literature scholar Arnold Band writes: "More often than not, the 'shtetl' is an imagined construct based on literary description either in Hebrew or in Yiddish, and even when treated by historians, it is the product of historiographic reconstruction, by no means free of imagining."[43] Folklorist Barbara Kirshenblatt-Gimblett argues that the multiple meanings of *shtetl* are inherent in these sites' history. She suggests distinguishing between notions of "the Jewish town" in the East European context (which might include communities that would not readily be thought of as *shtetlekh*) and of the *shtetl* as a "hermetic Jewish world," the product of numerous literary and other renderings.[44]

Although scholarly struggles to define a *shtetl* are a recent development, Jews' understandings of provincial East European towns as sites with distinct, defining communal value have an extensive and dynamic history. This is manifest in Jewish legends about the origins of some of these towns, including folk etymologies for their names, based on Hebrew (or, occasionally, Yiddish) glosses. Thus, Ostróg (Yiddish: *Ostre*) is said to originate from the phrase *os torah* ("mark of the Torah"); the root of Kolomyya (Yiddish: *Kolomey*) is purportedly the phrase *kol miya*, meaning "voice of God"; Shebershin, the Yiddish variant of Szczebrzeszyn, is explained as being derived either from *shev rishon* ("settle first") or from *shever shin*, meaning "broken tooth."[45] In addition to Judaizing Slavic town names, these legends also position Jews as defining forces in these towns' creation, which is sometimes conceptualized as fulfilling Jews' divinely directed mission. These legends resemble the Jewish folk etymology of Poland (Yiddish: *Poyln*) as *po lin* (Hebrew: "stay here"), a divine mandate to Jews to make Poland their home.[46]

Town names reflect a relationship to *shtetlekh* that not only is marked as distinctly Jewish but also has significance for Jews beyond these locales. Yiddish variants of town names (e.g., Kuzmir versus Polish Kazimierz) signify a sense of place that, while close to that of their neighbors, is particular to Jews. A number of towns achieved vernacular renown beyond their borders, as evinced in Yiddish folk sayings. For example: "In Skvire iz itlekher a khosid, in Yarmolinets iz itlekher a ganev" [In Skvyra everyone is a hasid, in Yarmolyntsi everyone is a thief]. "A gorzder ferd-ganef hot oykh moyre far Got" [Even a horse-thief from Gargždai fears God]. "Ven nit di lukniker yidn, voltn di shkotsim keyn shteyner nit gevorfn" [Were it not for the Jews of Luokė, gentiles wouldn't throw stones]. "Der grester latskever nogid hot nit mit vos shabes tsu makhn" [The richest man in Leckava doesn't have the means to celebrate the Sabbath]. "In Mezeritsh sharbt keyn oysher nit" [No rich man dies in Mezhyrich].[47] Often uncomplimentary, these folk sayings reflect internal localized rivalries among Jewish communities and allude to general anxieties about class, piety, and moral integrity.

Town names figure as locative appellations in Jews' personal names, especially rabbis and other prominent figures, from as early as the sixteenth century (e.g., Efrayim Shelomoh ben Aharon of Lunshits [Łęczyca], 1550–1619; Shimshen ben Peysakh of Ostropolye [Staryy Ostropil], d. 1648). Following mandates beginning in the late eighteenth century to acquire surnames, many East European Jews adopted family names that reference towns, perhaps as an extension of this earlier naming practice. The surnames Broder, Chomsky, Dubnow, Felstiner, Golub, Hrushovski, Kobrin, Lasker, Miropol, Rohatyn, Salant, Tartakoff, and Umansky, among dozens of others, continue to identify Jews with these towns, though, for many people with such names, any association with these locations may have disappeared, attenuated by generations of relocation and replaced by an association with kin. (Conversely, the "discovery" of an ancestor's *shtetl* through genealogical research can reposition the town as a locus of origin in family history.)

More extensive and lasting is the symbolic value of town names associated with hasidic groups established since the turn of the nineteenth century, including Belzer, Chortkover, Gerer, Kotsker, Lubavitsher, Munkatsher, Pupover, Skverer, Tasher, among others. What probably started as another extension of traditional locative appellations became an enduring nomenclature with enhanced meaning. For generations of hasidim, these names have signified the origins of their particular rebbe, his court, his lineage, his school of hasidism, and his followers. After World War II, these town names serve as enduring reminders of the East European fountainhead of a spiritual movement that now thrives elsewhere in the international networks of hasidic communities. Their particular towns of origin were, and sometimes still are, sites of return journeys for hasidim seeking spiritual enhancement.

Whereas hasidim imbued particular towns with a level of sanctity, *maskilim* conceptualized the *shtetl* as emblematic of a Jewish way of life and endowed this social geography with a divergent meaning. In contrast to the hasidic attraction to particular *shtetlekh*, even as many hasidim moved further away from these towns, *maskilim* strove to distance themselves from the *shtetl*, understood as an abstraction, even as it remained geographically immanent. This was, in part, a riposte to the identification of certain towns as central to hasidism's new order of spirituality. Moreover, as *maskilim* grappled with the challenges that modernity posed to Jewish life, they identified the provincial towns that were then home to most of East European Jewry as the proving ground for this encounter.

The maskilic intellection of the *shtetl* took place not in activities that paralleled hasidism's embodied practices of travel to these sites or its oral traditions (storytelling, singing) identified with particular towns; rather, *maskilim* detached from the *shtetl* by establishing it as a discursive subject. They brought a new self-consciousness, albeit a fraught one, to this social geography, by construing a familiar and often immediate locus as both markedly Jewish and decidedly problematic. *Maskilim* offered a selective and forthrightly polemical reading of the *shtetl*, even though some of the provincial communities they disparaged had, in fact, nurtured their scholarly and ideological aspirations. (Consider, for example, the relationship between the *maskil* Mendl Lefin and his patron, Prince Adam Kazimierz Czartoryski, a magnate whose latifundia included the town of Mikołajów, in which Lefin spent an important part of his life.)[48] The maskilic problematizing of the *shtetl* proved a threshold event in its intellectual history and had an enduring impact on its conceptualization, even as the significance of the *shtetl* changed.

As literature scholar David Roskies notes, *maskilim* wrote about the *shtetl* "as if they were on the outside looking in," even though they often were "but one step removed" from their subject.[49] Moving away from and back to *shtetlekh* has figured prominently in their conceptualization in works of modern Jewish culture, the distances traversed having a defining value for the meanings invested in these sites. Even as the emblematic *shtetl* often repelled *maskilim*, it loomed large in their worldview as the point of departure, and they scrutinized Jewish life in small towns with unprecedented attention. *Maskilim* critiqued such fixtures of East European Jewish life as local religious folkways, disparaged as superstitions; communal governance by the *kohol*, derided as hidebound and corrupt; a traditional Jewish pedagogy centered (for males) on the Talmud, abjured as sophistry; and Yiddish, dismissed as less than a proper language—even as *maskilim* sometimes wrote in it. Though these objects of cultural critique could be found in other settings, in maskilic discourses the *shtetl* emerged as its primary locus. Indeed, repudiation not only drove this new relationship with *shtetlekh* but also intensified it.

Maskilim expressed the defining ambivalence of their relationship with the *shtetl* as the locus par excellence of auto-critique in an expanding East European Jewish print culture. Secular belles-lettres emerged as an important new vehicle for engaging this readership. Maskilic literary works frequently took the form of satire, a genre that ably accommodated the double-edged nature of self-scrutiny. *Shtetlekh* provided not only the setting for many of these works but also the analytic rubric for the authors' polemics. A case in point is Yisroel Aksenfeld's *Dos shterntikhl* (The Headband); written at some point between 1820 and 1840 and first published in 1861, this early maskilic novel is a landmark of modern Yiddish fiction. *Dos shterntikhl* opens with a mock taxonomy of urban Jewish communities of different sizes—a *kleyn shtetl* (a small town), a *shtot* (city), and a *groyse shtot* (a large city)—thereby acknowledging but also ridiculing the challenge of distinguishing a *shtetl* from larger or smaller communities. Aksenfeld also derides the inflated self-image of a provincial town's inhabitants as cosmopolitanites: "If someone were to slip up and impulsively call the city [*shtot*] a town [*shtetl*], he'd be thought either a boor or a lunatic."[50]

Maskilim employed other playful literary strategies in their *shtetl* satires. Writers frequently offered critiques of the social order of provincial Jewish communities in set pieces within prose narratives. Exemplary are disquisitions in pioneering works of modern Yiddish fiction by Isaac Mayer Dik and Sholem Yankev Abramovitsh. Tirades by Abramovitsh's recurring narrator and authorial persona, Mendele Moykher-Sforim (Mendele the Bookseller), against some institution of *shtetl* life, especially Jewish communal leadership, regularly conclude with the tag line, "*Ober in dem bin ikh nisht oysn*" (But that's beside the point). This indirection is strategic, creating a rhetorical distance from what the author conceived as experientially immanent for his readers—even as Abramovitsh was writing in Odessa, and many of his readers were middle-class urbanites.[51]

Similarly, maskilic satires seldom directly identified particular towns as the subject of their prose. Aksenfeld named one of the towns in *Dos shterntikhl* Loyhoyopoli, a mock-Hebrew name meaning "Nosuchville," and the setting for his drama *Der ershter yidisher rekrut* (The First Jewish Recruit), published in 1862, is the town of Nibivale, a play on the Russian word for "imaginary." Yosef Perl's epistolary novel *Megaleh temirin* (Revealer of Secrets, 1819), an early work of maskilic Hebrew prose, encrypted the names of actual towns in pseudonyms that could be decoded through *gematria*, the traditional Jewish practice of ascribing additional meaning to Hebrew words through the numerical value of their letters. This device exploits the mystical sophism employed by the hasidim that Perl's satire targeted. Abramovitsh popularized the practice of identifying the towns in which maskilic works of fiction are set with comical, faux-indigenous names. His Glupsk, Tuneiadevke, and Kabtsansk attach Slavic geographical suffixes to Russian or Yiddish words (Russian *glupy*, "foolish," and *tuneiadets*, "mooch"; Yiddish *kabtsn*, "pauper"). Yiddish writers continued to use this device, from the Kasrilevke—another "Pauperville," and the most famous example of a *shtetl* pseudonym—of Sholem Aleichem (pen name of Sholem Rabinovitsh), to the Mistifke ("Trashville") of Soviet modernist Dovid Bergelson (in his short story "Der letster roshashone" [The Last Rosh Hashanah]). Even when these town names encrypted actual locales (Abramovitsh's Glupsk as Berdichev, where the author lived in the 1860s; Kasrilevke as Rabinovitsh's hometown, Voronko), they function as archetypes, marking fictional Jewish communities as exemplars of collective abjection: poverty, foolishness, moral or physical decline.

As modern Jewish letters continued beyond the Haskalah, the *shtetl* remained a subject of literary attention. To some extent, differences in Jewish writers' approach to this subject coalesced around their choice of language. In this complex multilingual environment, language choice directed authors' words to a particular audience and, increasingly, related their work to a particular ideology. An important distinction emerged between writing in Jewish languages versus writing in the languages of non-Jewish neighbors. Hebrew and Yiddish texts each targeted distinct readerships within an exclusively Jewish audience. Writing in German, Polish, or Russian made Jewish authors' work available both to more acculturated Jews and to non-Jewish readers, thereby positing a cultural common ground for Jewish and Christian intellectuals.

Given this different agenda, *shtetl* life does not figure as prominently in Jewish literature written in non-Jewish languages, nor, when it does appear, is the *shtetl* used primarily as a locus for the sort of internal Jewish critique found in maskilic writing in Hebrew or Yiddish. Osip Rabinovich's *Shtrafnoi* (The Penal Recruit, 1859), an early landmark of Jewish prose in Russian, portrays the Jewish leadership of a town grappling with the daunting challenges posed by Russia's military conscription policy under Tsar Nicholas I. With both Christian and Jewish readers in mind, Rabinovich's novella exposes the moral dilemmas Jews faced under Russia's paradoxical policies of promoting Jewish russification (in part through military service), on one hand, and Russian antisemitism—or at the very least, indifference to the circumstances of Russian Jewry—on the other hand.[52]

Nineteenth-century Jewish writing in German centered its portraits of *shtetl* life on the disparity between Westjuden and Ostjuden (Jews of Western and Eastern Europe, respectively). This rubric shaped the prose of Karl Emil Franzos, born in Czortków, who received a Western education in his youth and ultimately settled in Berlin. Though a native of eastern Galicia, Franzos viewed Jewish life there at a distance defined by his commitment to Western culture and liberal German nationalism. In his travel writing Franzos characterized Jews and other peoples of Eastern Europe as "half-Asian" and therefore racially different from indigenous West Europeans. Franzos's prose about *shtetl* life (including works set in the fictional town of Barnow, believed to be based on his native Czortków) portrays Jews there "with a mixture of sympathy and distaste," according to historian Steven Aschheim. Popular in its day, Franzos's fiction advocated for reforming Ostjuden through modern Western education.[53]

East European Jews writing in Hebrew and Yiddish pursued increasingly distinct literary agendas as the twentieth century approached. In each language writers evolved an aesthetic protocol associated with different audiences and ideologies. Hebrew writers addressed a small, intellectually elite, and largely male readership. Although some Hebrew fiction by *maskilim* assailed *shtetl* life, such as Abraham Mapu's *'Ayit tsavu'a* (The Hypocrite, 1857–1864), these writers generally focused on other subjects. Besides reflecting the maskilic agenda of engaging modern Western ideas, Hebrew writers were committed to forging a new Jewish culture centered on a vaunted ancient past, exemplified by the "revival" of Hebrew. As Hebrew was not then used as a vernacular, writers' ability to reproduce the speech of Jews in provincial Eastern Europe and draw on the idioms of colloquial storytelling was limited, compared to writing in Yiddish. Thus, Micah Yosef Berdyczewski wrote monologues and simple sketches of *shtetl* life in Yiddish, while reserving Hebrew for more aesthetically ambitious literary efforts. By the turn of the twentieth century, Hebrew literature was increasingly associated with Zionism, which informed much of what was written about the *shtetl* in the language. Hebrew writers settling in Palestine during the early decades of the twentieth century generally avoided the subject, save to position the *shtetl* as an exemplar of diaspora abjection. Hence, Dvora Baron's compatriots regarded her nuanced explorations of traditional Jewish life in provincial Eastern Europe from a gendered perspective, written in Hebrew while she lived in Tel Aviv in the 1920s to 1950s, as exceptional and eccentric.[54]

Yiddish writing, by contrast, employed a vernacular that addressed a rapidly expanding readership, despite the fact that *maskilim* had often derogated the language as a vehicle for belles-lettres. The tension between this low regard for Yiddish and authors' aspirations to create a modern literature for a growing Jewish middle class energized their writing. Provincial life proved a ready venue for this literature, which associated *shtetlekh* with linguistic and cultural tenacity, contrasted with signal shifts in East European Jewish life in rapidly expanding new urban and immigrant communities. Though their work often critiqued aspects of *shtetl* life, some Yiddish writers positioned these towns not as sites of abjection but as defining points of origin—even if they were ultimately to be transcended. This literary turn coincided with the advent of Yiddishism and diaspora nationalism, which transvalued Eastern Europe and its Jewish vernacular as central to a modern secular Jewish culture. Far from abandoning or ridiculing Yiddish, the advocates of these movements argued, the language should be cultivated as a cultural touchstone.[55] The burgeoning Yiddish press at the turn of the twentieth century was instrumental to both literary and ideological developments. Not only did newspapers disseminate wide-ranging content to a rapidly growing readership; but the Yiddish press also fostered new cultural practices, centered on reading, discussing, advertising in, and writing to these publications, which realized a new, modern Jewish culture on a scale of unprecedented scope.[56]

At this time, Sholem Aleichem emerged as the most popular champion of Yiddish as a literary language and the creator of some of the most widely read *shtetl* fiction. His Kasrilevke became the center of the author's literary world, home to two of his major fictional characters—Menakhem-Mendl and Motl Peysi dem khazns (Motl Peysi the cantor's son), both of whose narratives center on their protagonists' abandoning the town. Revisited in works of serial fiction and dozens of individual short stories, Kasrilevke is portrayed with an affection qualified and ironized by the author's frequent pointing up of the Jewish community's limitations, especially in response to the challenges posed by modernity. The distance between Sholem Aleichem's literary topos and his primarily middle-class, increasingly urbanized readership with cosmopolitan aspirations (the author himself lived in Kiev; his family spoke Russian, not Yiddish, at home) informed the literary strategies at work in his Kasrilevke stories. Primarily concerned with the Jewish community's humblest figures—widows, orphans, abandoned wives, servants, ne'er-do-wells, and the like—they play with folk narrative forms, whether by evoking traditional storytelling devices, such as local legends, or by crafting folksy versions of "high" culture's literary genres: the epistolary novel (*Menakhem-Mendl*, 1892–1909), the *Bildungsroman* (*Motl Peysi dem khazns*, 1907–1916), and the travelogue (*Dos naye Kasrilevke* [The New Kasrilevke, 1901] and *Kasrilevker progres* [Progress in Kasrilevke, 1914–1915], in which the author reports on Kasrilevke's modernization, to the point of becoming unrecognizable as his hometown).[57]

Yiddish authors' continued writing about the *shtetl* evolved an implicit polemic on modern Jewish life and letters generally. The *shtetl* became an intertextual common ground where new generations of writers invoked and responded to works by precursors as well as contemporaries. This is exemplified by two novellas, both named *A shtetl* and written early in their respective author's careers: the first, published in 1904, by Sholem Asch; the second, appearing in 1906, by Isaac Meyer Weissenberg. Asch's novella, set during the second half of the nineteenth century, presents *shtetl* life in lyrical terms, the town's rhythms in harmony with the changing seasons and the surrounding landscape, its Jewish citizens prosperous and committed to communitarian values. The *shtetl*'s halcyon image is only slightly complicated by intimations of changes that will, with time, disrupt it: a modernizing economy, hinted at with the advent of bookkeeping and the sewing machine, and internal communal divides, with the arrival of hasidism to the town. Weissenberg's *A shtetl* can be read as a riposte to Asch's idyllic *shtetl*.[58] The later novella is set in the immediate past, the period of political unrest around the 1905 Russian Revolution. Whereas Jewish community life in Asch's *A shtetl* is harmonious, the Jews in Weissenberg's novella are riven with internal conflicts, especially along generational and class lines, marked by violence culminating in murder. In contrast to Asch's image of the *shtetl* as having an organic social integrity of its own, Weissenberg positions the town as a provincial backwater in relation to the city, the center of new political and intellectual life.[59]

Literary portraits of the *shtetl* flourished alongside popular lore circulating among East European Jews in folksongs, legends, and sayings. The interrelation of literary and folkloric engagements with the *shtetl* is complex. As literature scholar Dan Miron notes, early maskilic satires that mocked traditional customs—such as local practices tied to observing religious holidays, arranging marriages, or curing diseases—nonetheless documented them with "felicitous, circumstantial, and detailed" descriptions. *Maskilim* thereby implied that, while local Jewish customs "should be eradicated," they should also "be preserved in memory and in literature."[60]

At the turn of the twentieth century, Jewish authors drew on personal experience, family lore, or their own research to craft richly detailed portraits of provincial Jewish life. At the same time, individual enthusiasts, scholars, and cultural organizations collected and published folk materials as a demonstration of Jewish patrimony. Occasionally these materials coalesced around a particular town, most famously in the case of folktales about the "wise men" of Khelem (Chełm), which emerged in the nineteenth century as the archetypal fools' town in Yiddish folklore.[61]

Though non-Jewish authors writing in German, Polish, or Russian occasionally made Jews their subject, attention was seldom on the *shtetl* per se. Jews appeared more often in these works either as an exotic people or as individual characters involved with non-Jewish protagonists. Exemplifying the latter case is the most famous Jewish character in nineteenth-century Polish literature: Jankiel the innkeeper in Adam Mickiewicz's 1834 narrative poem *Pan Tadeusz*.[62] These authors' portrayals of Jews, benign or otherwise, were as resident Others within Austrian, Polish, or Russian society. During the Enlightenment, Polonsky notes, Polish writers were more likely to portray Jews as responsible for the "backwardness and destitution of Polish towns."[63] By the 1870s, Eliza Orzeszkowa, the first major woman writer in Poland, addressed the place of Jews in Polish society more sympathetically in her fiction. Orzeszkowa's novels *Eli Makower* and *Meir Ezofowicz* offer detailed, informed portraits of East European Jewish life, exploring Jews' relationships with the Polish aristocracy as well as internal religious conflicts among Jews, and advocating for Jewish integration into Polish society.[64] Leopold von Sacher-Masoch's fiction about Galician Jews combines the author's firsthand observations—notably, an account of his visit to the Sadagorer rebbe's court, among the earliest narratives by German-language writers about visiting hasidim—with research of secondary sources on Jewish lore and custom to produce romanticized stories of a culture understood as an exotic, atavistic curiosity.[65] By the turn of the twentieth century, some authors, especially prominent members of the Russian intelligentsia (Anton Chekhov, Maxim Gorki, Leo Tolstoy), showed greater interest in the plight of Eastern Europe's Jews; as in other philosemitic literature about antisemitism, their works are ultimately less concerned with Jewish culture in its own right, or even with Jews' suffering, than with the moral implications of antisemitism for non-Jews.[66] Complementing these efforts by non-Jewish authors are works dealing with provincial East European life by Jewish writers who avoid the *shtetl* as a literary subject centered on Jewish experience. Short stories by Isaac Babel (in Russian) and L. Shapiro (in Yiddish) examine antisemitic violence from the perspective of the perpetrators. Bruno Schulz took inspiration from life in his native Drohobych for his modernist fiction, written in Polish during the interwar years, without addressing the subject of local Jewish communal life.

Visual representations of *shtetl* life appear within a configuration of creators, audiences, and means of circulation different from that of literary works on this subject. Christians portrayed provincial East European Jewry in works of visual art earlier and more readily than did Jews, as seen in landscapes and genre scenes by Jan Piotr Norblin de la Gourdaine, Wincenty Smokowski, Alexey Ivanovich Trankowsky, Zygmunt Vogel, and other artists working in the eighteenth and nineteenth centuries. By the turn of the twentieth century, images of East European Jews appeared frequently in a rapidly growing popular illustrated press and on picture postcards, which often portrayed their subjects as exotic or risible. At the same time, East European Jews are represented in a different light by the first generations of the region's academically trained Jewish artists. Paintings by Maurycy Gottlieb, Samuel Hirszenberg, Isidor Kaufmann, Maurycy Minkowski, and Maurycy Trebacz range from idealized depictions of religious observance to poignant representations of Jewish victims of poverty and persecution.[67] These works advocated for innovation on two fronts: first, making the case for Jewish subjects as worthy of representation in European salons, galleries, and museums where works of fine art were viewed; second, championing this form of "high" art as an important vehicle for creating modern Jewish culture. Jewish photographers began to document *shtetl* life as early as 1880, when Michael Greim opened his studio in Kamenets-Podolsk and traveled to the provinces to photograph traditional Jewish subjects.[68] These works of visual culture—especially those that were mass reproduced, including images published in the press and on postcards—crossed boundaries defined by language and presented provincial East European Jews in new mass media understood as inherently modern.[69]

Visual engagement with the *shtetl* extended beyond these depictions to include new attention to the indigenous material culture of East European Jews. As was also the case with Jewish folklore and folk music, artists and scholars began gathering or documenting Jewish folk art in the late nineteenth century, following larger efforts to collect and celebrate the folkways of Eastern Europe's national and ethnic cultures. Among the earliest such undertakings are Matthias Bersohn's collections of Polish Jewish artifacts, first exhibited publicly in 1875, and photographs of Polish wooden synagogues, the subject of his pioneering study published in 1900.[70] The extensive scope of East European Jewish visual culture includes synagogue architecture and decoration, ritual objects for home and synagogue, tombstone carving, domestic decorations (e.g., cut-paper ornaments for Shavuos), graphic arts (ornamental title pages for *pinkeysim* [communal chronicles], woodcut prints, amulets, mystical diagrams), clothing (including ritual garments), and foodways (special forms for baking bread or molds for cookies). Documenting and collecting this visual culture isolated it from its imbrication within Jewish communal or domestic life, enabling these objects and images to be situated within newer forms of Jewish culture. Collected as artifacts of Jewish heritage, these items were eventually displayed in ethnographic museums and served as sources of inspiration for artists seeking to create a modernist Jewish visual idiom, realized in both fine and applied art, especially graphic arts and stage design.[71]

These efforts to document Jewish folkways were disrupted by World War I, the Bolshevik Revolution, and the Russian Civil War, which both ravaged and galvanized modern East European Jewish culture. Isaac Babel's *Konarmiia* (Red Cavalry) stories, written in Russian between 1923 and 1926, offer the most widely read account of Jewish persecution and degradation during this period, though they center on the experiences of the First Cavalry of the new Soviet Red Army. At the same time, the destruction of the *shtetl* emerged as an important new rubric for Jewish writers and visual artists in Eastern Europe and America, for whom the devastation of an entire town's Jewish community is synecdochic for the roiling of provincial Jewish life. A new generation of Yiddish writers addressed the war's impact on local Jewish communities in prose fiction: L. Shapiro's "Di yidishe melukhe" (The Jewish Kingdom, 1919), Oyzer Warshawski's *Shmuglares* (Smugglers, 1920), Leyb Olnitzky's *In an okupirt shtetl* (In an Occupied Town, 1924), Itsik Kipnis's *Khadoshim un teg* (Months and Days, 1926). Other works portray the *shtetl*'s demise not as a consequence of warfare but in terms of more intimate, introspective forms of undoing. Dovid Bergelson's fiction about the stifling nature of middle-class provincial Jewish life on the eve of World War I centers on individual acts—such as a suicide or conversion to Christianity—as emblems of the untenable nature of these communities.[72]

This motif of the *shtetl*'s destruction engages a range of emotions, from glee (Sholem Aleichem's young Motl delights in wrecking Kasrilevke in a series of comic episodes) to horror, especially in nightmarish pogrom poems, exemplified by Moyshe-Leyb Halpern's "A nakht"

(A Night, 1916–1919) and Peretz Markish's "Di kupe" (The Heap, 1921–1922).[73] Some works depart from naturalist or expressionist idioms to depict the *shtetl* as a doomed locus by invoking the supernatural, drawing on—and transforming—traditional Jewish mysticism and folklore about the paranormal. Y. L. Peretz's play *Baynakht afn altn mark* (Nighttime in the Old Marketplace, 1907–1915) fills the deserted center of an anonymous *shtetl* with a procession of ghostly archetypal figures; in S. An-ski's drama *Der dibek* (The Dybbuk, 1912–1917) the *shtetl* is a place where the dead are present among the living, culminating in the exorcism of a woman possessed by the soul of her deceased beloved.[74]

These works conceptualize the *shtetl* as not only remote in time, space, or sensibility, but also losing its viability. By contrast, *maskilim* had critiqued the *shtetl* as the locus of a way of life they regarded as, regrettably, all too vibrant. Writers of the World War I era conceptualized *shtetlekh* as embodying an existence that the advances of modernity were leaving behind and, therefore, was incapable of providing for a Jewish future. These works imply that, to the extent *shtetlekh* continued to exist, they would do so as ghost towns.

Literati were not the only ones to conceptualize the *shtetl* as a locus of destruction; the interwar years witnessed the production of the first *yizker-bikher*, memorial books that mourn the destruction of a local East European Jewish community. These volumes were collaboratively produced by immigrant *landslayt* (fellow townspeople). This remarkable genre of collective remembrance would burgeon in the post–World War II era—indeed, *yizker-bikher* are generally thought of as works of Holocaust remembrance. But the first of these anthologies appeared in response to the destruction of Jewish communities during World War I and especially the Russian Civil War, as the title of the earliest example, published in New York in 1924, indicates: *Khurbn Proskurov: tsum ondenken fun di heylige neshomes, vos zaynen umgekumen in der shreklikher shkhite, vos iz ongefirt gevoren durkh di Haydamakes* (The Destruction of Proskuriv: In Memory of Those Holy Souls Who Were Murdered in the Terrible Massacre Carried Out by the Cossacks).[75]

Interwar portraits of the *shtetl* generally reflect a prevailing sense that World War I marked an unprecedented rupture in European life generally and for Jews in particular. Having come to epitomize a Jewish communality whose future was precarious, the *shtetl* was superseded by a rapidly expanding range of alternatives for Jewish community life: immigration—to the Americas, Western Europe, South Africa, or Palestine—which had been underway for a generation before the war started; cosmopolitan life, including major new centers of Yiddish-speaking Jews in such cities as Berlin, Buenos Aires, London, Moscow, New York, and Paris; and, conversely, experimental agrarian collectives: Jewish farming colonies in the United States and Argentina, kibbutzim in Palestine, the Soviet *kolhoz*, and Territorialist settlement plans, which ranged from Madagascar to New Caledonia, British Guiana, and Kimberly, Australia.[76] Along with these new political and social possibilities, Jews encountered new cultural practices—including avant-garde visual art and theater, film, tourism, scholarship—that afforded a modernist perspective on the *shtetl*.

Among the most distinctive modernist engagements with the *shtetl* was the work of avant-garde visual artists of the early twentieth century—including Nathan Altman, Marc Chagall, El Lissitzky, Abraham Maniewicz, Issachar Ryback, and Yosef Tchaikov—who presented the *shtetl* in the new idioms of cubism and expressionism as a distorted, fragmented landscape. The physical actuality of *shtetl* landscapes, often replete with sloping walls and sagging, steep-pitched roofs, conformed to the angular, fractured aesthetic of contemporary art. Artists extended this visual idiom to the depiction of *shtetl* inhabitants, portrayed as hunched, deformed extensions of a crippled landscape. Some of these works both invoke and subvert conventional representations of East European Jewish life. Ryback's *Shtetl, mayn khoreve heym: a gedekhenish* (Town, My Destroyed Home: A Remembrance), an album of thirty large-format graphic works, published in Berlin in 1923, depicts established genre scenes of traditional small-town Jewish life—including *kheyder*, a wedding, blessing Sabbath candles—refracted through the skewed, prismatic spatiality of cubism and the distorted perspectives and grotesque exaggerations of expressionism.[77] The title page of Ryback's album evokes the form of a traditional carved tombstone, thereby both celebrating provincial Jewish folk art as aesthetic inspiration and positioning the artist's work as an elegy.

Before immigrating to Western Europe, Ryback began his career in Russia and contributed to Soviet Jewish avant-garde visual culture during its first years. There, writers, artists, actors, and filmmakers offered the most radical visions of *shtetlekh* dismantled and transformed. Perhaps the best-known work to emerge from this brief period of fervent creativity is Yevgeny Vakhtangov's 1922 staging of An-ski's *The Dybbuk* for the Hebrew-language troupe Habimah, then based in Moscow. This landmark production, widely admired by audiences worldwide (Habimah toured this staging of the play for years) featured expressionist settings by Nathan Altman and music by Joel Engel. This production exemplified the transformation of *shtetl* folkways into a thoroughly aestheticized, rarefied terrain in the hands of modernist artists, including the poet Hayyim Nahman Bialik, who had rendered An-ski's Yiddish text into a modern literary Hebrew that few in the audience (including its Jews) could fully understand.[78]

Working with unprecedented government support and an equally unparalleled state-mandated aesthetic agenda, Soviet Jewish artists and writers engaged the *shtetl* as the proving ground for transforming Jews into Soviet citizens. Much as it had for *maskilim* a century earlier, the *shtetl* of the prerevolutionary era served as a negative model and a point of departure, from which the socialist transformation of the Jews would be measured. "The councils [i.e., soviets] are an instrument for rebuilding the town [*shtetl*] on socialist foundations," proclaims a 1930 Yiddish propaganda poster exhorting Jews in the USSR to embrace compulsory education, industrialization, and the establishment of collective farms, so as to eradicate "capitalist elements."[79] Reminiscent of how *maskilim* used this locus in their polemics, Soviet artists and writers found that, in staging the "dying Jewish shtetl," they brought about "its reanimation in a Russian literary and cultural space." Literature scholar Harriet Murav argues that, in Soviet films of the 1930s repudiating traditional Jewish life, "the shtetl Jew steals the show. The emblematic figure of the past haunts the project of the future."[80]

Many of the most consequential conceptualizations of the *shtetl* began far from Europe during the final decades of the nineteenth century, as hundreds of thousands of Jews immigrated from the Russian and Austro-Hungarian Empires, most settling in the United States. In order to establish themselves in their new homes, recent East European Jewish immigrants often sought out earlier settlers from their hometowns and, in turn, offered these *landslayt* news from their former homes. The steady arrival of new immigrants prompted the establishment of hometown mutual aid societies, known in Yiddish as *landsmanshaftn*. Fusing Old World and New World idioms, these institutions reflected the hybrid nature of immigrants' relationship with the *shtetl*. *Landsmanshaftn* took on some of the traditional roles of the *kohol* (especially providing financial aid) but did so within the protocols of American fraternal orders, including parliamentary procedure, induction ceremonies, and regalia.[81] Complementing these secular organizations were synagogues established by *landslayt*, so that they might worship according to a familiar Old World local tradition. Such a synagogue was sometimes referred to as an *anshey*, as the names of these institutions often included this Hebrew word, meaning "the people of" (as in the New York City synagogue Adas le Israel Anshei Meseritz). Similar institutions were established in other immigrant enclaves in cities in Canada, Latin America, South Africa, and Western Europe.[82]

As the *landsmanshaft* and *anshey* extended the interpersonal connections and familiar sounds (the local Yiddish dialect and modes for chanting worship) of hundreds of East European towns to new, remote settings, these institutions reconstituted individual *shtetlekh* "in exile."[83] The *landsmanshaft* and *anshey* transformed Jewish communities, each defined for generations by a particular geographic locus, into social networks found at great distance from their sites of origin and in the radically different setting of immigrant urban neighborhoods, where Jews from many different East European towns lived side by side among an array of other immigrants. As *landsmanshaftn* became fixtures of immigrant life, they developed into symbolic homes in their own right, and the relationship of *landsmanshaftn* with their respective *shtetlekh* changed with the dynamics of immigration. The end of mass immigration to the United States, due to restrictive quotas enacted in the mid-1920s, transformed immigrants' ties to their hometowns, prompting a new role for *landsmanshaftn*. During the interwar years, they provided economic relief to European *landslayt* struggling to recover from the devastations of World War I. After World War II, the mission of *landsmanshaftn* changed once again, centering on resettling surviving *landslayt* and memorializing those murdered during the Holocaust. Today, some *landsmanshaftn* continue to function as burial societies.

The immigrant context shaped how American Jews engaged the *shtetl* in creative cultural practices, including a burgeoning literature in both Yiddish and English. Immigrant memoirs and autobiographical fiction typically begin with the departure from the protagonist's hometown, which continues to serve as a point of reference in evaluating the immigrant's new home. In the writings of Mary Antin and Anzia Yezierska, the transition from Old World to New World frames the self-realization of modern cosmopolitan women moving away from provincial, traditional mores and patriarchal authority.[84] Occasionally, immigrant authors describe return journeys to Eastern Europe that point up the disparity not only between Old and New Worlds but also between the *shtetl* as remembered and its actuality upon revisiting (e.g., Abraham Cahan's 1898 novella *The Imported Bridegroom*).[85] Some American Yiddish poets explored the complexities of immigrants' alienation from both former and current homes in works that recall the *shtetl* with a complex of charged emotions. For example, Moyshe Leyb Halpern's 1924 poem "Zlotshev, mayn heym" (Złoczów, My Home) ironizes the nostalgia implicit in the poem's title, which also becomes its refrain, with a portrait of his hometown in disarray. At the end, the poet proclaims: "There's only one comfort for me, it's true, / That when I am buried, it won't be in you— / My home, my Złoczów."[86]

The end of mass immigration to the United States attenuated American Jews' connections to *shtetlekh*, which relied increasingly on some kind of mediation, whether letters from European relatives or works of immigrant popular culture, including reportage in the Yiddish press and portrayals of *shtetlekh* in fiction, song, theater, and film. Popular culture soon became American Jews' most widely familiar source of information about the *shtetl*. Immigrants' personal ties to individual towns yielded to shared engagements with representations of generic *shtetlekh*. These works structured the affective significance of the *shtetl* for American Jews, especially those who had never lived in or visited one. During the interwar years, the general trend of this affect shifted. Whereas in the 1920s, American Jewish popular culture frequently portrayed the *shtetl* comically, as a provincial backwater, the 1930s witnessed a turn to more sentimental images of *shtetlekh* as objects of longing. This trend may reflect other concomitant changes, including the end of mass emigration from Eastern Europe and rising concerns about European Jews' political and economic welfare, in the wake of international economic depression and the rise of fascist parties. The era's Old World sentimentality is exemplified by Alexander Olshanetsky and Jacob Jacobs's 1932 song "Mayn shtetele Belz" (My Little Town, Bălţi), in which nostalgia for this Bessarabian town is articulated as a generalized longing for the family home and childhood innocence. The song's popularity inspired a spate of imitations (e.g., "Mayn shtetele Molev" [My Little Town, Mogilev]), consolidating *shtetl* nostalgia as a trope of American Yiddish popular culture.[87]

A considerable number of immigrant Jews made return visits to their hometowns in the interwar years, informing and complicating American Jews' increasingly mediated image of the *shtetl*. Undertaken for a variety of reasons, these trips all entailed symbolic engagement with *shtetlekh*, albeit often implicitly. This engagement was defined by the nature of visiting itself: finite, planned, bracketed by lengthy journeys, culminating with return to the travelers' new homes. Some travelers documented their visits in memoir or travel writing, artwork, photography, or even, on occasion, film. (It is thanks to several dozen such travelers, who went abroad equipped with movie cameras, that most of the documentary footage of actual life in these town exists.) Typically, records of these trips were personal undertakings, shared only with family or friends. Some efforts addressed a larger public, ranging from fundraising films made for *landsmanshaftn* to reports and photographs run in the American Yiddish press.

Central to the symbolic value that visitors from abroad assigned to *shtetlekh* is their understanding of these towns as chronotopes—that is, as conceptual interrelations of time and place.[88] Writers and artists living in interwar Western Europe visited Ostjuden as vestiges of a premodern way of life: on one hand, less sophisticated and viable; on the other hand, more vibrant, intense, and authentic in its Jewishness. In some instances, these visitors obscured their personal connections to the East. Thus, the Austrian writer Joseph Roth's essay "Das jüdische Städtchen" (The Jewish Small Town), a description of visiting a Galician *shtetl* in the mid-1920s, conceals from readers that the unnamed location is, in fact, Roth's native town of Brody.[89]

For immigrants returning from the Americas, these trips followed a rubric that juxtaposed the Old World against the New World. This pair of chronotopes, which links the continents of Europe and America with the past and the future, respectively, construed immigrants' return journeys as travels back in time and related personal travel to a cultural dynamic on a grand scale. [90] Literary and artistic documentations of travels reflect this conceptualization of the immigrant journey. Chone Gottesfeld, for example, chronicled a trip to his hometown of Skała in the mid-1930s, after having established himself as a Yiddish writer in New York. While Gottesfeld appeared to his former neighbors in Skała to be a prosperous American, they impressed him as specters of an abject existence that he had managed to escape.[91] Travel writing regularly recounts the disparities between the actuality of *shtetl* life and how authors had remembered or imagined it, thereby measuring both personal transformation and the growing divergence between *shtetl* Jews and immigrants as well as their perceptions of one another.

Although most immigrant Jews' visits to *shtetlekh* were personal journeys, centered on reunions with family and childhood acquaintances, other Jews undertook these trips on behalf of charities. These organizations included *landsmanshaftn*, bringing aid to *landslayt* in their respective hometowns, and larger philanthropies, such as the American Jewish Joint Distribution Committee and the Jewish Colonization Association, which assisted Jews throughout the region. Economic disparities between America and Eastern Europe provided both the motive for these expeditions and the organizing rubric for their documentation, which focused on the material needs of the Jewish communities visited and the amounts of money collected and distributed. These trips reinforced American Jews' image of the *shtetl* as a locus of Jewish poverty and vulnerability.

A small number of Jews who traveled from America to Eastern Europe were immigrants' children motivated by a desire to engage its Jewish culture as a touchstone of authenticity, whether religious or secular. Some immigrant Orthodox families sent their sons to attend yeshivas in Poland, in order to receive a more rigorous rabbinical training than was available in the United States.[92] Performers who traveled to Eastern Europe include actress Molly Picon, who did so to improve her command of Yiddish and enhance her professional reputation on the American

Yiddish stage, which was dominated by European-born artists. Picon eventually became one of the most popular portrayers of *shtetl* life, drawing on her visits and on the theatrical conventions of more established performers rather than on any "native" experience of small-town Jewish life.[93]

Some of Picon's performances are preserved in the feature films about *shtetl* life made during the interwar years in Eastern Europe and the United States. These films offer the most elaborately realized mediations of the *shtetl* made before the Holocaust. Often based on stage or literary works, these features provide visions of provincial Jewish life rooted in established conventions of its representation, while remediating this accumulation of characters, narratives, sounds, and images through the new medium of motion pictures. As film critic J. Hoberman notes, these films are inherently "Janus-faced"; both progressive and retrospective, they hover "between two worlds" artistically as well as culturally.[94]

Made in the United States, Austria, Poland, and the Soviet Union, interwar Yiddish films reflect the range of notions of the *shtetl* in these different centers of Jewish life. The 1923 silent film *Ost und West* (East and West), made in Austria and released in the United States with Yiddish and English intertitles, preserves Picon's earliest extant screen performance. The film portrays a wealthy American Jewish immigrant's return to his native *shtetl* in Galicia, accompanied by his headstrong, American-born daughter, played by Picon. Within the genre of romantic comedy, *Ost und West* portrays a complex of Jewish culture clashes—pious, though narrow-minded and inhibited *shtetl* Jews versus boorish, frivolous, and wanton American Jewish parvenus, as well as primitive, "oriental" hasidim versus sophisticated, cosmopolitan Viennese Jews. In both contests, *shtetl* Jews are depicted as exotic, atavistic figures, objects of ethnographic curiosity and, ultimately, of anti-nostalgic mockery.[95]

After a spate of early American silent shorts, made between 1908 and 1918, depicting pogroms against East European Jews, the *shtetl* appears as a locus of Old World poverty and prejudice in the occasional Hollywood feature-length film of the 1920s, notably *Hungry Hearts* (the 1922 adaptation of Anzia Yezierska's eponymous novel) and *Broken Hearts* (1926). Like much immigrant Jewish literature of the early twentieth century, these films juxtapose *shtetl* life against both immigrant aspirations and the challenges posed by life in America.[96] Silent films made in Soviet Russia in the mid-1920s depict the *shtetl* as epitomizing a Jewish way of life that Marxism would transform. They include the documentary *Evrei na zemle* (Jews on the Land, 1925) as well as adaptations of major works of Yiddish and Russian fiction: *Skvos slezy* (Through Tears, 1925, based on Sholem Aleichem's *Motl Peysi dem khazns*), *Evreiskoie shchastie* (Jewish Luck, 1925, adapted from Sholem Aleichem's *Menakhem-Mendl*), and *Benya Krik* (1926, based on stories about the title character by Isaac Babel, who also wrote the screenplay). These films were produced by the state-run studio VUFKU (All-Ukrainian Photo-Cinema Administration), which continued throughout the silent era to make films about Jewish life in the final days of the Russian Empire and early days of the Soviet Union. Among these films are *shtetl* melodramas that examine class conflict within the Jewish community—*Zemlia zovet* (The Land Is Calling, 1928), *Glaza katorie videli* (Eyes That Saw, 1928)—or repudiate antisemitism, such as *Kvartaly predmestia* (Suburban Quarters, 1930).[97]

With the advent of sound motion pictures, Yiddish cinema's brief heyday in the late 1930s produced a spate of *shtetl* dramas made on both sides of the Atlantic. Yiddish films shot in Poland that are set in *shtetlekh* range from romantic musical comedy (Joseph Green's *Yidl mitn fidl* [Yidl with His Fiddle, 1936], starring Picon) to gothic tragedy (Michał Waszyński's 1937 film version of *Der dibek*). Whereas these features were shot, at least in part, on location in Polish towns, American Yiddish films staged *shtetl* life either in studios or on location in rural Pennsylvania, Long Island, or New Jersey—where, for example, Edgar Ulmer shot *Yankl der shmid* (Yankl the Blacksmith, 1938) on a set that he also used for a Ukrainian film, *Cossacks in Exile*. American Yiddish films typically depicted *shtetl* life with nostalgic affection for a bygone way of life recalled as ethnic heritage. Some of these films portray the *shtetl*'s cultural and moral integrity as trumping urban or immigrant Jewish life. Thus, in the 1937 musical *Dem khazns zindl* (The Cantor's Son) the protagonist, played by Yiddish theater star-cum-cantor Moishe Oysher, rejects success on the American Yiddish stage for the life of a cantor back in his Old World hometown. Only occasionally do these films address the *shtetl*'s limits, most notably in Ulmer's 1939 film *Di klyatshe* (The Mare, also known in English as *The Light Ahead*), based largely on Sholem Yankev Abramovitsh's *Fishke der krumer* (Fishke the Cripple). To dramatize this late maskilic novel, which decried *shtetl* life as superstitious, narrow-minded, and divided by internal class conflict, Ulmer staged the film on angular sets that recall the aesthetics of European expressionism. At the same time, *Di klyatshe* voices heartfelt fears for the future of these communities in "agonized monologues," delivered by Isidore Cashier in the role of Mendele the Bookseller, "on the dangers faced by the Jews of Eastern Europe." As Hoberman notes, these speeches were powerfully resonant with European politics on the eve of World War II.[98]

By the mid-1930s, *shtetl* life was increasingly represented as imperiled, at the mercy of larger political forces—even in works not set in the present. Isaac Bashevis Singer's 1935 debut novel, *Sotn in Gorey* (Satan in

Goraj), recounts a seventeenth-century Jewish community's descent into mass hysteria in the wake of the fervor surrounding Shabetai Zevi's purported messianism. Literature scholar Ruth Wisse argues that the novel can be read as an allegory that obliquely critiques the "failed messianism" of "revolutionary ecstasies" embraced by some Jews in the first decades of the twentieth century.[99] In Hebrew novels published in the 1930s about *shtetlekh* destroyed during World War I—Yehuda Yaari's *Ka-or yahel* (Like a Dazzling Light, 1937) and S. Y. Agnon's *Oreah natah la-lun* (A Guest for the Night, 1938–1939)—Zionism figures as the only hope for the vanquished *shtetl*. Thus, in Agnon's novel, the narrator brings the key that opens the *besmedresh* of Shibush (the author's encrypted name for his actual hometown of Buczacz) to Jerusalem as a symbolic act of redemption for diaspora Jewry.[100]

Responding to the worsening political and economic circumstances of the late 1930s, portraits of *shtetl* life as endangered both echoed images of destroyed towns created in the wake of World War I and were soon read as prophetic in ways unimagined by their creators. A case in point is Mordecai Gebirtig's song "Undzer shtetl brent" (Our Town Is Burning), composed in 1936, following a highly publicized outbreak of anti-Jewish violence in the Polish town of Przytyk. During World War II the song became something of an anthem, mourning the ongoing destruction of European Jewry; since the war, "Undzer shtetl brent" has remained a fixture of Holocaust remembrance.[101] Similarly, Roman Vishniac's photographs of Jewish life in East European towns and cities, taken during the late 1930s at the request of the American Jewish Joint Distribution Committee for use in public relations campaigns to raise awareness of Jews suffering economic and political persecution, became documents of "a world that might soon cease to exist," according to the photographer's own postwar accounts.[102]

From the 1880s until World War II, growing numbers of Jews who never lived in or even visited these communities engaged *shtetlekh* with increasing frequency through texts, performances, and works of visual culture. Symbolic engagements with the *shtetl* flourished during this period due to a rapidly growing and dispersing Jewish population. By 1939, there were an estimated eleven million Yiddish speakers worldwide, about half of them living outside of Eastern Europe. Complicating the *shtetl*'s expansive mediation was the presence of millions of Jews still residing in Eastern Europe's provincial towns, increasingly mindful of the continued difficulties of living in these locales and of the promise of a better, "newer" life somewhere else.

Inherent in this development is a defining paradox: with greater distance, the *shtetl* became a more potent symbolic presence in modern

Jewish life, whether admired by Jews seeking to claim an East European cultural patrimony or disparaged by people committed to remaking these environments (the Soviet Union) or their Jewish inhabitants (both Soviets and Zionists). More than a social geography, the *shtetl* had become a public idea, widely familiar and increasingly mediated through new cultural practices that could unite or divide Jews in new configurations. These diverse notions of the *shtetl* demonstrate that its conceptualization was neither straightforward nor simply utilitarian. Alongside public notions of the *shtetl* were private ones that often complicated or contradicted more familiar images, while remaining largely unknown.

Even the grimmest prewar visions of the *shtetl's* demise did not anticipate the intensity, vastness, and brutality of the Holocaust. Within larger postwar efforts of mourning and memorializing Jewish victims of Nazism, Jews initiated a new era of engaging individual towns or the *shtetl* in general. Even as they drew upon the substantial foundation of prewar engagements, post-Holocaust efforts forged a new relationship with these towns. No longer a place Jews left behind, whether voluntarily or otherwise, the *shtetl* was now a paradigmatic locus of communality understood as abruptly appropriated from Jewish experience and brutally annihilated.

Beginning immediately after the end of World War II and continuing into the twenty-first century, Jews have commemorated prewar *shtetl* life in a surge of memoir literature, including both individual autobiographies and collaboratively produced *yizker-bikher*, published by the hundreds in the Americas, Europe, and Israel. Alongside this literature are films and audio- and videotaped oral histories documenting Jews' memories of prewar life in *shtetlekh*, as well as works of visual art in which former *shtetl* residents depict both personal recollections and representative genre scenes from their prewar hometowns. Some former *shtetl* residents have devoted much of their postwar lives to memorializing their towns' Jewish past in multiple projects.

Concomitant with the memory practices of former *shtetl* residents are the engagements of other people with individual *shtetlekh* or the *shtetl* as an archetype in the mode of postmemory—that is, what literature scholar Marianne Hirsch characterizes as "a very particular form of memory precisely because its connection to its object or source is mediated."[103] Postmemory of the *shtetl* predates World War II. But prewar mediations of *shtetl* life existed in a relationship, if an imagined one, with an ongoing actuality that could at least in theory authenticate or challenge these representations. After the Holocaust, *shtetl* mediations exist without any such touchstone. The genocide overtakes notions of the *shtetl* as living, albeit abjectly or in decline. What shifts, then, is the relationship of postmemory to memory. The loss of the remembered *shtetl* leaves its postmemory bereft of its defining referent. This shift distinguishes post-Holocaust engagements with the *shtetl*, diverse as they are, forging yet another new kind of relationship with this locus.

The *shtetl* has long been engaged not simply as a social geography in which East European Jews lived alongside their non-Jewish neighbors but as a social space to think with—akin to Walter Benjamin's nineteenth-century arcades, Jürgen Habermas's eighteenth-century coffeehouses, or, to cite a Jewish example, Louis Wirth's ghetto.[104] But whereas these were all individual intellectual projects (at least initially), conceived with broad implications for Western culture, thinking with the *shtetl* has been a widely shared vernacular activity, largely undertaken as a means of Jewish self-realization. Participants in this activity have included people living in these provincial East European towns, former residents, visitors, as well as people with no direct experience of these places. For the most part, this undertaking has not been an academic exercise. Scholarship comes relatively late to the *shtetl* and has had, ultimately, a limited impact on its conceptualization. Rather, engaging the *shtetl* has mostly been a subjective, often imaginative, impassioned, and at times explicitly polemical activity. It is the scholar's challenge to acknowledge—and to respect, even while critiquing—the difference between the agendas of most of these engagements and an academic method.

This task calls for rethinking scholarly approaches to the *shtetl*, especially those that look askance at vernacular engagements with the subject. Some historians seek to retrieve the actuality of Jewish life in provincial East European towns from its popular discourse. Conversely, literature scholars often privilege the *shtetl* as a creative construct and evaluate its mediations according to aesthetic criteria, thereby usually derogating works deemed sentimental or stereotypical rather than striving to understand them in their own right. Studying the *shtetl* as a site of Jewish vernacularity requires approaching "phenomenon" and "concept" not as opposed but as inherently interdependent rubrics. At the same time, their interrelation is not straightforward, especially as shifting notions of what constitutes the vernacular in Jewish life have rendered the *shtetl* increasingly unfamiliar, exemplified by postvernacular use of the term *shtetl* itself.

As a case study in Jewish vernacularity, examining the *shtetl* entails addressing a series of intellectual challenges. First, the relationship of the *shtetl* to historical time is often problematized, especially in discussions of East European Jewish encounters with modernity. Jewish settlements in these provincial towns began as an early modern proving ground, only to yield to newer forms of modernity, so that Jewish life in *shtetlekh* came to be regarded as vestigial. A consequence of this dynamic is temporal slippage between the *shtetl* as a subject of discourse and the actuality of East European Jewish life. Antony Polonsky notes that images of the *shtetl* in modern Jewish literature tend to be retrospective—for example, dwelling on the figure of the Polish nobleman well after this aristocracy had faded from the scene as a political force.[105] Conversely, there are works, such as An-ski's *Der dibek* or Gebirtig's "Undzer shtetl brent," that come to be seen as prescient of the *shtetl*'s dissolution and demise. This slippage continues, as the Jewish past sometimes overwhelms encounters with present-day life in East European towns where Jewish communities once thrived. Thus, historian Glenn Dynner describes a visit to present-day Kock, once the seat of the Kotsker rebbe: "I felt my mind was playing tricks on me—mournful strains of a Hasidic melody (*niggun*) seemed to drift along the breeze. But on closer inspection, the sounds were real. They were coming from the Catholic mass."[106]

In tandem with this temporal slippage is a spatial disparity, as engaging the *shtetl* entails shifting dimensions of physical distance from the subject. The challenges posed by this disparity are also tied to articulating the *shtetl*'s relationship to the modern, in which distance played a defining role. Just as it was possible to seek intellectual distance from the *shtetl* while still living in a provincial East European town, champions of the *shtetl* as a redoubt of an authentically premodern Jewish culture often did so at some remove. This distance, originally more intellectual than geographic, increased over time and eventually traversed continents. Following World War II, this remove also spanned the intractable breach of genocide. Distance shapes engagements with *shtetlekh* even when visiting these sites. These travels have long been described as journeying "back"—including trips undertaken by first-time visitors. (In this regard, the *shtetl*'s conceptualization diverges from that of other important Jewish sites, notably the modern State of Israel, which was constructed around the Zionist rubric of an elevated ingathering well before it came into existence and is still understood in these terms, even by many Jews moving away from it.) These temporal and spatial disparities reveal the extent to which the familiarity and ordinariness of the *shtetl*, as the epitome of Jewish vernacular culture, has been displaced. Rather than view these disparities as inherently problematic, they are better understood as defining the values invested in the *shtetl* as a fountainhead of vernacularity. It is precisely these disparities that compel so many people to undertake journeys, actual and imagined, striving to breach the distance between these towns and themselves.

Current scholarship on the *shtetl* centers on challenges that in themselves call for interrogation. First, there is no consensus, scholarly or otherwise, as to what constitutes a *shtetl* in terms of population size, location, or other criteria, in part because the nature of these towns ranges widely and shifts over time. Indeed, if anything defines them, it is their intermediate status—diminutive in relation to cities, larger and distinctly urban in relation to nearby rural settlements. Moreover, what comes to be codified as *shtetl* life is characterized by other kinds of between-ness: in its traditional social order, town residents were situated between the nobility and the peasantry; these towns constituted a strategic social and cultural meeting place between Jews and Christians; the nature of the towns' original economy, and especially Jews' role in it, hovered between the feudal and the industrial; Jewish community life in Eastern Europe before World War I existed somewhere between subjection and autonomy, and so on. The *shtetl*'s contingent, intermediary nature should be seen as a core feature and, moreover, as key to understanding the *shtetl*'s ongoing value as a locus of Jewish vernacularity. The difficulty of defining the *shtetl* should not be regarded as an intellectual obstacle but as an opportunity for gaining insight into what has been at stake when attempting to do so. Both the undertaking and the difficulty are symptoms of modernity, confronting the challenges posed by a vernacular sensibility in which establishing such criteria is irrelevant. Moreover, the ambiguous nature of the *shtetl* has afforded great flexibility to its cultural engagement—indeed, its power as a cultural icon lies, to a considerable extent, in its amorphousness.

Much recent scholarship on the subject also voices concern that the *shtetl* has been conceptualized as centrally, if not exclusively, Jewish, notwithstanding the more diverse demography of these towns. Jews are neither the only ones to claim *shtetlekh* as Jewish sites nor have they done so consistently; non-Jews may regard individual towns or the region in which they are found as Jewish phenomena (e.g., the notion of Poland as Paradisus Judaeorum—the "Jews' Paradise"—so termed by their Christian neighbors in response to the flourishing of provincial Jewish life there in the sixteenth century).[107] Recent scholarship often critiques popular representations of *shtetl* life as problematically selective in their elision of non-Jews. But it is worth considering what motivates this widespread impulse to portray these towns as a saliently Jewish locus, for it is both a key aspect of vernacular engagement with the *shtetl* and a discursive strategy adopted by many modern writers and artists. This portrayal may, for example, have served to repudiate the frequent denigration or omission of Jews' presence in the European landscape by others. Thus, Sholem Aleichem wrote in 1904 of the Jews of Kasrilevke:

> However small and poor and alone and remote it may be, [Kasrilevke] is still tied to the rest of the world, as if by some sort of wire, which, if you tap it at one end can soon be felt at the other end! . . . Why, then, does Kasrilevke feel the troubles and pains of everyone else in the world, and no one whatsoever feels the pain of Kasrilevke? No one whatsoever takes any interest in Kasrilevke? Kasrilevke is something of the world's stepchild, and if it were, heaven forbid, to come into misfortune, . . . no one, you can be sure, would notice.[108]

The discourse of the *shtetl*'s Jewishness associates this locus, if sometimes implicitly, with Yiddish. Jews, of course, spoke Yiddish elsewhere and spoke other languages in these towns. In the decades before World War II, those who championed Yiddish envisioned it as a Jewish national language with the capacity to be cosmopolitan, a vehicle of both mass and highbrow culture for an international diaspora increasingly centered in cities. At the same time, shifts in Jews' language use away from Yiddish to other vernaculars informed its symbolic value, increasingly associated, whether positively or negatively, with provincial Eastern Europe as its heartland.

After the Holocaust, equating the *shtetl* with Yiddish became even more prominent, epitomizing signal shifts in the language's use as a postvernacular. As I have noted elsewhere, in the postwar era "the tautology of language, culture, and people that [Yiddish] once evoked for the majority of world Jewry is no more. However, far from devaluing Yiddish, the undoing of this tautology has transformed the very nature of the language's worth, often endowing it with greater significance and, at times, with higher esteem than it enjoyed before World War II." Thus, on one hand, the meaning of the term *shtetl* in the postvernacular mode has become more particularized, referencing not just any town but a prewar East European Jewish community. On the other hand, *shtetl* has acquired greater significance as a metonym for a bygone way of life and for values—intimacy, communality, piety, provinciality, insularity, rootedness—variously associated with it. Moreover, postvernacular Yiddish is distinguished by a self-consciousness that "may mark it as suspect in the eyes of some observers, as a painful consequence of the loss of an 'automatic' traditional vernacularity, or even as inimical to 'authentic' *yidishkeyt* [Jewishness]." However, this deliberateness might also be seen as "a development that . . . enables and enhances, rather than hinders, cultural innovation."[109] The postvernacular value of the term *shtetl* epitomizes this development.

Spanning the divergent understandings of the significance of the *shtetl* is a desire to engage its displaced vernacularity. The tension across these engagements, especially between freewheeling popular notions of the *shtetl* and the deliberate efforts to situate this locus in an actuality, not only complicates but also enriches and animates the value invested in the *shtetl*. Nowhere is this tension more evident or paid more attention than in scholarship on the *shtetl*, and its intellectual history is the subject of the next chapter.

2 *Forsht ayer shtetl!*

In the history of Jewish studies, scholarship on the *shtetl* per se is a relatively recent phenomenon, coalescing in the early twentieth century and flourishing in the post–World War II era. Explicit study of the *shtetl* follows an extensive and varied precedent of writing about Jews in East European provincial towns that dates back at least to the seventeenth century. This chapter examines the intellectual history of non-belletristic writing about *shtetlekh*, broadly defined, in order to track both the evolving understanding of the topic and the dynamics of this writing as a practice of self-scrutiny for Jews and others.

Although the advent of modern scholarship effects noteworthy changes in writing about *shtetlekh*, these developments are not completely separate from earlier efforts. Rather, much scholarship on the *shtetl* up to the present interrelates devotional or communally affirmative motives, which are typical of early writing about *shtetlekh*, with modern projects of scholarly documentation and empirical analysis. This tension between methods and agendas is emblematic of a larger phenomenon in Jewish studies, in which scholars often strive to produce work that is not dispassionate but rather is forthrightly engagé. Scholarly writing on the *shtetl* therefore entails a complex, dynamic engagement with vernacularity. Beyond informing what aspects of provincial East European Jewish life scholars examine and how they do so, this engagement reflects changing valuations of the vernacular culture of the *shtetl*, whether in relation to intellectual or "high" culture, political ideologies, or other, newer vernacular practices.

Early Writings

During the early modern period, Jewish communities in East European towns produced an indigenous local historiography in the form of *pinkeysim*. These chronicles were usually maintained by a local *kohol* or a particular society, such as a *khevre kdishe*, to document events of note as they happened. As the Jewish counterpart to records kept by municipal authorities, *pinkeysim* enabled East European Jews to document local history on their own terms and in their own languages. The volumes in which these chronicles were written were prized objects and believed by some Jews to have magical powers.[1]

Whereas *pinkeysim* recorded ongoing activity incrementally, accounts of the massacres of thousands of Jews in dozens of towns during the Ukrainian uprisings of 1648–1649 offer crafted narratives of the past. Historian Adam Teller observes that these texts evince a shift in established practices of remembering other attacks on Jewish communities, departing from the composition of *piyyutim* (liturgical poems), which were recited as part of ritual days of remembrance for these persecutions. *Piyyutim* typically situate the particular events being remembered within a panhistoric recollection of Jewish suffering. Offering little in the way of specifics, these poems emphasize what the commemorated events have in common with earlier tragedies. By contrast, Jewish narratives of the Ukrainian uprisings center on particular incidents, times, and places. Written in prose, these accounts were not incorporated into liturgical practices but circulated through a new East European Jewish print culture. Though these accounts are more specific in their historicity, their reach was broader, establishing remembrance of the massacres of 1648–1649 within a regional network of communities.

The best known of these accounts, *Yeven metsulah* (Abyss of Despair) by Natan Neta of Hannover, narrates these attacks in a series of episodes, each set in a different town. Unlike *pinkeysim*, which chronicle single localities, Hannover's text concerns a region, defined not merely by geography but by a common experience and, moreover, a shared remembrance. Rather than recounting individual attacks within an overarching chronology, *Yeven metsulah* offers each episode as an exemplar of a different kind of martyrdom.[2] Towns serve both as sites where atrocities took place and as narrative units, rooting the martyrology in a particular time and place as well as using this geography to articulate a typology of Jewish responses to persecution. Though the chronicle offers some early history of individual communities, more telling is the establishment of towns as landmarks of remembrance reaching beyond these locales. Thus, Teller argues, *Yeven metsulah* conceptualizes the Jews of Eastern Europe as distinct among other Jewish communities.[3]

East European Jewish intellectuals' turn toward modern scholarship during the late eighteenth century did not engender studies of their own history, especially in provincial towns. Though *maskilim* advocated pursuing a modern Western education, this did not entail applying its methodologies to their own milieu. On the contrary, the Haskalah directed Jews' intellectual life beyond the *shtetl*. *Maskilim* did devote considerable attention to *shtetl* life, but largely through non-scholarly forms of writing, especially satire, as noted in chapter 1, and memoir. Far from viewing *shtetlekh* as subjects worthy of scholarly analysis, *maskilim* skewed the notion of studying the *shtetl* in works of what literature scholar Dan Miron terms "anti-folklore," which offer mock disquisitions on *shtetl* mores as if the very notion that they were worthy of intellection is risible.[4]

The memoir became a major genre of Haskalah literature, in which *maskilim* chronicled their intellectual development as a prototype for fellow Jews. Like *pinkeysim*, some of these memoirs later emerged as important resources for scholarship on the *shtetl*, a frequent setting of these works. Maskilic memoirs might also be considered a kind of indigenous historiography, in which the subject is not the traditional Jewish community but the evolving modern Jewish self. The emplotment of these memoirs tracks personal development through a series of challenges and revelations that provide readers with an exemplary or cautionary tale for scrutinizing their own lives. Because of their self-reflexive nature, maskilic memoirs configure their authors' environments according to different strategies that support the exposition of personal development.

Among the earliest East European Jewish memoirists of the maskilic period is Dov Ber Birkenthal of Bolechów, a wine merchant and amateur Jewish historian. Birkenthal's memoir was written in Hebrew sometime in the final decade of the eighteenth century, shortly before his death in 1805. Though Birkenthal's motive for writing his memoir is not known, historian Gershon Hundert observes that its "value as an historical source is, by now, incontestable."[5] Birkenthal's narrative shifts from personal and family history to discussions of larger topics, such as the instability of the Polish monarchy in the mid- to late 1700s. Though at one point he does describe the text as being, in part, "the narration of what was happening in our community in Bolechow,"[6] Birkenthal does not relate the local Jewish community's history in a systematic way. Rather, as the memoir chronicles Birkenthal's life experiences, it follows his itinerant career as a merchant to other locales in eastern Galicia and Hungary, where he traveled frequently to purchase wines. In his narrative, Bolechów serves as the social and geographic center of Birkenthal's activities and, perhaps, his thinking. The town figures as the node from which his extensive interactions with non-Jews and with Jews in other locations radiate, rooting the author's journeys and disquisitions in his cultural as well as geographic home.

By contrast, Solomon Maimon's *Lebensgeshichte* (Autobiography, 1792–1793) positions the author's youth in Poland (he was raised near Nieśwież) as the point of departure for his life's journey, moving from the traditional Jewish world of Eastern Europe to the Haskalah in Berlin. Extended descriptions of provincial East European Jewish life anchor the memoir's polemic. The narrative traces Maimon's intellectual development, which parallels his coming of age and his travel from East to West.

The author's fraught portrait of his childhood milieu serves as the base from which Maimon's realizations of his intellectual ambitions (as well as frustrations) are to be measured. *Maskilim* hailed Maimon's *Lebensgeshichte*, which was written in German, as advocating Christian Germans' acceptance of modernized Jews and the reform of East European Jewry. Later scholars championed this work as the "first modern Jewish autobiography,"[7] which provided a model for subsequent generations of Jews' personal narratives, especially those in which provincial East European Jewish life serves as the foil for the authors' transformation through secular education and urban life. Among these autobiographies are Mordekhai Aharon Gintsburg's *Avi'ezer* (published posthumously in 1863) and, most famously, Moses Leib Lilienblum's *Hat'ot ne'urim* (Sins of Youth, 1873).[8]

The earliest modern scholarly studies of Jews in Eastern Europe, appearing in the latter half of the nineteenth century, generally paid scant attention to provincial life per se. The first historians of East European Jewry, including both non-Jews and assimilationist Jews, were primarily concerned with studying the Jewish past in order to advocate for Jewish emancipation and integration into a political and cultural mainstream.[9] Studying Jewish life in provincial Eastern Europe as a topic in its own right required both a recognition of its value and a commitment to gathering primary research materials. Among the first individuals to do so was an amateur historian with a strong commitment to local Jewish communal life—the author, book dealer, bibliographer, and activist Ephraim Deinard, who collected documents from Jewish communities during his extensive travels throughout Eastern Europe in the 1870s.[10] A decade later, Simon Dubnow, a pioneering figure in modern East European Jewish historiography, initiated calls for the organized, institutional collection of documents pertaining to Jewish life throughout the region. For Dubnow, individual communities exemplified a Jewish national culture, which called for a historiography that narrated Jews' social and political life on a grand scale. From studying records of local Jewish communities throughout Eastern Europe, Dubnow argued that their activities realized an autonomous internal governance equivalent to a national system.[11] Dubnow envisioned both collection efforts and scholarship as projects of defining value for East European Jewry as a national entity, for whom the study of history and a historically informed consciousness would serve as the secular equivalent of religious tradition, inspiring modern Jewish politics and culture.

Historians studying local East European Jewish communities typically focused not on smaller towns but on major cities, which had become important centers of Jewish life in the region. These studies include

Shmuel Yosef Fuenn's pioneering history of Jewish life in Vilna, *Kiryah ne'emanah* (The Loyal City, 1860), as well as the early work of a generation of East European Jewish historians whom Dubnow had inspired, such as Majer Bałaban's *Żydzi lwowoscy na przełomie XVIgo i XVIIgo wieku* (The Jews of Lvov at the Turn of the Sixteenth and Seventeenth Centuries, 1906). These efforts reflect larger trends in nineteenth- and early-twentieth-century historiography in Europe, which as a rule paid little attention to small communities and marginalized populations in favor of elite figures, major events, and leading political and cultural centers.

In response to modern Jewish historiography, Orthodox Jews in Eastern Europe began writing their own works of history, centered on chronicling the lives of religious leaders. Even as these works presented a counter-narrative of the East European Jewish past, they emulated some of the formal features of secular historiography, including its predilection for writing about great men and major urban centers. Though details of provincial Jewish life can be gleaned from some of these works, especially hasidic hagiographies of *rebeyim*, these authors did not directly address the subject in their works.[12]

Thus, scholarship on Jewish Eastern Europe at the turn of the twentieth century generally ignored provincial communities—or, if these were addressed, cited them as a model of abjection. Consider, for example, the following passage from Leo Wiener's landmark study of nineteenth-century Yiddish literature, published in 1899:

> The beginning of this century found the Jews of the Russian Empire living in a state bordering on Asiatic barbarism. Ages of persecution had reduced the masses to the lowest condition of existence. . . . Incredibly dirty in their houses and uncleanly about their persons, ignorant and superstitious, . . . they presented a sad spectacle of a downtrodden race. . . . One need only go at this late hour to some small town, away from the railroads and highways, where Jews live together compactly, in order to get an idea of what the whole of Russia was a century ago, for in those distant places people are still living as their grandfathers did.[13]

Shortly after Wiener's study was published, some of the authors it discusses offered a markedly different valuation of the *shtetl* in their writings, especially as they turned to autobiography and reflected on the provincial towns in which they had spent their formative years. In the early twentieth century, Jewish authors more often depicted *shtetlekh* as the locus of a bygone communal existence that should not be deprecated but appreciated, if at a distance. Among the first to do so was poet and critic Avraham Ya'akov Paperna, who published a memoir of his childhood and youth in the Belorussian town of Kapyl (also the hometown of Sholem Yankev

Abramovitsh) in the Russian Jewish annual *Perezhitoe* (The Past) in 1910 and 1911.[14]

The landmark work of this type is Yekhezkel Kotik's *Mayne zikhroynes* (My Memoirs, 1913–1914). Like Maimon, Kotik chronicles larger changes in Jewish life, as the author, a popular restaurateur and community activist in Warsaw, looked back from this urban vantage at the age of sixty-five to his mid-nineteenth-century childhood in the town of Kamenets-Podolsk. Yet whereas Maimon's hometown serves as the author's intellectual point of departure, Kamenets-Podolsk figures as "the spatial axis" of Kotik's memoir and, notes historian David Assaf, as a "microcosm . . . of Eastern European Jewish history."[15]

Writing in Yiddish, Kotik addressed a mass readership in its vernacular, which by then had become the vehicle for a modern Jewish literature of unprecedented scope. This use of a shared vernacular echoed the memoirist's assumption that he described a widely familiar experience of growing up in "a typical small town," in which Jewish life was central not only demographically—in the late nineteenth century, Jews were the majority population in Kamenets-Podolsk—but also culturally (Kotik also characterizes settlements like Kamenets-Podolsk as "*yidishe shtetlekh*"—"Jewish towns").[16] At the same time, Kotik acknowledges that this common experience was removed in time and further distanced by the consequences of modernity—in particular, immigration and increased antisemitism. One could add to these the consequences of moving to large cities, which Kotik exemplified, and a new cultural self-consciousness about this localized past as something lost, to be retrieved through narrative.

Kotik's memoirs were admired by leading Yiddish writers of the day, some of whom were simultaneously writing about their own provincial childhoods in more deliberately literary works. During this period, each of the three "classic" Yiddish writers of Eastern Europe published autobiographical works: Sholem Yankev Abramovitsh's *Shloyme Reb Khayems* (written intermittently between 1894 and 1914, and also appearing more or less simultaneously in Hebrew under the titles *Ba-yamim ha-hem* [In Those Days] and *Haye Shlomo* [The Life of Solomon]), Y. L. Peretz's *Mayne zikhroynes* (1913–1914), and Sholem Aleichem's *Funem yarid* (From the Fair, 1913–1916). Like Kotik, these three authors revisited their provincial childhoods from the vantage of an advanced age in a major city: Odessa, Warsaw, New York. As literature scholar Jan Schwarz notes in his study of Yiddish autobiography, these works use *shtetlekh* as both geographical and cultural settings for narratives centered on their authors' emergence as writers, for whom *shtetl* life served as a prime subject of literary attention "as both insider and outsider."[17]

Activist Scholarship

The first scholarly efforts to document contemporary Jewish life in provincial Eastern Europe as a subject in its own right were not works of dispassionate research undertaken as ends in themselves. Rather, they were produced by activists committed to improving or transforming East European Jewish life in some way—whether demonstrating the worthiness of Jewish folkways as the basis of an indigenous national culture, creating new works of modern culture, or enhancing East European Jewish life by alleviating poverty, expanding educational opportunities, or combatting antisemitism. Though wide-ranging in subject and methodology, these efforts are all works of applied, engaged scholarship.

A noteworthy early example is an 1890 expedition to collect statistics on Jews living in provincial towns in Congress Poland. This mission—underwritten by Jan Bloch, a financier and economist who, though a convert to Catholicism, remained a dedicated Jewish philanthropist—was intended to mitigate accusations that Jews were economic parasites and draft evaders. Among those collecting statistics was Y. L. Peretz, then a young Jewish writer and socialist activist. Peretz wrote about his experiences on this mission in *Bilder fun a provints-rayze in tomashover povyat um 1890 yor* (Scenes from a Provincial Journey in the Tomaszów District in 1890). This prose narrative recounts the challenges Peretz faced as an urban, secularized Jew visiting Tyszowce, Łaszczów, and other towns in the region. There, local Jews, some of whom suspected the writer of being a government agent, flouted or ignored his efforts to collect demographic and economic data. Gradually, Peretz's narrative shifts to an account of these Jewish communities' dissolution through impoverishment, infighting, immigration, and moral decline. Several years after this work's initial publication in 1891, Peretz added an ending that offers an otherworldly portrait of a "dead town," where ghosts of deceased Jews gradually replace a declining population of the living. All other records of Bloch's expedition having been lost, Peretz's haunting narrative remains its sole legacy.[18]

Among the earliest extant statistical studies of Jews in a small town in Eastern Europe is "Statistikah shel 'ayarah ahat" (Statistics of One Town), a 1903 article by Jakob Lestschinsky, published under a pen name in the Hebrew journal *Ha-Shiloah*. Perhaps anticipating readers' skepticism about the worthiness of this undertaking, the author writes: "We know that there is no producing a comprehensive scholarly history of Jewish life in Russia according to any one small, insignificant town." However, he argues that—following the principles of biology, according to which one can extrapolate from isolated cells to the entire organism—it should be possible to use information from the many small towns in Russia "to understand the state of our people in general." Similarly, a note from the editor explains that the statistics on this town were collected not to produce a report on the location itself but to inform a general study.[19] (Lestschinsky eventually played a leading role in the statistical analysis of East European Jewish demography and economics.)[20]

Other researchers surveyed provincial East European Jewish communities not to address economic deficits but to celebrate cultural assets. This scholarship was initiated from without; as historian Kalman Weiser notes, the first people to collect Polish Jewish folkways were Poles, not Jews, beginning in the 1880s.[21] By the turn of the twentieth century, Jewish interest in collecting folklore coalesced among circles of urban intellectuals. A group of folklorists and musicians in St. Petersburg called for the documentation and study of Jewish folk music, eventually establishing the Society for Jewish Folk Music in 1908.[22] Scholars contributing to the Russian *Evreiskaia entsiklopediia* (Jewish Encyclopedia, 1906–1913) include pioneers in the study of Jewish folklore (S. An-ski), folk music (I. Kaplan), and art (Rachel Wischnitzer, née Bernstein, whose early work in the history of Jewish art includes studies of Polish and Russian synagogues).[23]

At the same time, a cadre of Jewish political and cultural activists based in Warsaw began to collect and publish examples of Yiddish folklore—stories, sayings, verses, riddles, and the like. These researchers regarded folklore as key to establishing a new Jewish national culture in Eastern Europe, in which Yiddish played a strategic, and sometimes central, role as the common vernacular. Some Jewish folklorists regarded *shtetlekh* as the "breeding ground" of Yiddish folklore, but, as folklorist Itzik Gottesman observes, this was not the only rubric that informed their understanding of what distinguished "the folk" from other Jews and "folkways" from other forms of Jewish culture. These folklorists avidly collected material from urban informants as well as from Jews living in the provinces. As East European Jews did not have a peasant class, the focal population of classic European folkloristics, "Yiddish folklorists never questioned the 'folkness' of Jews in the urban centers" of Eastern Europe.[24]

Aspiring to authenticate Jewish culture within the rubric of folklore, these folklorists—who were often secular, cosmopolitan urbanites, educated in mainstream Russian or Polish culture—revalued provincial Jewish life. From their perspective, small towns and surrounding rural communities localized a longstanding, distinctive East European Jewish culture, given both the age of these settlements (some of which dated back to the late Middle Ages) and a prevailing notion that these places were largely unchanged by modernity. Precisely that which had once stigmatized *shtetlekh* as backwaters among urbanized Jews now distinguished these towns as heritage sites—even though they were often becoming vibrant local centers of modern secular culture, while cities were home to growing enclaves of traditionally observant Jews.

Individual towns were not, as a rule, of special interest to these folklorists; rather, they focused on the aggregate of Jewish communities and their collected lore. Amassing folklore materials was an important new cultural endeavor in itself, demonstrating a common culture on a grand scale. Nor did folklore collectors attend to the local context of how folkways figured in informants' daily life. (Indeed, the notion of extracting "folkways" from an integrated vernacular culture, where they are bound up with what might be distinguished as "religion," "commerce," or some other ostensibly discrete sphere of activity, is an inherently modern concept.) Rather, collectors viewed folklore as a means toward a new end: the fabrication of a modern Jewish culture, which would legitimate Jews as the equivalent of a nation, validate their longstanding presence in Eastern Europe, and demonstrate their ability to create works of "high" art, thereby contributing to modern Western culture.

This aspiration demanded the cultivation of skills—scholarly research and analysis—that were newly valued as definitional practices for modern Jews. These skills, in turn, required new institutions—libraries, archives, academies, museums, scholarly presses—and new authority figures: researchers, educators, librarians, archivists, curators, critics, editors, publishers. Within this new cultural economy, the practices identified as folkways were no longer autochthonic phenomena, transmitted mimetically—indeed, they were no longer meant to be part of daily life. Rather, they would become objects of intellection through modern modes of scholarship, pedagogy, exhibition, performance, and belles-lettres. The scholarly scrutiny of provincial Jewish life, which *maskilim* had portrayed as a risible notion in literary works of mock erudition, became a project in earnest.

This new cultural economy situated *shtetlekh* less as subjects of interest in themselves than as sites for gathering material that would inform projects of political action and cultural innovation. Much as the provinces provided raw goods from the countryside to urban centers and foreign lands, provincial Jewish communities provided "raw" folkways for "export." Although provincial Jews supplied these cultural resources, they required urban-based scholars, writers, composers, curators, performers, and artists to process the raw goods—into books, articles, plays, artworks, exhibitions, compositions, and the like—for consumption by a modern Jewish constituency of middle-class urbanites (and those aspiring to this stature) as well as by non-Jewish cosmopolitanites.

This cultural disparity between urban and provincial Jews in Eastern Europe emerged as a defining rubric in some of the first scholarly attention to cultural work about the *shtetl*. In 1911, Baal-Makhshoves (né Israel Isidor Elyashev), considered the first significant Yiddish literary critic, published a pioneering essay titled "Dray shtetlekh" (Three Towns). Baal-Makhshoves declares the provincial town the basis of Yiddish literature, parallel to the central role of the city in West European belles-lettres and the rural village in Russian writing. At the same time, he notes, "Today's Jew is no longer a provincial [*kleyn-shtetldiker*]," and, as a result of mass urbanization and immigration, especially by the young, Jewish life in small towns "is dying. In a few generations, it will only exist as a historical remembrance." Nevertheless, Yiddish writers, both new and established, "have not escaped from this milieu," which stands "at the center of their creative fantasies." Baal-Makhshoves then offers a comparative reading of Peretz's *Bilder fun a provints-rayze* and the *shtetl* novellas of Sholem Asch and I. M. Weissenberg (discussed in chapter 1), proclaiming them "the best artistic tombstone for provincial Jewish life."[25] The critic configures the *shtetl*'s imminent demise as not simply an inevitable consequence of modernization but a foundational transformation for Jewish life and culture, a notion others would iterate in their reflections on the *shtetl*'s changing meaning.

Early-twentieth-century efforts to document provincial East European Jewish folkways and convert them into works of modern scholarship and culture were most fully realized in the work of S. An-ski (the pen name of Shloyme Zaynvl Rapoport). Like Peretz and Dubnow, An-ski was equally interested in modern scholarship, cultural creativity, and social activism, which he regarded as integrated, rather than discrete, pursuits. Moreover, An-ski was similarly inspired by political, aesthetic, and intellectual models in the larger culture—in his case, Russia's *narodniki* (populists) and the politics of the Socialist Revolutionary Party.

With support from the Gintsburgs, a family of Jewish philanthropists in St. Petersburg, An-ski initiated what was then the most extensive and programmatic effort to collect East European Jewish folklore and related materials. This initiative entailed a series of expeditions by a small team of researchers, who visited some seventy locations in what are now Ukraine and Belarus, from 1912 until the start of World War I. These expeditions yielded thousands of texts (folktales, legends, lyrics), hundreds of musical examples (songs and melodies, some recorded on wax cylinders), manuscripts, examples of material culture, as well as photographs of architecture and other subjects. An-ski's collecting expedition was rooted in an elaborately conceived understanding of Jewish folkways, manifest both in extensive questionnaires for researchers to administer, which he had prepared in advance of the expedition, and in plans for future use of the collected materials in works of "high" art and public culture. The expedition conceptualized folkways in relation to modernist outcomes—artworks, musical compositions, literary publications, and theater pieces, exemplified by An-ski's own play *Der dibek* (discussed in chapter 1)—as well as a planned network of ethnographic and art museums throughout the western provinces of Russia and scholarship based at an institute for higher education.[26]

World War I both disrupted and repurposed An-ski's project. He shifted his efforts to aiding Jews under assault and documenting the wartime destruction of provincial Jewish communities, resulting in his book *Khurbn Galitsye* (The Destruction of Galicia), published posthumously in 1920. As Peretz had done in his *Bilder fun a provints-rayze*, An-ski treated these communities' dissolution as a subject of interest in its own right, albeit from a more radical political perspective, and he also addressed the limits of modern cultural aspirations to refashion Jewish life on the basis of collected folklore. An-ski's expeditions in the prewar years had centered on collectibles in the aggregate: visiting dozens of locations; amassing hundreds of examples of tales, songs, artifacts, etc.; compiling answers to a questionnaire with thousands of individual questions. Paradoxically, the wartime shift in An-ski's agenda focused his attention on individual Jewish communities, by dint of their persecution. *Khurbn Galitsye* recounted not only assaults on these communities but also how they responded to destruction. Destruction called new attention to these communities, and, as in *Yeven metsulah*, new narratives were created from their undoing. But whereas Hannover's account constructs a martyrology that affirms Jewish piety in the face of attack, An-ski's is a secular—and increasingly pessimistic—narrative. Though at first An-ski admired the Jewish resilience he witnessed in the face of persecution as ennobling, possessing "a severe beauty that transformed these human sorrows and sufferings into an epic tragedy," he eventually "no longer encountered the earlier sublime and beautiful drama. Tragedy was commonplace," and it left Eastern Europe's war-torn Jews in a degraded state.[27]

Looking Forward, Looking Back

Following World War I, new kinds of scholarship on the *shtetl* flourished, a consequence of threshold developments in East European Jewish life during the war's immediate aftermath. As citizens of newly constituted nations, these Jews had unprecedented opportunities to research and publish scholarship on European Jewry, past and present. Increasingly this work came from professionally trained scholars informed by current methodologies in the humanities and social sciences. Although important scholarship was still done by autodidacts, the interwar years witnessed the establishment of new academic institutions dedicated to the study of East European Jewish life. In Poland, these were independent entities, led by the Institute for Jewish Studies in Warsaw and the YIVO (acronym for Yidisher visnshaftlekher institut [Institute for Jewish Research]) in Vilna. In the USSR, these institutions were underwritten and regulated by the state. Much of this scholarship reflected the ideologies of new Jewish political agendas: the diaspora nationalism of Dubnow, the Folkism of linguist Noah Prylucki, the Labor Zionism of historian Emanuel Ringelblum, the Bundism of some YIVO scholars, the Marxism of scholars working in the Soviet Union.[28]

Scholarship on contemporary East European Jewry during the 1920s and 1930s reflected a pervasive sense that World War I had been an epochal watershed. Scrutiny of prewar life entailed new attention to *shtetlekh* as synecdoches of the war's devastating impact on East European Jews and their radically new postwar existence. Prewar attention to provincial Jewish life as a vestigial source of premodern folkways intensified, even as some scholars and activists studied these communities as proving grounds for a new, modern Jewish society. Regarded as longstanding repositories of local Jewish culture, *shtetlekh* acquired greater value as sites manifesting Jewish rootedness in an increasingly destabilized Eastern Europe. At the same time, this presence was contested, both from without by right-wing nationalist movements, notably in Poland in the late 1930s, and from within by Zionists. In addition to these ideological challenges, Jews' continued urbanization and immigration complicated the new esteem for the *shtetl*.

During the interwar years, East European Jewish scholars paid greater attention to provincial towns, reflecting growing interests in local history and the social sciences. At the University of Warsaw, historian Majer Bałaban held the only professorship in Jewish history in the Polish Republic, then home to Europe's largest Jewish population. Bałaban supervised dozens of master's theses, many of them local histories.[29] Studies of individual towns in interwar Poland also appeared idiosyncratically, the work of independent scholars or local communities. These studies reflect commitments both to contemporary scholarly methods and to enriching Jews' appreciation of local history as emblematic of their cultural tenacity. A case in point is "A litvish shtetl (in tsifern un lebn)" (A Lithuanian Town [in Numbers and Life]), a 1925 essay by Hirsz Abramowicz, an educator and community activist, who specialized in fostering vocational training for young Jews. His essay appeared among a series of reports of "ethnographic, statistical, and economic research" on local communities in the 1931 anthology *Af di khurves fun milkhomes un mehumes* (On the Ruins of Wars and Upheavals), issued by EKOPO, the Jewish Committee for the Relief of War Victims.[30] In the wake of the war's devastation, scholarship was mobilized by grassroots efforts to rehabilitate Polish Jewry.

Abramowicz characterizes his essay on Wysoki Dwór, a town he had known well since childhood, as a model case study: "The *shtetl* was the economic basis of East European Jewish life; it sustained us the way the village sustained Russian, Polish, and Lithuanian peasants. Until now, there have been few attempts to study the *shtetl*, as has been done, for example, with the Russian village, which has been analyzed comprehensively. I should like to make a beginning, in the hope that it will inspire others to undertake similar endeavors."[31]

The essay does not foreground Abramowicz's personal connection to Wysoki Dwór but roots his methodology in a questionnaire and additional data he and a student assistant collected. As its title indicates, the essay integrates statistics, direct observations, anecdotes, and lore. Abramowicz notes the war's detrimental impact on the town in reports on employment, educational institutions, religious customs, and the like, citing examples of decline ranging from the size of families to the scope of wedding celebrations. An ardent secularist, Abramowicz also championed the modern over the traditional, especially regarding education. The essay manifests both his affection for Wysoki Dwór and his awareness of its limitations, especially in its ability to respond to the economic demands of modernity. Extrapolating from his case study, Abramowicz concludes that the *shtetl* "remains a great source of uniqueness, originality, and folk creativity." At the same time, he characterizes the *shtetl* as "a great Jewish problem, with which we will have to grapple for a long time."[32]

Innovations in secular Jewish education in interwar Poland sometimes entailed studying local history. A remarkable example is *Pinkes fun der shtot Pruzshene* (Chronicle of the Town of Prużany), published in 1930.[33] What began as a student project in a local secular Yiddish school in 1926 became a comprehensive study of the town, including its history, based on primary sources; its current economy, based on statistics; and its local culture, based on interviews with community members. After the students' work attracted public interest, a committee was formed to publish this volume of some 300 pages, including photographs, maps, drawings, and numerous tables. While the book's overview of contemporary community institutions focuses on the Jewish population, which formed the town's majority in the interwar years, the historical narrative situates Jewish settlement and development within the general history of Prużany, and economic studies compare Jews' employment, housing, and other data with that of their Catholic and Russian Orthodox neighbors.

The Jewish physical presence in the provincial East European landscape attracted newfound attention during the interwar years. Both Polish and Jewish scholars at the Institute of Polish Architecture, established in 1923, documented the country's synagogue architecture with photographs, color renderings, and architectural plans.[34] Polish Jews' interest in local history and geography was popularized and institutionalized through the *landkentenish* ("land knowledge") movement. The Jewish Society for Knowing the Land, founded in Warsaw in 1926, promoted learning about local environments—through excursions, sports, lectures, reading, and photography—as a fixture of Polish Jewish culture. Targeting Jewish youth in particular, the movement was both inspired by and a polemical response to the equivalent Polish *krajoznawstwo* movement. Whereas this movement's publications and tours of sites in Poland often either neglected or disparaged Jewish landmarks, *landkentenish* strove to demonstrate that Jews had long been integral to Poland's physical as well as social landscape. The *landkentenish* movement exhorted Polish Jews to embrace their place in this landscape actively. Doing so, notes Samuel Kassow, was meant to strengthen Jews' sense of at-homeness in Poland and thereby enhance their mental and physical well-being, as well as demonstrate that Jews were both citizens and "settled inhabitants" in Poland and not "aliens or guests," as some right-wing Polish nationalists (and Zionists) contended.[35]

The *shtetl* figured in this movement's rhetoric as emblematic of Jews' longstanding presence in Poland. The author Michal Bursztyn wrote in the premiere issue of the periodical *Landkentenish* in 1933: "All along the Polish rivers lie towns and settlements with a rooted and diverse life that stretches back hundreds of years. The shtetl with its little forest and little stream, surrounded by neighboring villages, signified the direct, unmediated ties to nature, as far as that was possible, given the specific circumstances under which we [Jews] lived."[36] Through tourism and amateur ethnography, the *landkentenish* movement encouraged an increasingly urbanized Jewish population not to inhabit these provincial towns but to visit them as heritage sites.

Despite this increased popular interest during the interwar years, professional historians seldom published an in-depth monograph on the Jewish community in a single town in Eastern Europe. A notable exception is Isaiah Trunk's 1939 book *Di geshikhte fun yidn in Plotsk, 1237–1567* (The History of the Jews of Płock, 1237–1567), the first volume of a projected comprehensive history of the town, which was underwritten, in part, by the Committee to Commemorate the 700th Anniversary of Jewish Settlement in Płock. In a preface, this committee explains the volume's larger political significance: "This book appears at a time when the rights of the Jewish population in Poland are being questioned—a time when reactionaries consider Polish Jews, who have lived in this country for centuries, to be foreigners. This book demonstrates that Jews are not foreigners in Poland, who arrived only yesterday. It demonstrates that the thread of the history of Polish Jewry runs back many centuries, to the creation of this country's economy."[37] In his own prefatory remarks, Trunk explains that his history of Płock was motivated neither by local loyalty nor by a larger political polemic. Rather, as part of his interest in Jewish life in the province of Mazowie, this book exemplifies the importance of regional studies to the emerging field of Polish Jewish historiography, contributing new information and correcting longstanding mistakes about this history.

Trunk's book was published by YIVO, an independent research institute inaugurated in 1925 by a group of scholars of European Jewry, who were trained in various disciplines, including history, literary studies, linguistics, economics, and folkloristics. YIVO carried out the most wide-ranging efforts to study East European Jewish life in interwar Poland. In addition to creating a central library, archive, and research center, YIVO established a network of branch offices throughout Poland, with satellite offices in major centers of East European Jewish immigration around the world. The institute fostered public involvement in its efforts to document and study Yiddish folklore and language use, as well as East European Jewish history, economics, sociology, and pedagogy. Like precedent undertakings, YIVO was committed to using humanities and social science methodologies to conduct research parallel to the Western academy, which largely ignored East European Jewish life, past or present. At the same time, YIVO scholars understood their mission as benefiting East European Jewry by enhancing its self-image and nurturing cultural creativity. In the words of Max Weinreich, one of YIVO's founders, it approached *visnshaft* (modern scholarship) as *"visn vos shaft"* (knowledge that creates).[38] In contrast to Zionists or assimilationists, YIVO championed the legitimacy and value of a distinct Jewish way of life in Eastern Europe, epitomized by the institute's commitment to cultivating Yiddish as a language of scholarship, pedagogy, and "high" culture.[39]

In a 1929 pamphlet titled *Vos iz azoyns yidishe etnografye?* (Just What Is Jewish Ethnography?), YIVO exhorted the public to help collect ethnographic materials. Doing so, the pamphlet explains, will support YIVO's mission of documenting and analyzing Jewish folkways, which the institute vaunts as a "holy" legacy: "Customs, songs and tales that continue to live to this day among the people clearly transmit the sounds of long-forgotten echoes to us. And that is precisely why we must research the life of our people, to learn everything that has come down to us thanks to the strength of our tradition." Noting that "other peoples have already done a great deal in this area of study," YIVO points the would-be ethnographer to the best sources of material, which resides with *folksmentshn* ("common folk"), "as well as those who live near [them], who have their trust, who are familiar with their lives." These *folksmentshn* live "in remote little towns and villages," which are characterized as the last refuge of Jewish folkways: "Much has already been disrupted by modern culture, much has been driven out to the most remote towns, where it is on the verge of disappearing. We must collect what can still be saved."[40] Thus, YIVO configured its constituents in a new role as a conduit between scholars and resources, material as well as human. Implicit is a geographic and demographic configuration of Jewish culture, in which Polish Jewry is plotted on a spectrum, with YIVO's secular, cosmopolitan, professional researchers in Vilna on one end, and, on the other end, the traditional, provincial, common folk, untainted (and unenlightened) by modernity.

In the Soviet Union, state-sponsored research on the *shtetl* was conducted under various rubrics, including the Jewish divisions of academies in Minsk (the Jewish Department of the Institute for Belorussian Culture) and Kiev (the Institute for Jewish Culture at the Ukrainian Academy of Sciences) established in the 1920s. Part of a larger Soviet program of scholarship on national minority cultures, this research had political as well as intellectual importance for creating a multinational socialist state, in which proletarian class solidarity would ultimately transcend ethnic, religious, or national loyalties. While providing unprecedented recognition and support for studying East European Jewish life, past and present, the Soviet government mandated that this research conform to Marxist scholarly principles and advance the establishment of a socialist state.

Jewish life in towns in the Belorussian and Ukrainian Soviet Socialist Republics figured in pioneering works of scholarship on Yiddish language (e.g., the dialect research of Mordkhe Veynger and L. Vilenkin), literature (Meir Viner's analyses of nineteenth-century Yiddish literature), and music (Moyshe Beregovski's studies of folksongs and traditional instrumental music).[41] Other scholars scrutinized *shtetlekh* as the proving ground for a new Soviet Jewish way of life. This attention included promoting health and physical fitness, exemplified by the 1925 publication *Baveglekhe un sportive masn-shpil in shtetl* (Calisthenics and Team Sports in the [Jewish] Town), which includes instructions for 132 physical exercises and team athletics to foster a proletarian collective spirit.[42] However, Soviet research on *shtetlekh* centered on their economic future.

Though many Jews had moved eastward or resettled in major cities, a considerable number still lived in provincial towns of the Belorussian and Ukrainian SSRs, most in a state of economic instability. The new socialist government regarded these towns as exemplifying an abnormal and untenable economy. Scholarly attention focused on the socioeconomics of these sites, which was termed the "*shtetl* problem." The word *shtetl* indexed a socioeconomic actuality, despite the impossibility of either defining clearly what constituted a *shtetl* or providing consistently reliable data on these locations' demographics or economics. Historian Deborah Yalen notes that, notwithstanding these problems, the "perceived significance [of the *shtetl*] as the bedrock of Jewish economic dysfunction . . . remained unambiguous in the eyes of Soviet Yiddish activists."[43]

Other Soviet scholars championed the *shtetl* as key to popular engagement in regional studies, exemplified by the 1926 booklet *Forsht ayer shtetl!* (Research Your Town!) by historian and literature scholar Hillel Aleksandrov. A comparison to YIVO's guide to the amateur Jewish ethnographer, which appeared a few years later, is instructive. Both booklets promote the grassroots gathering of ethnographic materials as vital to developing modern, secular scholarship on Jewish life. Collecting and studying this material are conceived as new definitional Jewish practices that, while localized, contribute to larger social and political projects that will foster constructing a new Jewish life. In contrast to the concomitant Zionist agenda of making "new Jews" through settlement in Palestine, both the YIVO and the Soviet plans approach studying East European Jews' vernacular life as instrumental to building the Jewish future in situ.

Aleksandrov's guidebook differs from YIVO's by characterizing the study of these Jewish communities as helping to solve the "*shtetl* problem"—that is, reforming the economy of provincial Jews whose livelihoods as petit-bourgeois middlemen are inimical to a socialist state. Like YIVO, Aleksandrov stresses the importance of collecting a wide variety of materials, including vintage documents, statistics, and press accounts. But unlike YIVO's acclaiming of traditional folkways as sacred, *Forsht ayer shtetl!* characterizes *shtetl* culture as consisting of both "the remnants of a moldy past (religious schools, preachers, etc.)" and manifestations of "a new way of life," which included, among other phenomena, the communist youth organization and scouting movement. Prerevolutionary *shtetl* life, Aleksandrov explains—its capitalist economy, religious institutions and movements, legends of origins, and so on—should be systematically documented and analyzed, with an eye toward addressing current concerns of the regional economy. Similarly, local Jewish life should be studied not separately from that of neighbors but as integral to the larger socioeconomic environment. Amateur scholarship could serve a larger cause of national importance: "Keeping in mind the great interest currently in the problems of the town [*shtetl*], we hope that our activists—teachers, agronomists, workers in social institutions, students, etc.—will take up the task of researching their towns, thereby simultaneously helping government, social, and scholarly institutions."[44]

Rather than documenting folkways as an exercise in preservation or to provide inspiration for new cultural creativity, Soviet scholars scrutinized *shtetlekh* to measure Jews' advance toward integration into the Soviet mainstream. Socioeconomic data, Yalen notes, was "expected to demonstrate the self-disintegration of the shtetl as an obsolete artifact of the old regime. In fact, these Soviet Jewish narratives inadvertently highlighted the endurance of the shtetl in Soviet life at both the concrete and discursive levels."[45]

Indeed, literature scholar Anna Shternshis notes in her study of interwar Soviet Jewish popular culture that state-run publications on Jewish life in *shtetlekh* sometimes reported an increase in traditional Jewish religiosity following the Bolshevik Revolution, in contrast to Jews living in major cities. However, she argues, these reports "may have exaggerated the level of religious observance among Jews" so as to "justify further antireligious propaganda." Moreover, her research reveals that, instead of realizing the state's envisioned steady, unidirectional progress through a transitional Marxist Yiddish culture toward *korenizatsiia* ("nativization")—or, conversely, simply resisting state efforts to eradicate traditional Jewish mores—Soviet Jews evolved their own vernacular culture. This self-styled hybrid of old and new, official and unofficial, public and private was, as one person described it to Shternshis, a way of being both "Soviet" and "kosher."[46]

Interest in East European Jewish life extended beyond the region during the interwar years, in part due to new encounters with these Jews through immigration or during wartime. Among German-speaking Jews in Western Europe the "cult of the Ostjuden" flourished anew. Historian Steven Aschheim notes that, though German Jews' fascination with their East European coreligionists as ostensible embodiments of a premodern Jewish authenticity dates back to the early nineteenth century (Aschheim cites Heinrich Heine as an important precedent), the political and social changes wrought by World War I brought German Jews into much closer contact with larger numbers of East European Jews than previously and did so under more pressing circumstances.[47]

Interwar German Jewish writing on East European Jews included works for general audiences, exemplified by travelogues, such as Arnold Zweig's *Das Ostjüdische Antlitz* (The Eastern Jewish Countenance), published in 1920 with illustrations by Hermann Struck, and Alfred Döblin's 1925 *Reise in Polen* (Journey to Poland). For Zweig and Döblin, the protocols of the travelogue, as an account of a journey to an exotic place, were complicated by the particular nature of their travels to observe a Jewish counterpart whom German Jews had long contemplated as a foil for self-scrutiny.

Even among those German Jews who held Ostjuden in low regard—deeming them unsophisticated, parochial, superstitious, ill-mannered, slovenly, indigent—were many who felt that East European Jewry maintained a more comprehensive and genuine Jewish life, against which assimilated Western bourgeois Jewishness seemed pallid and ambivalent. Zweig characterized the East European Jew as having "a life that is lived to the fullest" and asserted that "Jewish ideas live in him and through him." At the same time, Zweig feared that an encroaching modernity, in the wake of war and revolution, would compromise East European Jewry, as had already happened among the Westjuden. What, he wondered, "will become of this eternal people . . . —will there still remain this Eastern Jewry in its ethnic richness and authenticity? For this is the last part of the Jewish people on earth which has created its own new songs and dances, rituals and myths, languages and forms of community . . . —and which continues to keep them alive and at the same time vigorously preserves the old traditions in all their validity."[48]

Like Zweig, Döblin traveled to Poland in order to experience a Jewish existence he regarded as thoroughly authentic. Reporting on his visit, along with a companion, to the town of Góra Kalwarja, the seat of the renowned Gerer rebbe, Döblin describes the complex ambivalence of the encounter for both Eastern and Western Jews, each gazing judgmentally upon the other: "How proudly these men, youths, boys stride along in clean black caftans, in high shiny black caps. They look romantic, rapturous, medieval. . . . At every step we take, we are surrounded by men . . . who gape at us. . . . New ones keep sizing us up. I feel as if I've come upon an exotic tribe; they do not want me, me or my companion, they regard us as intruders."[49]

Zweig and Döblin traveled primarily to major cities in Poland and Lithuania, rather than the provinces, and they generally paid less attention to their particular destinations than to the Jews encountered there as exemplars of an archetype. ("One Jew is barely distinguished from the next," Zweig asserts, by dint of their living in an environment of "tumultuous confinement" that he likens to fish in a restaurant aquarium.)[50] The self-reflexive nature of German Jewish writers' interest in the Ostjude is exemplified by their frequent use of the term *ghetto* to describe East European Jewish life, either in a particular setting or as a whole. In its original meaning as an externally restricted Jewish residential neighborhood, *ghetto* does not apply to the circumstances of East European Jewry until Nazi Germany established ghettos in occupied East European cities and towns during World War II. Rather, the ghetto is a phenomenon of early modern Western Europe (though by the turn of the twentieth century the term was used to refer to an urban Jewish enclave anywhere, including the United States).[51] German Jews esteemed emancipation from ghettos as defining events that inaugurated Jewish cultural and political integration into the West European mainstream during the nineteenth century. Referring to East European Jews as living in a ghetto implicitly situated them as atavisms for their German coreligionists.

Accounts of travels to East European Jewish sites also proved popular among Yiddish-speaking immigrants in the United States during the 1920s and 1930s. Travelogues appeared in the American Yiddish press and in book form. As the titles of some of these books suggest—Moyshe Olgin's *Mayn shtetl in Ukraine* (My Town in Ukraine, 1921); Yitskhok Blum's *A shtetele in Poyln* (A Small Town in Poland, 1939)—authors offered personal journeys to their hometowns as emblematic of immigrant Jews' larger interest in their birthplaces. Like the travelogues of German Jews, these accounts were exercises in self-scrutiny through reflection on the *shtetl* as chronotope.

Olgin (né Moyshe-Yoysef Novomiski), an important voice in radical Jewish politics during the first decades of the twentieth century, emigrated to the United States in 1914. Six years later, he traveled back to Eastern Europe and wrote a series of reports on his travels for the *Jewish Daily Forward*.[52] At about the same time that the newspaper ran this series, which championed Soviet Russia's early successes, Olgin published *Mayn shtetl in Ukraine*, an account of a prewar visit to his hometown, referred to as "B."[53] (Though Olgin had planned to revisit Ukraine during his postwar visit, ill health prevented him from doing so.) Olgin's account of visiting B. is structured less as a travelogue than as an ethnography of the town's Jewish types, their folk creativity, religious life, education, and relations with their Ukrainian neighbors. In contrast to his account in the *Forward* series lauding the Bolshevik Revolution's accomplishments, Olgin concludes *Mayn shtetl in Ukraine* by voicing concern about the uncertain future of both Jews and Ukrainians in Russia. Read in relation to his postwar travelogue, the book proffers travel back in time to a way of life left behind not only by Olgin and his readers though immigration, but also by Eastern Europe's Jews due to war and revolution.

Blum (né Y. Krivonogi), a poet and fiction writer, centers his account of traveling to his hometown of Ciechanowiec, after living in America for twenty-five years, on the powerfully affective impact that his visit had on him and the townspeople he encountered. In a preface to Blum's book, the *Forward*'s editor, Abraham Cahan, extols the work's authenticity while highlighting its emotional value: "Each of us holds dear his memories of the Old World [*alte heym*—literally, "old home"]. We each have the most tender feelings for everything connected with the years when we were still in the place where we were born and raised. Each one of us thinks of visiting our former homes; it is among the most precious of our wishes and sweetest of our dreams."[54] The book's focus on emotions stirred by the journey may reflect growing concerns among American Jews in the late 1930s for the future of fellow Jews in Eastern Europe, as they struggled with a depressed economy, growing anti-Jewish political movements, and looming concerns about war in Europe.

In addition to reflecting on their former homes through travel, immigrant Jews were themselves sought out as resources on Old World culture. Folklorist Yehuda Leyb Cahan began collecting folksongs and tales in Poland before immigrating to London and then, in 1904, to New York, where he spent most of the remainder of his career. A leading figure in YIVO's folklore research, Cahan conducted most of his fieldwork among fellow Yiddish-speaking immigrants, from whom he collected Old World folktales and songs. Cahan produced pioneering scholarship on Yiddish folk materials, which he analyzed according to taxonomies of form and region.

Cahan maintained strict standards for what constituted "authentic" folk material, as opposed to the popular or the *folkstimlekh* ("folksy"—i.e., fabricated in the manner of folkways). He identified songs collected from immigrants according to their East European hometowns, without regard to how these songs were maintained, shared, or transformed in immigrant settings, nor did he attend to the contingencies of these songs' performance in Eastern Europe. Rather, Cahan, like other Yiddish folklorists of the day, conceptualized Eastern Europe as Yiddish culture's heartland, its dimensions measured by geographic regions and Yiddish dialects. The analysis of folkways demonstrated that Yiddish folk culture was substantial and orderly; its comparison with other European folk traditions revealed the longstanding interrelation of Yiddish-speaking Jews and their East European neighbors. Cahan's approach to researching this folklore in America suggested that East European Jewish folkways had a resilience that endured beyond the impact of immigration.[55]

The most extensive American studies of East European Jewry were commissioned by various relief agencies seeking information on the economic well-being of Jewish communities, large and small, recovering from the upheavals of war. This research was forthrightly engagé, intended to help determine the most effective approaches to aiding East European Jews and bolster their public image, especially in the face of rising antisemitism.

Much of this research was conducted for the American Jewish Joint Distribution Committee (AJJDC), established in 1914 to provide financial aid, vocational training, health care, and other services to Jewish communities abroad struggling against poverty and discrimination. The AJJDC commissioned numerous studies of East European Jews' economic life, scrutinizing communities' prewar social history and collecting reports and statistics on contemporary conditions. Research was both conducted on a national scale and focused on individual towns as case studies, such as collecting statistics on competition between Jewish and non-Jewish businesses in Kalisz,[56] or surveying the health and education of children in Ostróg. This study revealed that "out of a sample of 386 Jewish children in four out of fifteen 'Jewish' streets, 262 were of school age but only 109 attended school. Of the other 153, 12 were ill, 3 were retarded, 6 had no documents for registration, 9 had not enrolled in time, 6 were not accounted for, and 117 could not go to school because they had no clothes or shoes. Of the total of 386, only 67 were healthy; 196 were weak or anemic, 61 were scrofulous. A total of 71 percent of the children were in various stages of undernourishment down to and including starvation."[57]

Scrutinizing the socioeconomic circumstances of Polish Jews generally, AJJDC analysts focused on key trends: the continued urbanization and increased cultural Polonization among the young, the creation of new cultural institutions and attraction of new political possibilities, as well as a lack of adequate training among Jews in viable vocations and growing concern over anti-Jewish discrimination. Consequently, the AJJDC devoted considerable resources to establishing professional and vocational schools in cities and promoting Jewish agricultural settlements, especially in the USSR. The AJJDC's vision of East European Jewry's future assumed that the economy once widely maintained in provincial towns was being left behind and that this abandonment should be supported. As Yehuda Bauer notes in his history of the AJJDC during the interwar years, the Jew as "the traditional middleman . . . no longer fitted into the economic picture" of Eastern Europe.[58]

These various transatlantic engagements between American and East European Jews reflect signal shifts in their relationship after World War I: the curtailing of mass immigration to the United States in the early 1920s; the maturing and flourishing of an immigrant-based Yiddish culture far from Eastern Europe; the rising prosperity of many immigrants, while East Europeans suffered widespread economic instability and impoverishment. Writing about East European Jewish life—whether personal narrative, analysis of Old World folkways, or statistical study of economic need—emerged as an important vehicle of retrospection for immigrants, after several decades of largely unilateral movement away from their former homes. Epitomized by the travel narrative, all these efforts examine the distance between Old and New World Jewry as a defining relationship in flux. The *shtetl* served as one of several rubrics for articulating this relationship. In particular, as new political, economic, and cultural interests invited attention to East European Jewry on a grand scale, personal attachments to hometowns remained affectively potent and acquired a new emblematic character of vernacular Jewish tenacity in the face of unprecedented challenges. This attachment was soon subjected to a much more extreme challenge, one that could scarcely have been imagined before World War II.

Remarkably, efforts to study Jewish life in *shtetlekh* continued into the war's first years. Emanuel Ringelblum's underground archive documenting Jewish life and death under Nazi occupation, though based in the Warsaw Ghetto, also recorded the demise of Jewish life in small towns in Poland, collected during the first two and a half years of the war. The archive created a detailed guide for reporting on the German invasion of provincial towns and collected reports from Jewish eyewitnesses in several hundred locales. Samuel Kassow notes that these reports differ from postwar accounts of the same events; during the war's first years, "most Jews still had no knowledge of the Germans' intention to destroy European Jewry. Although the writers were uprooted refugees, they were still a part of a living community." Many accounts recall the venerable history of these towns' Jewish settlements, while others offer candid reports of internal conflicts within the Jewish community—a subject, Kassow observes, often elided in "elegiac" postwar writing.[59] Similarly, these reports reflect the complex and often contradictory relations between Jews and Poles in the immediate prewar and early war years. With the onset of mass extermination of Polish Jewry, these relationships deteriorated, and the mission of documenting Jewish life in Polish *shtetlekh* was moot.

Postwar Collecting and Recollecting

Writing about the *shtetl* after World War II, whether scholarly or popular, is distinguished from prewar work by a pervasive sense of loss of Jewish lives and sites and, moreover, of a comprehensive way of life embodied by what had been destroyed. The "eleventh-hour" alarms that researchers had long sounded about the plight of East European Jewish culture seemed to have finally struck with unanticipated swiftness, thoroughness, and cruelty. The subject of their research had apparently become what Barbara Kirshenblatt-Gimblett terms the "ethnographic phantom."[60] Writing about the *shtetl* in the post-Holocaust era is therefore inevitably, if often tacitly, bound up with mourning and coming to terms with loss.

Postwar scholarly writing about the *shtetl* also responds to a new instrumental concern—namely, the need to craft some strategy of engaging with East European Jewry alternative to the lost option of direct observation of a thriving culture in situ. Multiple distances—of place, time, population, language, literacy, sensibility—have to be breached, and negotiating these disparities becomes integral to the writing. Postwar reconfigurations of Jewish life prompted new questions regarding the place of Eastern Europe: What did the East European Jewish past mean for American Jews, now suddenly the world's largest and most secure Jewish community in the world, albeit by default? What could the centuries of Jewish life in Eastern Europe mean for the new country of Israel, founded on a Zionist conviction that the diaspora constituted a fallen state for Jews, rendered politically powerless and bereft of a culture authentically their own? What did the prewar past mean to the many Jews still living in Eastern Europe, who had to contend with postwar communist regimes and were largely inaccessible to the West? What might this Jewish past mean to non-Jews, as they began to contemplate the enormity of the Holocaust?

In response to these new concerns, the *shtetl* emerged in the West as the paradigm par excellence for East European Jewish life. This new focus on the *shtetl*, not merely as a subject of interest but as a key matrix for writing about the life—or death—of East European Jewry, was not an inevitable development. Rather, the attraction of the *shtetl* paradigm indicates in part what resources, motives, and possibilities informed postwar contemplation of the East European Jewish past, its destruction, and its uncertain future. To begin with, the *shtetl* was a readily available idiom in Yiddish popular culture, an established subject of fiction, memoirs, plays, songs, and films. The vernacular of the preponderance of East European Jews murdered during World War II, Yiddish quickly became a signifier of these Jews and, moreover, of their destruction, especially among those Jews for whom it was no longer a language of daily life.[61]

Postwar attraction to the *shtetl* paradigm suggests a desire for a vestigial, premodern model of East European Jewish life that is both integral and intimate in scale. This rubric relegates the considerable cosmopolitan trending of East European Jewry, who had been flocking to cities, trade unions, and universities, and likewise ignores the extent to which its traditionalists had adopted modern educational, cultural, and political practices as means of maintaining their religiosity. *Shtetl* also provides the postwar discourse on East European Jewry with an abstracted locus that transcends the complex dynamics of national and regional boundaries. When construed as a distinctly Jewish geographic idiom, *shtetl* implies an alternative Jewish mapping of sites of persecution.

At the same time, the use of *shtetl* as a paradigm—a small-scale unit of social geography reproduced hundreds of times over an expansive territory—complements another important postwar conceptualization of prewar East European Jewish life as a "world." This term codifies the subject on a grand scale and as comprehensive in scope, taking in urban as well as provincial communities, modern as well as traditional practices. As a post-Holocaust idiom, the "world of East European Jewry" has also frequently been modified as "lost" or "vanished."[62] By contrast, the *shtetl* model connotes modesty of scale and avoids direct reminders of destruction. Indeed, given its paradigmatic nature, the *shtetl* can reference something transcendent, which might endure or be replicated elsewhere.

The first sizeable corpus of postwar writing about the *shtetl*, individual memoirs and collaborative *yizker-bikher* produced by Jews who had lived in prewar Eastern Europe, centered on personal memories of individual towns. Hundreds of memorial books were created for East European Jewish communities large and small, beginning shortly after the war and continuing for several decades. Anthropologists Jack Kugelmass and Jonathan Boyarin characterize *yizker-bikher* as a spontaneous, "genuinely collective response to the Holocaust." At the same time, these books reflect precedent Jewish memory practices, including "the long tradition of Jewish mourning literature," extending back to the Book of Lamentations. Though the style and format of *yizker-bikher* vary widely, they have in common the larger purpose of using writing as "a means of preserving and establishing living memory" and a substitute for "the task of a proper burial" of one's dead, rendered impossible by the Holocaust.[63]

Kugelmass and Boyarin note that "the preponderance of memorial books are for *shtetlekh* rather than major cities," disproportionate to "the demographics of prewar Polish Jewry, over one third of whom lived in Poland's three largest cities."[64] This characteristic may also account for the distinctive intimacy typical of these books, which entail an unusually high correlation among their authors, subjects, and audiences. *Yizker-bikher* were largely written either in Yiddish, their authors' most common native tongue, or (especially for books published in Israel) in Hebrew, the state's official Jewish language. Thus, these books were not meant for a general readership; usually printed in limited editions, *yizker-bikher* were funded and purchased by subscribers, who were almost exclusively the Jewish former residents of the town in question.

As titles sometimes indicate (e.g., *Kalush: hayeha ve-hurbanah shel ha-kehilah* [Kałusz: The Life and Destruction of the Jewish Community]; *Yizker-bukh tsum fareybikn dem ondenk fun der khorev-gevorener yidisher kehile Voyslavits* [Memorial Book for Preserving the Memory of the Destroyed Jewish Community of Wojsławice]),[65] a *yizker-bukh* is nominally devoted to recalling a *kehile*—that is, a local Jewish community, as articulated in traditionally religious terms—even though much of what is recollected concerns secular and non-Jewish phenomena. The rubric of the *shtetl* emerges, if implicitly, as the organizing principle for these books. Many of them feature maps, usually drawn from memory, which configure the town as the Jewish community's geographic unit. These maps recall the physical town as experienced by Jews—for example, identifying streets and other landmarks with the names Jews used to refer to them (e.g., in Yiddish rather than Polish). The maps also typically include non-Jewish landmarks—municipal buildings, churches, Christian cemeteries, etc.—relevant to recalling local Jewish life. This characteristic extends to the texts in *yizker-bikher*, which recount local history, geography, and non-Jews as they relate to remembering the Jewish past. Local geography orients discrete memories proffered in a *yizker-bukh* to one another, situating various individuals, social institutions, and events, as recalled by different writers, within an integral space. Beyond mapping memory, *yizker-bikher* reconstitute textually what was displaced or eradicated from its original, indigenous physical place.

The act of documenting these destroyed communities created, if temporarily, new virtual communities, by establishing a network among the former Jews of each town, now living scattered throughout the Americas, Europe, Africa, Oceania, and Israel. Creating these books under daunting circumstances—locating and coordinating a recently dispersed constituency of contributors and subscribers, raising funds for publication, gathering texts and illustrations, editing, printing, and distributing—was as much a project as the documentation of memories. Indeed, the books' realization marked the conclusion of this commemorative process; once sent out to subscribers, these volumes often reposed, forgotten, on "the bottom shelves of the book cabinet."[66] Other social networks—*landsmanshaftn*, congregations, personal or professional ties, affiliations with Jewish political or philanthropic organizations—might continue connections among the new diasporas of these localities, but *yizker-bikher* as a rule mark the end of their communal writing.

Concomitant with these collaborative projects, numerous individuals published memoirs of prewar Jewish life in East European provincial towns. Many of these works are by Holocaust survivors, who juxtapose their prewar life—whether construed as a period of innocence or of foreboding—with their wartime experience, which generally forms their narratives' centerpiece. These works typically interrelate personal history with a larger collective narrative of persecution and memorialization. The series *Poylishe yidntum* (Polish Jewry), issued by the Central Association of Polish Jews in Argentina from the mid-1940s through the mid-1960s, published more than 160 Yiddish books—including histories, novels, poetry, memoirs, biographies, memorial books, and translations—among which are several accounts of prewar Jewish life in *shtetlekh*. Within the context of this series, individual memoirs figure as examples of a collective enterprise of memorializing a vanquished people and their way of life.[67] Through these postwar publications, Polish Jewry was reconstituted as an entity in "exile"—both in Argentina and in the virtual realm of international Yiddish publishing.

Complementing the indigenous, localized works of *shtetl* remembrance found in *yizker-bikher* and memoirs are early postwar efforts, primarily through the written word and primarily in English, to recall prewar East European Jewish life on a grand scale for general audiences. Kirshenblatt-Gimblett terms these works—which include literary essays, anthologies, photo albums, performance works, and cultural anthropology—the "popular arts of Jewish ethnography."[68] These various projects all addressed two complementary challenges: memorializing what of East European Jewish life was lost and articulating what endured or might still be accessible despite mass murder, destruction of property, uprooting of survivors, and erasure of traces.

Among the earliest of these works is Abraham Joshua Heschel's 1950 book *The Earth Is the Lord's: The Inner World of the Jew in Eastern Europe*. The scion of a prominent Polish hasidic dynasty who became a scholar of Jewish philosophy in Berlin and eventually escaped to America during World War II, Heschel conceptualizes the life of prewar East European Jewry as an "inner world," eliding the historical and geographic specificity of his subject as he foregrounds its spirituality. Heschel repeatedly stresses the abstract and transcendent in East European Jewish life—for example, asserting that "the Jews in Eastern Europe lived more in time than in space." He mentions particular locales to render them paradigms of sanctity, tacitly invoking their symbolic value among hasidim: "Koretz, Karlin, Bratslav, Lubavitsh, Ger, Lublin—hundreds of little towns were like holy books. Each place was a pattern, an aspect, a way of Jewishness. When a Jew mentioned the name of a town like Miedzybosh or Berditshev, it was as though he mentioned a divine mystery."[69]

During the 1950s, several American academics undertook major research projects and produced key scholarly works on prewar East European Jewish life. Emblematic of American Jews' new importance as caretakers of the East European Jewish past, some of these efforts have had an enduring, international impact on how East European Jewry is remembered. In all these efforts the *shtetl* figures as a paradigm.

Perhaps the most influential of these works—and increasingly considered one of the most problematic—is the 1952 anthropological study *Life*

Is with People: The Jewish Little-Town of Eastern Europe by Mark Zborowski and Elizabeth Herzog. *Life Is with People* evolved from a scholarly endeavor that initially paid no particular attention to prewar East European Jewish life: the Columbia University Research in Contemporary Culture Project, a cross-cultural study initiated by anthropologist Ruth Benedict in 1946, with funding from the U.S. Office of Naval Research. This project extended wartime research Benedict had conducted in "anthropology at a distance"—that is, interviewing immigrants and refugees about their cultures of origin—for the Office of War Information. Among Benedict's informants were a considerable number of East European Jews. Eventually, she found their Old World culture to be a subject of interest in its own right, and she tasked a group of scholars to "delineate the East European Jewish culture area." By the time this study was published (under the supervision of anthropologist Margaret Mead), the *shtetl* had emerged as the organizing rubric for distilling a cultural system from the wide-ranging information researchers had gleaned from informants and other sources, bridging "the goals and methods of salvage ethnography and the study of living communities in situ." Kirshenblatt-Gimblett notes that, while it was not the study's point of departure, "*shtetl* became a textual way to achieve coherence, totality, and authority in the representing of East European Jewish culture," working from "the accounts of so many unrelated individuals" as well as an array of secondary sources that researchers had consulted, including memoirs, literary works, and films.[70]

Like the compilers of *yizker-bikher*, Zborowski and Herzog used the *shtetl* as a rubric to structure their descriptions of practices, mores, and beliefs, as well as people and institutions. But whereas each *yizker-bukh* recalled a particular community and its distinctive history, in *Life Is with People* the *shtetl* is generic and timeless. Moreover, following the model of observational anthropology, which was formulated in relation to the study of small, isolated, homogeneous communities (e.g., Benedict's studies of American Indian peoples or Mead's work on islands in the South Pacific), this rubric approached East European Jewish culture as "a self-contained entity," in which external forces, "however much impact they may have upon it, are treated as external to the system."[71]

In effect, *Life Is with People* conflated the living culture of prewar East European Jewry with its mediation, especially the memories of immigrants and refugees. The *shtetl* rubric followed not only the anthropological model of tribal village community but also modern Jewish cultural practices of representing *shtetl* life—in literature, memoir, performance, and the like—that had been in place among East European Jews for decades. The *shtetl* is therefore not a location or a population in *Life Is with People* (its title notwithstanding) but something abstracted from them: culture, understood as a closed, coherent system of ideas, realized in practices and beliefs. Within this approach, the specifics of geography and history are ultimately irrelevant; a *shtetl* could, in theory, be realized anywhere or at any time. As a "pattern of culture," to use Benedict's classic formulation,[72] the *shtetl* transcends the particular, including the destruction wrought by genocide or the international dispersal of immigrants, refugees, and Holocaust survivors. In this regard, *Life Is with People* resembles Heschel's *The Earth Is the Lord's*—and it is telling that both books' titles are affirmative sentences in the present tense.

Though it met with some scholarly opprobrium upon publication, *Life Is with People* proved to be quite popular, remaining in print for decades. The book familiarized many English-language readers with its conceptualization of the *shtetl* and, moreover, with the word itself. (Bernard Richard's review of the book includes the first use of *shtetl* by the *New York Times*.)[73] The influence of *Life Is with People* on popular images of East European Jewry is exemplified by *Fiddler on the Roof*. The book proved an important resource for the creators of this 1964 Broadway musical, which transforms Sholem Aleichem's Tevye—a rural Jew who lives with his family in a village among Ukrainian peasants, in relative isolation from other Jews—into a *shtetl* resident surrounded by coreligionists.[74] Remarkably, *Fiddler on the Roof* later directed people back to *Life Is with People*. The front cover of the book's 1974 paperback edition features an endorsement from Sheldon Harnick, the musical's lyricist: "*Life Is with People* told us about life in the Jewish villages as no other book. It should be read by all who have enjoyed *Fiddler on the Roof*."[75] More recently, the image that *Life Is with People* offered of the *shtetl* as a timeless paradigm, exclusively Jewish and rooted in traditional religiosity, was given graphic form in a 1984 cut-and-paste craft book, *The Paper Shtetl: A Complete Model of an East European Jewish Town*.[76]

Notwithstanding its popular format, *Life Is with People* has also had an enduring influence on scholars interested in the East European Jewish past, especially those unable to draw on primary sources. A case in point is anthropologist Barbara Myerhoff, whose 1978 study *Number Our Days* assesses immigrant Jews' remembrance of their East European birthplaces in relation to *Life Is with People*, even while acknowledging its flaws.[77] The book's conceptualization of the *shtetl* was canonized by an entry in the 1971 *Encyclopedia Judaica* (apparently the first comprehensive entry on *shtetl* in a Jewish encyclopedia), written by Zborowski.[78] Conversely, *Life Is with People* became a negative model for subsequent scholarly efforts and, eventually, a subject of scholarly scrutiny itself.

Like *Life Is with People*, Irving Howe and Eliezer Greenberg's 1954 *A Treasury of Yiddish Stories*, the first major anthology of Yiddish literature in English translation published after the Holocaust, remained in print for decades and has done much to inform the image of the *shtetl* in the English-speaking world.[79] Howe and Greenberg's collection focuses on the particular history and singular character of the cultural moment that created modern Yiddish literature and which it, in turn, is seen as embodying. To contextualize this literature, the editors provide extensive introductory materials, running over ninety pages. The introduction's first section, titled "The World of the East European Jews," characterizes the Yiddish speakers who produced and read this literature as a cohesive, self-contained social entity—"a kind of nation, yet without nationhood"—whose cultural patterns are "probably without parallel in Western history."[80] Howe and Greenberg conflate this "world" with its literature by organizing the anthology—containing over fifty prose works, plus a sampling of folktales and proverbs—into a hypertext that limns the emergence, efflorescence, and destruction of Yiddish modernism.[81]

Rather than ordering their selections by chronology, genre, geography, or author, the editors grouped and sequenced these works as chapters of a master narrative. Its epicenter is, as David Roskies has observed, the *shtetl*,[82] which Howe and Greenberg identify as the crucible of Yiddish modernism: "Modern Yiddish literature focuses upon the *shtetl* during its last tremor of self-awareness, the historical moment when it is still coherent and self-contained but already under fierce assault from the outer world. . . . Yiddish reaches its climax of expressive power as the world it portrays begins to come apart."[83] Situated at a historical and cultural crossroads, the *shtetl* also becomes the strategic locus for looking back at the "world" of East European Jewry.

Perhaps the most deliberately structured scholarly effort to collect information on the prewar lives of East European Jews is the *Language and Cultural Atlas of Ashkenazic Jewry* (*LCAAJ*), initiated by linguist Uriel Weinreich at Columbia University in the late 1950s. Whereas Ruth Benedict's project did not set out to study European Jewry, this was the subject of the *LCAAJ* from the start. And whereas *Life Is with People* was wide-ranging in its source materials and its authors struggled to find a methodological rubric that would integrate these diverse sources, the *LCAAJ* was conceived with a carefully delineated methodology. Centered on Yiddish language use, the *LCAAJ* charts both the configuration of Yiddish dialects of the immediate prewar period across Northern Europe and the language's historical structures in relation to both time and space.[84]

Working with responses from over 600 native informants to a 220-page questionnaire, the *LCAAJ* maps regional variations in Yiddish language and culture across the European continent, ranging from phonological, lexical, and grammatical differences in dialect to an array of folkloric beliefs and practices (e.g., whether it was local practice to put sugar in gefilte fish; what games of chance were played locally on Hanukkah). Each informant represents a different geographic site, the locations carefully chosen to represent the demography of Yiddish speakers across Europe.

The *LCAAJ* offers a structural approach to East European Jewish life ordered on a grand scale. But unlike *Life Is with People*, this approach is rooted in the physical geography of Europe, in which Yiddish language and culture articulate a set of boundaries, territories, and causeways different from the modern political map of Eastern Europe. Although the *shtetl* is not the subject of study, it is the implicit unit of research. The *LCAAJ* focuses on the geographic distribution of dialects, rather than linguistic variants' frequency of use, which would be tied more to the growing concentration of prewar Yiddish speakers in major cities. Therefore, most of the East European locations on the *LCAAJ*'s map are towns. The use of one informant per location—even when that location is Warsaw—implies a local uniformity of language and culture that is more in keeping with the scale of a small, provincial settlement than a large city. Moreover, the assumption that each site had a stable, local lect conforms to notions of the *shtetl* as culturally self-sufficient and minimally influenced by outside practices, rather than to the complex dynamic of urban culture.

In this respect, the *LCAAJ* resembles *yizker-bikher* as being implicitly scaled to the *shtetl*. The *LCAAJ* questionnaire implies a locally cohesive speech, situated in the prewar past, by repeatedly asking, "*Vi azoy hot geheysn in [X] . . . ?*" (How in [the locale of X] did you say . . . ?). The town is the elemental unit of which larger structures—regional dialects and customs—are composed as a result of the interrelation among neighboring sites. Although the *LCAAJ* maps a vast speech territory by documenting the use of Yiddish in a "European area second in size only to the Russian one,"[85] this territory is realized in constellations of linguistic features in hundreds of towns.

These were not the only works of scholarship on the *shtetl* produced in the United States in the early postwar years. For example, YIVO, its central headquarters now located in New York, published detailed studies of individual towns by former residents, such as Abraham Ain's overview of Jewish life in Świsłocz, focusing on its economic life and labor activism, and Yehiel Shtern's description of traditional Jewish education practices in Tyszowce.[86] In these closely focused, local studies, the larger "lost world" of East European Jewry goes unmentioned. Instead, the authors attend to the detailed, dispassionate documentation of a particular site.

The diffuse nature of early postwar scholarship on prewar East European Jewry reflects the war's atomization of the scholarly communities that had coalesced in Eastern Europe during the interwar years. Many leading scholars were murdered during the Holocaust; those who survived the war generally resettled elsewhere, especially in the United States and Israel, and sought new intellectual homes. (A noteworthy exception is the group of scholars—including Tatiana Berenstein, Artur Eisenbach, Adam Rutkowski, Szymon Datner, Danuta Dąbrowska, Bernard Mark, Ruta Sakowska—who remained in Poland and founded the Żydowski Instytut Historyczny [Jewish Historical Institute] in Warsaw in 1947.) In the United States, YIVO emerged as the leading center for research on East European Jewry, publishing works by Jacob Shatzky, Isaiah Trunk, Max Weinreich, and Mark Wischnitzer, among other scholars who had begun their careers in interwar Poland. Other scholars who survived the Holocaust—Ben Tsiyon Dinur (né Dineson), Shmuel Ettinger, Jacob Goldberg, Israel Halpern, Jacob Katz, Josef Kermish, Jakob Lestschinsky—settled in Israel and helped establish the study of East European Jewry in the nation's major universities. By contrast, American universities provided little opportunity in the early postwar years to scholars of this subject. A noteworthy exception is historian Salo Baron, on the Columbia University faculty since 1930. Baron arranged for Philip Friedman, who had been a historian of Polish Jewry in interwar Poland, to be appointed a lecturer at Columbia, where he undertook pioneering research on the Holocaust.

Israel's institutionalization of scholarship on East European Jewry reflected changing attitudes toward the culture of origin for the majority of the state's Jews. For example, in 1951, the Hebrew University inaugurated a chair in Yiddish Studies, first held by Dov Sadan, after Hebraists' vehement objections had quashed the plan when it was initially proposed in the 1920s.[87] In 1953 the Israeli government established Yad Vashem as both a research center and a site of Holocaust remembrance. As historian Roni Stauber notes, these two agendas—the "national objective of commemoration" and "independent Holocaust research . . . , disinterested and based on scientific principles"—conflicted with one another, a dilemma some scholars addressed early on.[88] To a considerable extent, the tension between these two agendas centered on the scholarly insights of an emergent Holocaust historiography that challenged established Zionist notions of diaspora Jewry as inherently powerless and Israel's championing of armed resistance during the Holocaust, epitomized by the Warsaw Ghetto uprising, over other responses to persecution.

This tension also informed Israeli documentation of Jewish life in East European communities large and small within the rubric of Holocaust studies. Yad Vashem's series *Pinkas ha-kehilot* (Chronicle of Jewish Communities), the first volume of which appeared in 1969, provides encyclopedia entries on hundreds of Europe's Jewish communities "from [their] foundation until [their] destruction," with "priority . . . given to the events and problems of the period of the Holocaust." The preface to the series' first volume on Jewish communities in Poland acknowledges that there "a particular Polish Jewish life was created, whose features may still be discerned throughout the Jewish dispersion," and valorizes "the characteristic features of the vitality displayed by Polish Jewry . . . in the armed resistance in the ghettos and concentration camps and in the ranks of the partisan movement." At the same time, the volume's introduction asserts that "the fact that the Jews were always discriminated against and the hostility of the non-Jewish environment to a large extent decided the fate of the Jewish population during the tragic period of the Holocaust."[89]

Shtetl Studies Comes of Age

A turn in postwar scholarship on the *shtetl* began toward the end of the 1960s, in tandem with the establishment of Jewish studies in the academic mainstream, especially in the United States (e.g., with the founding of the Association for Jewish Studies in 1969). Expansion of this field beyond work published in Hebrew or Yiddish situated East European Jewry as a subject of inquiry for an international scholarly community. The development of Jewish studies was also part of a larger expansion in subjects of research and methodological approaches in the academy, especially the flourishing of interdisciplinary area studies, which often attended to communities that scholars had previously neglected or derogated, such as women, ethnic and racial minorities, non-Western cultures, the poor, the disabled.

Growing academic attention to East European Jews and to Yiddish language, literature, and culture engendered new scholarship, primarily in English and Hebrew, on the *shtetl* as a subject of academic interest in its own right. Exemplary is the work of Dan Miron, who was trained in both Israel and the United States, on the image of the *shtetl* in key works by Sholem Yankev Abramovitsh and Sholem Aleichem. In a series of studies initiated in the 1970s, Miron identifies the *shtetl* as a literary topos where these and other Yiddish and Hebrew writers of the late nineteenth and early twentieth century essayed a synthesis of their "love-hate relationship" with premodern East European Jewish life. These writers, Miron argues, "managed to both look at [the shtetl] as an object and through it as a subject. . . . As an object, shtetl civilization was presented as anachronistic, solipsistic, and provincial. . . . As a subject, the shtetl image lyrically expressed its essence as the hub of true Jewish intimacy and spiritual self-sufficiency. . . . As both object and subject, it amounted to a tremendously potent myth that nourished and sustained an alienated, nostalgic, modern Jewish community."[90]

Several key works prepared by scholars for the general reader, published between the mid-1960s and mid-1970s in English, repositioned the *shtetl* as a subject of study, whether directly or obliquely, through the compilation of prewar materials. These works address what historian Steven Zipperstein describes as postwar Jews' "resurrection" of Eastern Europe "as a counterweight to America."[91] In their introductions, the editors of these anthologies articulate, sometimes explicitly, their concerns about the need of scholars to correct common misperceptions of the East European Jewish past, articulating a divide between the academy and the general public even as scholars strived to bridge this gap in knowledge and sensibility.

Historian Lucy Dawidowicz's 1967 anthology *The Golden Tradition: Jewish Life and Thought in Eastern Europe* traces the cultural achievements of East European Jewry from the mid-eighteenth to the mid-twentieth century through fifty-seven excerpts from the writings of religious leaders, secular scholars, political activists, educators, and literary figures, spanning the ideological spectrum from religious to secular, integrationist to staunchly Jewish nationalist. As Kirshenblatt-Gimblett notes, the focus in *The Golden Tradition* on elite figures engaged in historically specific circumstances "can be read as a corrective to *Life Is with People*."[92] The overall organization of the anthology is chronological, preceded by an extensive historical introduction to the "world of East European Jewry," arguing for its singular importance by virtue of its scope and achievement. Instead of the paradigm of *shtetl*, Dawidowicz invokes—and transforms—the paradigm of tradition, characterizing it as engaged in an ongoing series of dramas defined by the challenges of modern politics, economics, and culture. On the eve of World War II, she writes, "East European Jewry stood at the threshold of a new era in which traditional Judaism [was] at last ready to encounter the modern world. . . . But the new drama was not acted out; its dramatis personae were cut down forever."[93]

As English became the leading language for the international study of East European Jewish life, the demand for translations of primary texts grew, providing opportunities to create new literary canons and establish intellectual protocols for their engagement. Among these efforts is the 1973 collection *A Shtetl and Other Yiddish Novellas*, edited by Ruth Wisse. In her preface, Wisse cautions against reading these novellas as ethnographic, rather than literary works, "only because, in an understandable hunger for sheer information about the shtetl and the East European 'roots' of modern Jewry, the reader may be led too hastily to accept interpretation as fact, to read a story as sociology or anthropology." At the same time, she characterizes the literary attention to this subject as part of the actuality of the *shtetl*, which was "first and foremost, native ground" for Yiddish authors. Moreover, Wisse sees the attraction to the *shtetl* as literary subject being, in part, its ethnographic value as "a distinctly *Jewish* form of settlement, with a unique sociological and anthropological character," which, in turn, "could be exploited in literature to various mythological ends." Wisse characterizes this development as the continued fate of the *shtetl*: "As the actual world of the shtetl passed ever more completely into history, depictions of it in Yiddish fiction bordered increasingly on the mythical and metaphorical," culminating in the work of Isaac Bashevis Singer, whose literary *shtetlekh* "only appear to be grounded in history and fact but have actually passed into the metaphysical domain. The disappearance of the world of the shtetl doomed and freed the artist to make of reality a metaphor."[94] In this declinist view of the *shtetl* and its remembrance, literature no longer thrives in symbiosis with a living milieu but has become a false friend to those seeking ethnographic representation and is thus a symptom of the *shtetl*'s elusiveness.

Motivated by the pedagogical need to address this new attraction to the topic, Diane and David Roskies created *The Shtetl Book: An Introduction to East European Jewish Life and Lore*, a 1975 compendium of sources on the social history of the "everyday life of ordinary Jews" during the nineteenth and early twentieth centuries in the provincial towns of Eastern Europe. In contrast to *Life Is with People, The Shtetl Book* provides primary materials, focuses considerable attention on one town (Tyszowce), foregrounds the importance of Yiddish, and calls attention to such previously neglected topics as Jewish-gentile relations and "entertainment" (children's games, amateur theatricals). In addition to addressing the dearth of resources on this subject available to English-language readers, the Roskieses characterize their book as offering a corrective to "generalizations and sentimentalism" and assert, "Our book is about real places and events."[95]

The YIVO Institute's 1976 exhibition *Image Before My Eyes* and its attendant album use the medium of photography to portray a history of Polish Jewry from the mid-nineteenth century until the eve of World War II.[96] Photographs serve not only as primary documents but also as an implicit rubric, centering attention on the modernity of Polish Jewry as it engaged this exemplary modern medium. Though the album examines the use of photography to document traditional religiosity (synagogues, cemeteries, ritual preparations), attention centers on new institutions (modern schools, theater, public health organizations, political parties) and, as a consequence, on life in major cities. Though provincial towns are represented

1. Alexey Ivanovich Trankowsky, *Jewish Wedding* (1875). Trankowsky was one of a number of eighteenth- and nineteenth-century artists who depicted Jewish life in provincial towns in Eastern Europe. (See p. 33.) This painting of a wedding procession pays careful attention to details of dress and custom. The town's buildings and foliage frame the celebrants, rooting this ritual within its social geography. (Gift of Dr. and Mrs. Fritz Schmerl, in memory of Professor Hamilton Wolf. The Magnes Collection of Jewish Art and Life, University of California Berkeley.)

2. By the start of the twentieth century, postcards depicting life in provincial towns in Eastern Europe were produced for local markets. (See p. 33.) This World War I–era postcard depicting "Russian types" in the Lithuanian town of Virbalis was produced for German soldiers, writing home about their experiences in "the war in the East." (From the Archives of the YIVO Institute for Jewish Research, New York.)

3. A Jewish immigrant, traveling from America to visit his hometown of Nieśwież, Poland, in the 1920s, poses with his relatives. During the interwar years, a significant number of Jews who had immigrated to the United States traveled back to visit Eastern Europe. (See p. 39.) Photographs such as this not only document family reunions but also reveal the cultural divergence between immigrants and their European relatives, evident in differences in dress and even in the ways that people pose for the camera. (From the Archives of the YIVO Institute for Jewish Research, New York.)

4. Issachar Ryback, “Shul gas” (Synagogue Street), from his 1923 album *Shtetl, mayn khoreve heym: a gedekhenish* (Town, My Destroyed Home: A Remembrance). In this collection of graphic works, the artist memorializes traditional East European Jewish life, disrupted by the upheavals of World War I, through the modernist aesthetics of cubism and expressionism. (See p. 36.) (From the Library of the YIVO Institute for Jewish Research, New York.)

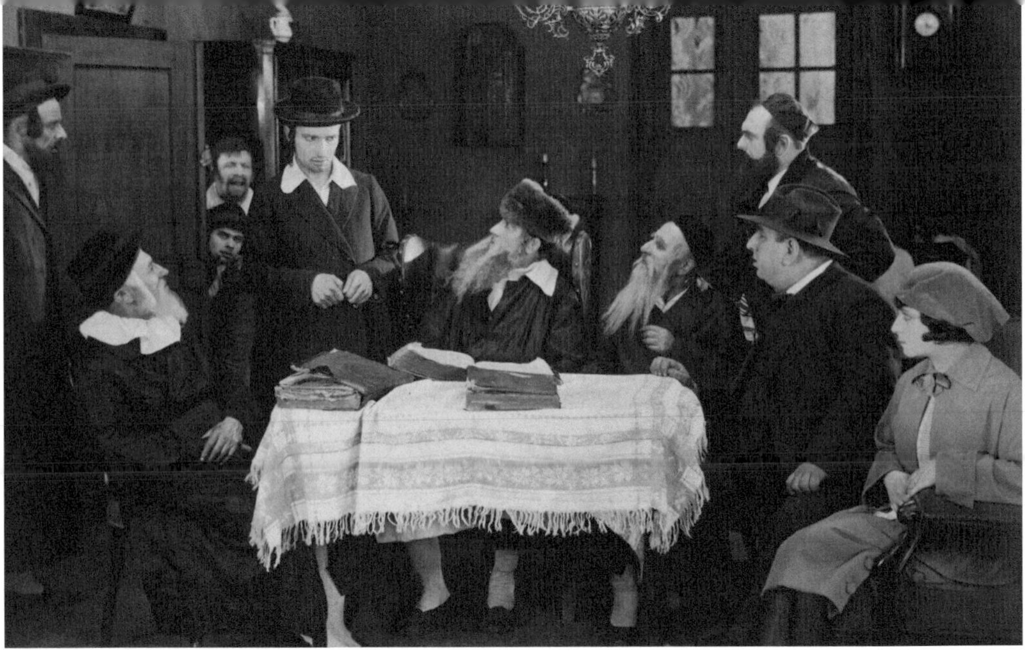

5. Production still for *Ost und West* (East and West), Sidney Goldin's 1923 silent film, in which the mores of an arriviste American Jewish immigrant and his daughter (played by Goldin and Molly Picon, on the right) clash with their Old World relatives during a fateful return visit to his hometown in Galicia. (See p. 41.) (Collection of American Jewish Historical Society.)

6. Scene from the dramatization of Sholem Yankev Abramovitsh's novel *Masoes Binyomin ha-shlishi* (The Travels of Benjamin the Third), staged by the State Yiddish Theater GOSET in Moscow, 1927. Early Soviet Yiddish culture presented *shtetl* life as the negative model of Jewish existence in tsarist times, to be replaced by Jews' transformation into citizens of the socialist state. (See p. 37.) This set design by Robert Falk depicts the *shtetl* in an exaggerated state of disrepair. (© Beit Hatfutsot Photo Archive, Zuskin Collection, Tel Aviv.)

7. Still from *Yankl der shmid* (Yankl the Blacksmith, released with the English-language title *The Singing Blacksmith*), Edgar Ulmer's 1938 film based on a 1906 play by Dovid Pinski. Like several other American Yiddish films set in a *shtetl*, this was filmed on a location near New York City—in this case, on the grounds of a monastery near Newton, New Jersey. (See p. 42.) (Courtesy of the National Center for Jewish Film.)

8. The front of Zalman Kaplan's photography studio in Szczuczyn, Poland, ca. 1930. Up to the start of World War II, Kaplan's had been the town's only photography studio for nearly half a century. (See p. 95.) The gateway to his establishment was flanked by two display cases, in which Kaplan posted recent photographs of his clients. (© mhmarvins@yahoo.com.)

9. Erecting a monument to the murdered Jews of the Polish town of Siedlce, shortly after World War II. Similar memorials, constructed from the remains of vandalized Jewish graveyards, can be found in cities and towns throughout Poland. These monuments both recall the Jewish communities that once thrived in these locales and testify to the extent of their destruction. (See p. 104.) (From the Archives of the YIVO Institute for Jewish Research, New York.)

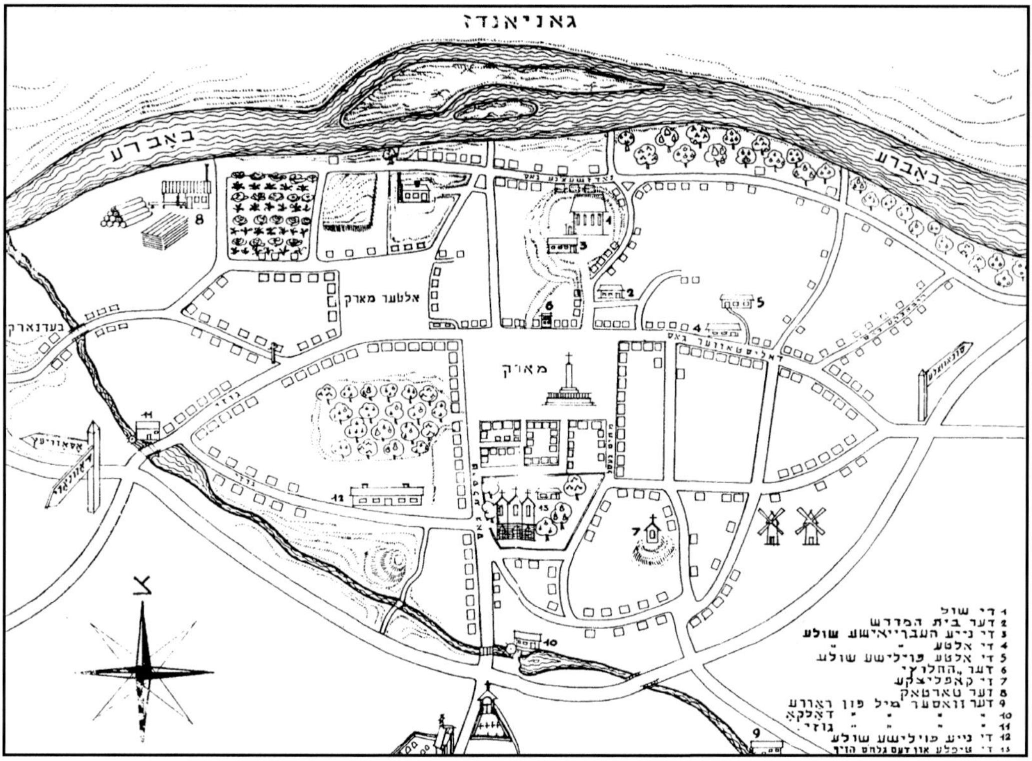

10. Map of Goniądz, drawn from memory by Tuvia Yevrei (Yevreyski), from *Sefer yizkor Gonyondz* (Memorial Book of Goniądz), published in Tel Aviv in 1960. Similar maps appear in many *yizker-bikher*, memorial books written primarily after the Holocaust by Jews who had once lived in East European towns. (See p. 75.) These maps recall the town's geography as it was meaningful to its prewar Jewish residents, labeling locations and using terminology, such as Yiddish street names, that would not be found on a municipal map of the same locale. *(Sefer yizkor Gonyondz*, issued by the Committee of Goniondz Association in the United States and Israel.)

11. Lithograph by William Gropper, from *The Shtetl* (1967). Gropper, best known for cartoons he drew for the left-wing press in the United States, created this series of twenty-four prints, depicting archetypal *shtetl* figures, in tribute to a personal cultural heritage he found both haunting and elusive. (See p. 98.) (William Gropper Papers, Special Collections Research Center, Syracuse University Library. Courtesy of the Gropper family.)

12. Frank Stella, "Grodno I" (1973), from his series *Polish Villages*. During the early 1970s, the artist, one of the leading figures in the American minimalist school, created over one hundred large-scale works such as this one, inspired by prewar photographs of wooden synagogues that had once dotted the East European landscape. (See p. 99.) (© 2013 Frank Stella / Artists Rights Society [ARS], New York. Photo: Art Resource, NY.)

13. Cover of *The Paper Shtetl: A Complete Model of an East European Jewish Town*, created by David Grupper and David G. Klein in 1984. This cut-and-paste activity book reflects notions prevalent in post–World War II America about the *shtetl*: an exclusively Jewish community, steeped in piety, and largely untouched by modern ideas or social and political change. (See p. 78.) While this model excludes the non-Jewish residents of these towns, it merges elements of rural Jewish life with *shtetl* practices. ("Book cover," copyright © 1984 by Random House, Inc., from *The Paper Shtetl: A Complete Model of an East European Jewish Town*, created by David Grupper and David G. Klein. Used by permission of Schocken Books, a division of Random House, Inc. Any third-party use of this material, outside of this publication, is prohibited. Interested parties must apply directly to Random House, Inc. for permission.)

14. Mayer Kirshenblatt, *Mother Giving Birth to My Brother Vadye* (1994), one of over two hundred paintings the artist made of his life growing up in Opatów, Poland, during the interwar years. Kirshenblatt began this series of memory paintings almost sixty years after leaving his hometown in the 1930s. (See p. 102.) Like other artists recalling the East European Jewish past, Kirshenblatt integrates personal and family history with depictions of traditional practices. Here, for example, he shows a key beside his mother's bed, because it was a custom to place a key beneath a woman in labor to help "open the gates" of her womb. (Collection of the Mayer Kirshenblatt family. Courtesy of Barbara Kirshenblatt-Gimblett.)

15. This fundraising brochure for the Shtetl Museum, printed at the turn of the twenty-first century, juxtaposes two approaches undertaken by Yaffa Eliach to represent *shtetl* life of the pre-Holocaust era: a monumental installation in the United States Holocaust Memorial Museum in Washington, D.C., which displays Eliach's collection of hundreds of photographs of Jews who once lived in her hometown of Ejszyszki (see p. 95), and Eliach's plan to reenact provincial East European Jewish life in the form of a living history museum, to be erected in Rishon LeZion, Israel. (See p. 115.) (Collection of Jeffrey Shandler.)

16. Visitors pose in the *shtetl* exhibition in the South African Jewish Museum, which opened in Cape Town in 2000. By photographing themselves in this environment, which merges reconstructed architectural elements with an enlarged photograph of a street in a Lithuanian town, tourists simulate prewar pictures taken of immigrants on return visits to their hometowns. (See p. 115.) (South African Jewish Museum, Cape Town.)

17. Frédéric Brenner, *Hanging of Haman, Purimspiel*, Tykocin, Poland (2002). At the turn of the millennium, residents of Tykocin—home to a restored Baroque-era masonry synagogue that had become a significant tourist attraction—began staging an annual Purim play. (See p. 106.) By enacting the story told in the biblical Book of Esther of Persian Jews' miraculous rescue from persecution, these Poles both recall the town's prewar Jewish community and, at the same time, obscure the history of its destruction during the Holocaust. (© Frédéric Brenner, Courtesy of Howard Greenberg Gallery, New York.)

18. *Kroniki sejneńskie* (Sejny Chronicles), a 2008 theater piece created and performed by young people from this town in northeastern Poland, commemorates Sejny's multicultural history. Central to the performance is a clay model of the town with which the players interact. This piece is one of a number of cultural initiatives undertaken by the Borderland (Pogranicze) Foundation, a nongovernmental organization based in Sejny, dedicated to promoting awareness and accord among Eastern Europe's multiple ethnicities, religions, and nationalities. (See p. 113.) (Photograph by Michal Moniuszko.)

19. Yelena Shmulevitch on the set of Joel and Ethan Coen's 2009 film *A Serious Man.* Shmulevitch played Dora, the "Shtetl Wife" in the film's Yiddish-language prologue. This opening scene haunts the rest of the feature, which is set in Minneapolis in 1967, suggesting oblique connections between Jewish storytelling, especially about the uncanny, in prewar Eastern Europe and postwar America. (See p. 135.) (Photograph by Allen Lewis Rickman.)

20. A poster for Sex and the Shtetl, a 2009 conference convened by the Graduate Theological Union and the Program in Jewish Studies at the University of California, Berkeley. Exemplary of recent academic trends, scholars attending the conference examined gender roles, sexual mores, and eroticism in East European Jewish culture of the nineteenth and early twentieth centuries. (See p. 89.) Here, the *shtetl* serves less as the topic per se than as a well-known point of entry to the East European Jewish past, whose presumed familiarity is being challenged. The poster features El Lissitzky's illustrations to Mani-Leyb's children's poem "Yingl Tsingl Khvat," originally published in 1918/19. (Graphic design by Lee Bearson.)

21. This replica of the ceiling of the eighteenth-century wooden synagogue that once stood in Gwoździec, Poland, was created by Handshouse Studio, a "not-for-profit innovative educational organization" based in Massachusetts, which "initiates adventurous hands-on projects as a way to explore history, understand science, and perpetuate the arts." Over three hundred professionals and students from around the world participated in the construction of this ceiling in 2011–2012. Built with the same technology used for the original synagogue, the ceiling is the largest artifact in the Museum of the History of Polish Jews, which opens in Warsaw in 2014. (See p. 113.) (Courtesy of Richard and Laura Brown, Handshouse Studio, Inc. www.handshouse.org; www.handshousestudio.org.)

amply in the volume, they are not distinguished as *shtetlekh* (e.g., Kazimierz nad Wisłą and Krzemieniec are identified as "cities," along with Lublin, Cracow, and Warsaw); rather, *Image Before My Eyes* uses the term "settlement" for the full range of Jewish communities in Poland. Whereas *Life Is with People* offers a composite, timeless, synthetic narrative, *Image Before My Eyes* is a bricolage work, composed of hundreds of photographs that are themselves inherently fragmentary and specific in their relation to time and place. In *Image Before My Eyes* the history of photography defines both the rise of Polish Jewry's encounters with modernity and, implicitly, its abrupt demise during the Holocaust. World War II marked the end of established photographic practices for Europe's Jews, replaced by photography under Nazism, whether as an instrument of surveillance by perpetrators or as an underground practice of resistance.

A curious barometer of scholarly attention to the *shtetl* is the frequency with which the term has figured in works whose subjects lie beyond Jewish life in provincial East European towns. Beginning in the 1970s, both academic and general publications have appeared with titles that begin "From shtetl to. . . ." These titles variously lead to geographic locations in the United States (*From Shtetl to Milltown: Litvaks, Hungarians, and Galizianers in Western Pennsylvania*), France (*De mon shtetl à Paris*), or Australia ("From the Shtetl to the Monash Soviet: An Overview of the Historiography of Jewish Radicalism in Australia"), as well as more abstract destinations: *From Shtetl to Suburbia: The Family in Jewish Literary Imagination; From Shtetl to Destruction: The Jewish Experience in Eastern Europe; From Shtetl to Socialism: Studies from 'Polin.'*[97] Ranging from a memoir tracing an actual journey originating in a small East European town to an anthology of scholarly essays on Polish Jewry, these works all invoke the *shtetl* as an archetypal locus of origin. At about the same time, another group of titles began to appear, in which diverse locations—Antwerp; Whitechapel; the East Bronx; Bessemer, Alabama; Gloversville, New York; Moises Ville, Argentina—are each identified as a *shtetl.*[98] This group of titles, in contrast with the previous one, conceptualizes the *shtetl* as a Jewish community with expansive possibilities for reproduction. These titles indicate not simply a wide familiarity with the *shtetl* but also its ready acceptance as an exemplar of Jewish social geography. Simultaneously the *shtetl* is understood as a nucleus of centrifugal movement and an enduring communal paradigm that readily reproduces itself.

By the turn of the millennium, scholarship on East European Jewry had become a fixture of the humanities and social sciences, burgeoning in quantity and variety. This development reflects larger trends in the fields of Jewish studies, East European studies, Holocaust studies, and Slavic studies and also responds to changes outside the academy, especially the collapse of communist governments in Eastern Europe and the USSR. This wide-ranging scholarship—including the work of historians, literature scholars, linguists, anthropologists, folklorists, sociologists, political scientists, art historians, ethnomusicologists, and others—is regularly presented at international conferences and colloquia and published in multiple languages. Several academic book series and journals are now devoted to East European Jewry in part or in their entirety.[99] The scope of scholarship on this topic is exemplified by *The YIVO Encyclopedia of Jews in Eastern Europe*, published in 2008, with contributions by over 450 authors from around the world.[100]

Within this larger expansion is a growth of scholarly attention to the *shtetl*, signaled by a new widespread use of the term in academic writing. As of September 2012, a major database on dissertations and master's theses in North America and Europe lists 377 citations for works that include the word *shtetl* in their texts. The earliest example was written in 1964; 1 more appeared in the 1960s, followed by 3 in the 1970s, 13 in the 1980s, 9 in the 1990s—and then 197 in the first decade of the twenty-first century. The upward surge appears to continue into the next decade, with 153 examples reported for the years 2010–2012.[101] Even allowing for less complete reporting in the database of dissertations from earlier decades, these figures suggest a remarkable contemporary embrace of the *shtetl* as a subject of academic interest and a term of scholarly discourse. *Shtetl* figures in contemporary scholarship in several ways: the term is sometimes used as a metonym for East European Jewry; individual towns or *shtetlekh* as a group are scrutinized as historical subjects in their own right; scholars examine creative work—especially literature, but also drama, film, music, and visual art—about the *shtetl*; scholars of contemporary culture analyze new attention to the *shtetl* in tourism and other practices; and *shtetl* has prompted a meta-scholarship on its use as a discursive phenomenon.

Former residents now seldom undertake close studies of an individual town; rather, they are usually the work of professional scholars with intellectual, rather than personal, interests in these sites. Exemplary is Gershon Hundert's *The Jews in a Polish Private Town: The Case of Opatów in the Eighteenth Century*, which examines relations between Poles and Jews during a crucial period in the history of both communities through the close reading of "one of the best-documented private towns" in eighteenth-century Poland. Addressing the question "Why Opatów?" Hundert explains its strategic importance for Polish Jewish history generally: Opatów's location in the region of Małopolska, the town's history of ownership by a series of magnate families, and its position as home to "one of the preeminent Jewish families of east central Europe," whose influence in Jewish communal life extended far beyond Opatów.[102]

An ongoing concern, especially for historians and literature scholars, is analyzing the actualities of past Jewish life in East European provincial towns in relation to representations of the *shtetl* in belles-lettres or popular culture. In addition to pointing up discrepancies between "image" and "reality" and challenging popular misconceptions about *shtetl* life derived from these representations, these studies sometimes address the rationale for this disparity. By the turn of the twenty-first century, a familiar roster of discrepancies had emerged, with the onus usually placed on representations, deprecated as sentimentalized, overgeneralized, hyper-Judaized, or ideologically driven. Historians such as Anthony Polonsky see their task as "recover[ing] a past which is as accurate a depiction as we can make of a world" in its diversity.[103] Literature scholars, conversely, argue for the centrality of the imaginary; thus, David Roskies characterizes the *shtetl* as "arguably the greatest single invention of Yiddish literature," exemplifying what he terms the "Jewish search for a usable past."[104] Some scholars relate the disparity between "image" and "reality" to a divergence in sensibility between the academy and the general public. Samuel Kassow writes, in his introduction to a 2007 collection of scholarly essays offering "new evaluations" of the *shtetl*, that, despite "gross generalizations and romanticized nostalgia" attending the subject, "serious students of history, anthropology, architecture, and literature have begun to apply their multidisciplinary insights to describing and understanding this most important facet of East European Jewish life."[105] At the same time, there is concern for a common unfamiliarity with the actuality of the *shtetl*, which, literature scholars Gennady Estraikh and Mikhail Krutikov note, is "a *terra incognita* not only for young students but often also for their lecturers."[106]

The distance separating scholars and others from the East European Jewish past changed radically in the last decade of the twentieth century with the fall of communism. Greater access to archives in Eastern Europe has brought to light materials unseen for decades—often to researchers in those countries as well as scholars in the West—presenting new possibilities for scholarship on the region's Jewish past, including new assessments of Jewish life in East European provincial towns. Some archival treasures have been made newly available to the general public; most notably, materials collected during An-ski's 1912–1914 expeditions, now housed in the State Ethnographic Museum in St. Petersburg, toured museums in Western Europe, Israel, and the United States in the early 1990s.[107]

Easier travel to Eastern Europe in the post-communist era has enabled a variety of new scholarly projects. Return visits to ancestral hometowns in Eastern Europe inspired historians Omer Bartov and Shimon Redlich to write monographs about these locales' histories either in the years culminating in the Holocaust (in Redlich's book on Brzezany) or during the war and its aftermath (in Bartov's book on Buczacz and environs), focusing in each case on non-Jews' relations with Jews and their destruction.[108] Expanded travel opportunities have also enabled new research on Jewish visual and material culture in provincial towns as well as opportunities for ethnographic work among Jews now living in these locations.[109] Projects to videotape elderly East European Jews, as Holocaust survivors or Yiddish speakers, also yield information about the experiences of those Jews who remained in the region's provincial towns after the war, unlike most other Jewish Holocaust survivors, who moved to larger cities or other countries.[110]

AHEYM, the Archives of Historical and Ethnographic Yiddish Memories (the acronym is Yiddish for "homeward"), was initiated in 2002 by two Indiana University professors, linguist Dov-Ber Kerler and historian Jeffrey Veidlinger, who journeyed to Eastern Europe to videotape interviews with over 300 Jews born in the first decades of the twentieth century. Kerler and Veidlinger prize their target population, who "remained in their native region" in the aftermath of the Holocaust, as an atavistic resource. These elderly Jews are valued informants both linguistically—as "Eastern Europe's last native speakers of Yiddish"—and historically, as Jews who had not, like most others in postwar Eastern Europe, "abandoned the shtetls and the Yiddish language and found instead a future in the larger metropolises, where they lost many of the local customs, beliefs, and practices that had defined Jewish identity in the prewar shtetl." The move "homeward" that AHEYM celebrates is therefore undertaken not by its subjects, who stayed in the region, but by its scholars and then others who will use its resources.

In promoting the project to North Americans who largely no longer speak Yiddish, AHEYM fuses the language's symbolic value with the *shtetl* of "popular imagination": "Whether it is borsht and knishes, klezmer, Jewish humor and Yiddish vaudeville, Chagall or wooden synagogues, contemporary notions of Yiddish culture are inseparable from the territory of Eastern Europe in general and the shtetl in particular." Although the project records life histories of elderly Jews who witnessed and participated in an extraordinary series of historical events, framed by the rise and fall of the Soviet Union, attention centers not on this dynamic but on what among these Jews endured despite these epochal changes, epitomized by their remaining in these provincial towns, manifest in Yiddish dialects and folkways.[111]

Recent ethnographic research on the *shtetl* among scholars in the former USSR offers a decidedly different approach from much of the work undertaken in the West, as seen in *Shtetl XXI vek: polevye issledovaniia* (The Shtetl of the 21st Century: Field Research).[112] The essays in this collection are based on fieldwork conducted in Ukraine between 2005 and 2007 by faculty and graduate students at Jewish studies centers in Moscow and St. Petersburg. As Deborah Yalen notes in her review of this anthology, it "poses a challenge to the prevailing image of the shtetl in Western Jewish culture as an irretrievably lost world" and offers instead examinations of "the 'post-Soviet shtetl' as a legitimate and viable object of present-day anthropological study." This work challenges Western scholarship not only by questioning "assumptions . . . that Soviet Jewish identity constitutes a departure from a 'normative' model of Jewish identity" but also by foregrounding the value of contemporary ethnography—on-site observations of material culture and interviews with living informants—over literary and archival research as central to understanding Jewish life in Eastern Europe in the past as well as the present.[113] Concurrently, scholars in the West, including Yalen, have been reassessing established understandings of Soviet Jewish culture, including its conceptualizations of *shtetl* life.[114]

Contemporary American scholarship on the *shtetl* often reflects larger trends in Jewish studies in the United States, from attention to gender to a focus on Jewish-Christian relations. American scholars have revisited canonical texts on *shtetl* life to offer new theorizations of their significance, whether positing that the Haskalah is a Jewish Romantic movement, centered in Eastern Europe (per historian Olga Litvak), or that "classic" Yiddish fiction exemplifies a postcolonial critique of modernism (per literature scholar Marc Caplan).[115] Holocaust historians have examined *shtetlekh* in case studies of how both Jews and their neighbors responded to German occupation. Most notable is Jan Gross's *Neighbors: The Destruction of the Jewish Community in Jedwabne, Poland* (2000), a study of local Poles' participation in the mass murder of the town's Jews during World War II, which roiled postwar memory on a national scale.[116] Historians of the war also turn attention to *shtetlekh* when examining the work of Einsatzgruppen, mobile squads that executed Jewish communities in or near provincial towns throughout Eastern Europe. The scale of these operations, defined by these towns' size and location (as opposed to the Holocaust's large urban ghettos or the industrialized murder of death camps) highlights the intimacy of this genocidal operation.[117] Even as these studies focus on persecution, they offer an oblique portrait of prewar relations between Jews and their neighbors through events that constitute a macabre unraveling of earlier life in these towns.

Attention in Jewish studies to memory practices has inspired scholars to examine works that study or recall the *shtetl* not for what they reveal about the actualities of an erstwhile Jewish way of life but for how these works are themselves of interest as cultural artifacts. In addition to more broad-based works of meta-scholarship, such as Steven Zipperstein's discussion of American imaginings of the *shtetl* in his reflections on "the relationship between history and metaphor in the ways in which the Russian Jewish past has been understood in the last century," scholars have examined *shtetl* remembrance in *yizker-bikher* and works of popular culture (such as *Fiddler on the Roof*), as well as the conceptualization of the *shtetl* in the intellectual histories of scholarly disciplines (exemplified by Mikhail Krutikov's survey of literary criticism on Yiddish *shtetl* fiction) or individual works (notably *Life Is with People*).[118]

The dynamic of studying the *shtetl* entails shifting notions of the value of writing about Jewish life in Eastern Europe's provincial towns. This writing begins with the proto-scholarship of *pinkeysim* and seventeenth-century martyrologies, local practices of remembrance that have a semi-sacred status, followed by the anti-scholarship of the Haskalah, which codified the *shtetl* as a defining Jewish locus, even as *maskilim* frequently repudiated the subject in memoirs or mocked it in satires. With the advent of modern scholarship on East European Jewry, writers turned to *shtetlekh* as sites providing the raw goods of research; historians, folklorists, social scientists, as well as literary and visual artists went to these provincial towns to find material for their endeavors. As *shtetlekh* attracted interest in their own right, especially in the wake of their destabilization during World War I, they became the subject of heritage scholarship, notably in interwar Poland and among immigrants in the United States. At the same time, *shtetlekh* in Soviet Russia served as the proving ground of state-sponsored scholarship, while concerns for the future of Jews in these towns also motivated researchers in the West working for Jewish philanthropies. In the early aftermath of World War II, scholars elevated the *shtetl* to the stature of a paradigm, central both to conceptualizing the "lost world" of East European Jewry and to postulating a transcendent Jewish cultural pattern or essence that endures beyond the Holocaust. A dispassionate scholarship now seeks to redress the "wrongs" of popular attention to the *shtetl* through work that is methodologically rigorous and strives to be non-ideological. Most recently, a poststructural scholarship has taken a more self-conscious approach to the topic, variously addressing the need to nuance, qualify, demystify, or interrogate *shtetl* discourses. Notwithstanding this new scrutiny, the importance of the *shtetl* endures. Indeed, this attention enhances—even as it problematizes—the *shtetl*'s significance.

Throughout these epistemological shifts in writing about *shtetlekh* run other dynamics that complicate this periodization. From *pinkeysim* to the interwar *landkentenish* movement to contemporary genealogists and local historians, one finds a recurrent attention to specificity, motivated by a close geographic, communal, or personal connection to a particular *shtetl*. Complementing this dynamic is another, which extends from maskilic satires to turn-of-the-century amassing of folklore materials to works of early post-Holocaust "popular ethnography," in which the *shtetl* is regarded at a distance and as an abstraction, structure, or exemplar.

These dynamics are further complicated by the continued repurposing of older writings. *Pinkeysim* acquired new significance in the late nineteenth century, when modern Jewish historians collected these chronicles as primary materials for their scholarship. No longer objects of internal, local interest, *pinkeysim* became resources for scholars of East European Jewish communal life as this informed a larger historical narrative. Similarly, interest in *yizker-bikher* has grown in recent years among researchers; as a result, some of these books, which were originally written for a cohort of the towns' surviving Jewish communities, have been translated into English or transformed into websites.

The geographic and cultural distances that define postwar study of the *shtetl* vary among its many scholars, posing different challenges according to where scholars are situated. Contemporary Israeli scholars can find it daunting to understand the *shtetl* as a Jewish entity thriving in diaspora, independent of a sovereign state or territorial demographic majority. For supporters of political Zionism, in Israel and elsewhere, the *shtetl* exemplifies the larger challenge of understanding how Jewishness could prosper, uncompromised in its difference or sense of Jewish pride, without "a land of one's own." Contemporary Polish scholars may find counterintuitive the notion of the *shtetl* as a locus within Poland, in which Jews flourished culturally both in relation to Poles and independent of them. As an epitomizing locus of a Jewish claim on Polishness, the *shtetl* can be unrecognizable to Poles in the postwar era. Engaging the *shtetl* is part of a larger challenge Poles face in understanding their multicultural past and their complicated roles in the undoing of a multiethnic Poland, whether as bystanders or as agents. Scholars in the former USSR confront the challenge of situating their study of the *shtetl* in relation to the complex layers of scholarship in prerevolutionary Russia and the Soviet era. In this regard, studying the *shtetl* is part of larger challenges these scholars face in positioning their work vis-à-vis both this fraught past and the expectations of Western scholarship. Contemporary American scholars can find the *shtetl* perplexing, as a place where Jews flourished largely without the benefits of democracy, citizenship, a socially open consumer culture, the possibility of assimilation (whether as opportunity or as threat), or the security that the existence of a Jewish state provides for the imagination, if not in actuality. The *shtetl* thus exemplifies the challenge for Americans to understand the possibilities of Jewish life in the diaspora outside the United States.

Studying the *shtetl* poses to all contemporary scholars the common challenge of thinking beyond the telos of the Holocaust. For decades, scholars have grappled with how to consider the *shtetl* in relation to its destruction and the intellectual onus of remembering Jewish life in relation to Jews' murder. These dilemmas not only haunt scholarly writing on the *shtetl*; they also inform the work of artists, writers, filmmakers, and others who have engaged the *shtetl* in a variety of creative endeavors, the subject of the next chapter.

3 *Shtetl* Fabulous

Scholarship and nonfiction writing on the *shtetl* flourished after World War II alongside an array of other engagements with this subject: fiction, poetry, and plays; musical compositions, works of visual art, films, videos, and other media works; museum exhibitions, festivals, and other tourist productions. At first, many of these endeavors were the work of Jews who had once lived in East European provincial towns, but increasingly these are the efforts of people with no experience of this way of life. Rather, they are projects of the imagination that both rely on older representations of *shtetl* life and respond to new attractions to this subject. In this changing relationship with the *shtetl*, inventiveness acquires a new primacy, in part due to a need to compensate for the lack of personal memories of this way of life. Moreover, as reactions to the massive loss of people, resources, and cultural literacy in the war's aftermath, these endeavors have value as productive acts. By dint of their creativity, these conjurings of the *shtetl* defy the destructive will behind the Holocaust, even though they often acknowledge its impact. They test the constraints of cultural breakdown and sometimes flout the strictures of scholarship. These imagined engagements with the *shtetl* demonstrate both the power and the limits of creative work in the subjunctive mode as a response to genocide and bereavement.

Image

Among early postwar efforts to engage Jewish life in prewar Eastern Europe, visual media—two- and three-dimensional artworks; photography, both still and moving; exhibitions and installations; collectibles and ephemera—reveal with particular urgency and poignancy the challenges faced by endeavors to conjure the *shtetl*. After the Holocaust, visual artists were abruptly bereft of sources, in some respects more so than postwar writers addressing the same subject. Much of prewar Jewry's visual culture was destroyed or inaccessible. Many artworks and artifacts, including those in museum collections, were lost, stolen, destroyed, or otherwise missing from their prewar provenances. Physical environments where Jews once lived had been looted, vandalized, and emptied of both inhabitants and their possessions. New political circumstances made visiting many of these sites difficult. Postwar visual engagements with the *shtetl* therefore grapple not only with the loss of people and their way of life but also with the disruption of visual mediation—and, moreover, of the visible. The postwar trope of characterizing prewar East European Jewry as a "vanished world" implies the loss of any visible traces of the past. Indeed, Jewish survivors' memoirs regularly recount discovering the absence of anyone or anything recognizable after the war. The void has since become emblematic of the Holocaust.

A key strategy among the earliest efforts to address this loss in visual terms is the repurposing of available prewar visual materials, exemplified by Raphael Abramovitsh's *Di farshvundene velt/The Vanished World*, a collection of 350 photographs of prewar East European Jewish life, published in 1947 by the Forward Association. This volume both mourns the Holocaust's millions of victims and commemorates Eastern Europe as having been "the religious and spiritual hegemony of World Jewry" for five centuries.[1] Abramovitsh calls attention to the transformation of the original prewar provenance of photographs now serving as memento mori, by explaining that they "were taken by people who could not foresee that they were photographing a people on the eve of their destruction."[2] *The Vanished World* is among the first efforts to use prewar photography toward this new end of memorializing East European Jewish life before the Holocaust. Despite (or, perhaps, precisely because of) the irony inherent in this undertaking, which strives to use photographs to make visible what can no longer to be seen, the practice has become widespread. Photographs documenting the routines of prewar East European Jews serve as commemorative artifacts in numerous publications, artworks, films, and museum displays, which at times imbue these pictures with the power of votive objects.

Efforts to collect and present photographs of prewar Jewish life have grown in scope, format, and symbolic gravitas. In the 1990s, Fundacja Shalom, an organization dedicated to promoting Jewish culture in Poland, collected from Polish citizens photographs in their possession of prewar Jews. This project yielded hundreds of images as well as stories of remembrance and loss of former acquaintances. These photographs and recollections eventually appeared in a book and exhibition, *And I Still See Their Faces: Images of Polish Jews/I ciągle widzę ich twarze: Fotografia Żydów polskich*.[3] Because many of the images came from Poles who did not know the identity of the subjects—only that they were Jews—the project derives much of its value not from the visual information that photography provides about prewar Jewish life, in contrast to the presentation of similar pictures in *Image Before My Eyes* (discussed in chapter 2). Rather, the impact of *And I Still See Their Faces* lies in the absence of information—as well as people and their culture—and the haunting power of lost, unidentified Jews.

In several recent memorial projects centered on similar prewar photographs, a single town provides the rubric for defining the collection of images and informing their significance. A cache of some 2,400 photographs confiscated at Auschwitz from Jews deported from Będzin in 1943 appears in two different albums, both published in 2001.[4] Whereas most such photographs were destroyed at the death camp, this collection—apparently taken from several families from Będzin who had been deported at the same time—remained intact, probably by accident. The pictures' postwar preservation, documentation, exhibition, and publication are characterized both as acts of Holocaust commemoration that testify to the void—"gestures of confrontation with a loss that cannot be nullified"—and as efforts at "recreating that lost world" in microcosm.[5]

Hundreds of photographs of life in Szczuczyn—taken by Zalman Kaplan, who ran the town's only photography studio from the 1890s through the 1930s—were collected decades later by his grandson Mike Marvins, himself a professional photographer based in Houston, Texas. In addition to offering a glimpse of life in Szczuczyn over nearly half a century, the collection provides insight into the photographer's role in a small East European town. Kaplan documented local landmarks and community organizations, both Jewish and Christian, as well as the people who visited his studio to be photographed. Kaplan's pictures, presented in exhibitions, a book, and online, demonstrate the medium's place in this and similar communities. Beyond documenting the lives of Szczuczyn residents, photography served them as a modern vehicle for self-fashioning and enacting communality.[6]

Most famously, personal photographs symbolically reconstitute a Jewish community destroyed during World War II in a monumental display, known as the Tower of Faces, in the United States Holocaust Memorial Museum in Washington, D.C., which opened in 1993. The installation features over 1,000 photographs of prewar Jewish residents of Ejszyszki. The images come from a collection initiated in the late 1970s by Holocaust survivor and scholar Yaffa Eliach, who was four years old in September 1941, when all but twenty-nine of Ejszyszki's 3,500 Jews were shot and buried in mass graves by members of an Einsatzgruppe and its Lithuanian collaborators. Eliach and her immediate family were among those who escaped this fate, and most of them survived the war in hiding.

The museum's exhibition designers lined the walls of a rectangular tower with oversized reproductions of photographs from Eliach's collection. The tower runs perpendicular to the museum's core exhibition, which is displayed on three floors, and intersects the exhibition's narrative at two strategic points. The first occurs just before visitors leave the exhibition's first, uppermost floor, which chronicles the Nazi rise to power before World War II. Here the tower is introduced as "a shtetl," depicting residents of a "typical" East European Jewish community.[7] As visitors pass through the tower near its top, they are surrounded by the photographs, which extend from the top of the tower down to the visitors' eye level and descend below their feet to the level beneath. Later, upon leaving the exhibition's second floor, which relates the implementation of the Nazi-led genocide, visitors encounter the tower again. At this point, they are at its bottom and can look up to see the images rise past the ceiling to the level above. Here the photos are identified as representing "the end of a shtetl."

Whereas the museum displays photographs elsewhere as evidence of crimes perpetrated by Nazi Germany and its collaborators, the images in the Tower of Faces are offered as objects—indeed, as icons—of memory. The photographs' significance is defined both by their massing on a grand scale—it is impossible to see all of the images at one time, and some are always at an elevation that prevents them from being seen up close—and by the installation's distinctive positioning within the core exhibition's master narrative. When first encountering the tower, museumgoers are offered a last glimpse of *shtetl* life, and all that it invokes, before it sinks out of sight (at this vantage, the photographs seem to be falling below one's feet). When encountered the second time, the tower provides a haunting look back at a community—and the way of life it exemplifies—that has ended. This time, the visitor views the images as they appear to rise up, heavenward. These perspectives recall literary tropes of the *shtetl* as declinist (e.g., An-ski) and as elegiac (e.g., Heschel). Though the tower is monumental in scale, it also resembles the intimate layout of a "family [photo] album," in which visitors "are situated right inside . . . a domestic space," according to Marianne Hirsch, thereby presenting the *shtetl* as though it were an extended family, frozen in time and universally familiar in the subjects' response to the camera's gaze.[8]

Drawings and paintings of the *shtetl* appeared in print and exhibition concomitant with early postwar publications of prewar East European Jewish photography. Collections of prewar portraits, genre scenes, and landscapes depicting *shtetl* life repurpose these works as memorial gestures, especially in relation to postwar artwork. In 1946 the Yiddish press Dos naye lebn (The New Life), based in Poland, issued *Dos shtetl* (The Town), a volume of forty artworks by Zinovi Tolkatshov. In the volume's preface, Mikhl Mirski—a writer who had been active in prewar left-wing publications and fought in the Polish Army during World War II—hails the collection as "the first significant artistic response to our national catastrophe." Tolkatshov, who had served in the Red Army, was then best known in Poland and the USSR for his drawings of the recently liberated death camps Majdanek and Auschwitz. His prewar artwork includes illustrations for Soviet editions of Sholem Aleichem's fiction.

Dos shtetl pairs paintings Tolkatshov had created in the 1930s with lithographs he made immediately after the war. Both pre- and postwar images depict characters from Sholem Aleichem's works as well as generic *shtetl* scenes and types. Mirski describes the pairings as our "old way of life . . . confronted by [our] national catastrophe." He notes, for example, that the book's first two images, portraits of the Yiddish writer, juxtapose "Sholem Aleichem of the past, standing before a view of his . . . town (albeit a stooped town of old cottages with roofs in disrepair), organically growing together with his environment" with an image of the author "today, not in the town, but on a field with bare trees and plowed-up earth. There is no longer a Jewish town, but something seen from a distance, a remnant." Mirski argues that the artist's postwar "turn to Sholem Aleichem is not a step backward," but that it follows the "movement of Sholem Aleichem and his protagonists on the road to Majdanek and Treblinka." Unlike Tolkatshov's images documenting the devastation he encountered in death camps, the postwar drawings in *Dos shtetl* obliquely reference Jewish losses (including the destruction of his original prewar paintings, reproduced in this volume from photographs taken before the war). Tolkatshov's postwar images visualize loss in relation to the diminished state of what remains, underscored by the shift from the richer texture of his paintings to his more spare postwar lithographs. As Mirski notes, "confrontation is the leitmotif"[9] that runs throughout these images or, more precisely, through their juxtaposition.

Lionel Reiss's drawings, etchings, and paintings of similar *shtetl* scenes figure within a more complex series of repurposings of prewar images in postwar contexts. A child immigrant from Jarosław to the United States at the turn of the twentieth century, Reiss worked as a commercial artist in New York before embarking on a sketching tour of Jewish neighborhoods across Europe, northern Africa, the eastern Mediterranean, and the Arabian Peninsula in the early 1920s. Reiss first published this work in the 1938 book *My Models Were Jews: A Painter's Pilgrimage to Many Lands*. The volume includes a selection of images of European Jewish neighborhoods in cities and towns, titled "Life in the Ghettos." Among these works are several *shtetl* scenes—including "The Muddy Stream, Tarnopol," "Market in Chelm," "Ghetto in Stryj"—as well as scenes of provincial East European Jewish life in unspecified locations ("Street Fiddler," "Fish Market," "Blessing the New Moon"). Historian Cecil Roth introduces these works as souvenirs of Reiss's journey to find Jewish "old worlds" in a race against the onslaught of modernity, noting that "in many cases, the solitary record of these rapidly-passing monuments of the past is now to be found in paintings and drawings."[10]

Many of Reiss's images of European Jews reappear, though configured differently, in his 1954 book *New Lights and Old Shadows*. Following images of the new State of Israel, this volume looks back to prewar European Jewish life as "A World That Has Vanished." Again, these works are introduced by Roth, who situates Reiss's subject not within the mission of the nostalgic traveler but as a scholar mourning the destruction of a traditional Jewish way of life. Roth elegizes Eastern Europe as this venerable culture's last bastion, notwithstanding the hardships that the region's Jews endured, possessed of "a dignity which no poverty or maltreatment could undermine." Though Roth hails Reiss's artwork as "irreplaceable historic document[s]" of this lost culture, they remind the historian of the destruction's scope, even as postwar communities strive to forge new relationships with this past: "It is not only that six million human beings were brutally done to death . . . but that an entire way of life and an entire civilization have been uprooted. . . . A handful of survivors have carried some pale shadow of their former existence to London, to New York, to Buenos Aires. . . . But whether in these centres it can endure is problematical, for the heart of that life is now stilled."[11]

Reiss's drawings of East European Jews were published yet again in 1971, this time in a book devoted exclusively to the topic: *A World at Twilight: A Portrait of Jewish Communities of Eastern Europe before the Holocaust*. Framing the artwork are texts by Isaac Bashevis Singer and literature scholar Milton Hindus that foreground the *shtetl* as a paradigm for Jewish life in prewar Eastern Europe. Whereas Roth termed European Jewish neighborhoods "ghettos," both Singer and Hindus refer to the region's Jewish settlements generally with the term *shtetl*. In keeping with its title, the volume's organization of images and texts presents this culture in crepuscular decline, with sections devoted to "Primitive Living Conditions," "Poverty," and "Negative Features" (which include "Superstitions," "The Bathhouse on Friday," and "The Heder"), and ends with a discussion of the "transplantation" of this culture as an attempt to "bridge the chasm between the Old World shtetl of eastern Europe and modern America."[12] Over the course of Reiss's three books, the *shtetl* comes into its own as a subject of artistic reflection, and an enduring declinist view of the *shtetl* is balanced by desires to span the gap between this past and the Jewish present.

Shortly before this last volume of Reiss's artwork appeared, another American artist, William Gropper, paid similar tribute to the East European Jewish past. In 1967, Gropper created *The Shtetl*, a set of twenty-four color lithographs drawn with an economical yet expressive use of line, similar to the left-wing political cartoons for which he is best known. Gropper described *The Shtetl* as a "personal" work: "I am still looking for my roots. . . . I suppose it is a desire for recognition, of belonging— . . . a voice from the dim past. A far off land—a village and people that no longer exists, but a faint memory."[13]

Unlike Reiss, Gropper relied not on direct observation but on earlier visual representations of the subject. His lithographs depict established, generic *shtetl* subjects—musicians, porters, dancing figures, scholars reading, women blessing candles and preparing food—as codified in nineteenth-century portraits of provincial Jewish "types" and genre scenes, which were subsequently revisited (and sometimes skewed) by prewar modern artists. Though Gropper characterizes the project as a personal quest for rootedness, his drawings do not depict one or more towns where his ancestors had once lived, nor does he portray the *shtetl* as a locus of radical politics. Rather, Gropper retraces the conventions of *shtetl* representation. These lithographs intimate a familiarity with vintage photographs and illustrations by earlier artists, such as Marc Chagall, for his and his wife's memoirs, and Ben Shahn, for Irving Howe and Eliezer Greenberg's *A Treasury of Yiddish Stories*.[14]

Among the more visually adventurous reworkings of prewar images of East European Jewish life in postwar artworks is American artist Frank Stella's series *Polish Villages*. Created over several years in the early 1970s, these 130 works were inspired by Maria and Kazimierz Piechotka's *Wooden Synagogues*. This 1959 book reproduces black-and-white photographs and architectural drawings of over seventy Polish synagogues, some dating back to the seventeenth century. Art historian Szymon Zajczyk had photographed the buildings during the interwar years for a planned comprehensive study of Jewish art at the Institute of Polish Architecture; students in the Polytechnic of Warsaw had created the architectural drawings. These images and accompanying historical information were published after the war as "vestiges of a destroyed world," a memorial to the "martyred buildings," which, like their prewar inhabitants, had been annihilated during World War II.[15] (In addition to prompting Stella's series of artworks, these buildings, perhaps the best-known examples of *shtetl* architecture, have inspired the design of some postwar American synagogues as well as the headquarters of the National Yiddish Book Center in Amherst, Massachusetts.)

Stella's *Polish Villages* are not figurative works depicting prewar East European Jewish architecture. Rather, the artist, who had emerged as a leading minimalist in the 1960s, responded within his established idiom to Zajczyk's photographs. *Polish Villages* are large-scale, irregularly shaped combinations of painting and low-relief wooden sculpture, formed of irregular, angular geometric shapes and thrusting diagonal, parallel lines. These compositions evoke elements of Polish synagogue exteriors, especially as represented in Zajczyk's photographs, which, art historian Mark Godfrey notes, emphasize the architecture's angularity. Stella acknowledged the inspiration for this series by titling individual works with the names of towns—Felsztyn, Lipsko, Ostropol, and so on—whose buildings appear in *Wooden Synagogues*, although there is no ready correlation between the architecture of the synagogue from a given town and the form of eponymous works. Rather, the connections between the artworks and their inspiration are more general. Echoing the Piechotkas, Stella described *Polish Villages* as being "about the destruction of an entire culture."[16]

The established repertoire of *shtetl* landscapes, genre scenes, and portraits of types that informs postwar professional artists' work recurs in a much larger, concomitant body of mass-produced images, including decorative prints, greeting cards, and book illustrations. This iconography also appears in the work of amateur artists and in artisans' production of collectibles, models, ritual objects, and the like. Although natives of Eastern Europe often create these amateur and craft works, they are sometimes inspired not only, or even primarily, by personal recollections but rather by other representations. A case in point is a series of scale models of Polish wooden synagogues built by Moshe Verbin. A native of Sokolka who emigrated to Palestine as a teenager in 1935, Verbin "'discovered' the wooden synagogues of early Poland when he found a book which was published . . . [in] 1957"—the Polish edition of the Piechotkas' book, which inspired Frank Stella—and then began making models based on its photographs and architectural drawings.[17]

Beyond merely revisiting a prewar stock of visual images of traditional East European Jewish life, these postwar works constitute a new kind of memory practice rooted in material culture and, for those that are mass-produced, commodification. Both this replication and the subject matter of many of these works—holiday celebrations, synagogue life, religious study—suggest that their creation is itself an act of devotion. The devotion is not to Judaism per se, however, but to a belief in the *shtetl* as a milieu in which a comprehensively Jewish life was once realized and which endures in public remembrance as a defining locus of Judaism. For some collectors of these works, owning and displaying images of religiosity replaces religious observance.

Some Jews who once lived in East European provincial towns before World War II have produced sizeable series of drawings, paintings, prints, sculptures, or models depicting personal recollections of *shtetl* life. The work of these largely self-taught artists and artisans typically fuses conventional subjects of Jewish customs (holidays, life-cycle events) with local history (such as depictions of the town's synagogue and other landmarks) and autobiography. For example, Rachel Faust, a native of Tomaszów Lubelski who immigrated to the United States in 1920, regularly incorporated portraits of her child self, always wearing a red dress, in genre scenes of rituals set in her hometown, such as celebrating Simchas Torah or blessing the new moon.[18]

Though much of this output has remained in the artists' private collections, some of their works have been exhibited or published.[19] Among the first of these memory artists to receive public attention after World War II is Samuel Rothbort, who was born in Volkovisk in 1882 and emigrated to the United States in 1904. A self-taught painter and sculptor, Rothbort began creating memory paintings of his native town in the late 1930s. Rothbort's *shtetl* paintings, which eventually numbered over five hundred, were the subject of a 1961 documentary film, *The Ghetto Pillow* (later retitled *Memories of the Shtetl*) by Harriet Semegram, and provided inspiration for Jerome Robbins's staging of *Fiddler on the Roof.*

Even as Rothbort's paintings were acclaimed as a cultural resource, they challenged some observers' notions of prewar East European Jewish life. When a selection of his work was exhibited in New York in 1962, journalist Alfred Werner struggled with the paintings' depiction of one of the "ghettos of Tsarist Russia" with "light and joyous color," explaining that "one should not argue with the veteran artist whose proper realm is not historicity but the honest expression of his amiable self." For Werner, the paintings, despite "loving emphasis on minute detail," aestheticize Rothbort's roseate view of his past: "Some of the pictures . . . give off the air of a fairy-tale world, tend to make us believe that the bagel sellers and fiddle players, the town criers and water carriers, the ice skaters and shoplifters could not have been real people but are sketches to be performed to the music of some 19th century Russian composer."[20]

In 1986, a book of memory paintings by Ilex Beller, a native of Grodzisko who immigrated to Western Europe at the age of fourteen in 1928, appeared in both French- and English-language editions. *Life in the Shtetl: Scenes and Recollections* presents Beller's paintings as exemplifying "a kind of resurrection" of prewar *shtetl* life in works of postwar remembrance, which is itself "gradually dying out." Beller's work thus "captures" an "imperiled world" that was first vanquished by the Holocaust and then endangered by the passing of prewar immigrants, such as Beller, and Holocaust survivors, who can recall their direct experience of *shtetl* life. The preface to *Life in the Shtetl* hails Beller's paintings as "accurate representations" that "possess the freshness and purity of an unspoiled childhood." The foreword, by French poet and journalist

Charles Dobzynski, argues that Beller's work constitutes "a foundation for sociologists" bent on studying *shtetl* mores, while also acknowledging the "magical" qualities of the paintings, some of which combine ethnography with fantasy.[21] For example, Beller's painting of a Passover seder depicts the biblical prophet Elijah floating in midair beside the table where the ceremony is being observed. Dobzynski's characterization implies that these paintings offer an authentic record not simply of daily practices but of a culture imbued with a childlike sense of the supernal as immanent.

Among *shtetl* memory artists, Mayer Kirshenblatt stands out, even as his work shares elements in common with other projects. Like Faust, some of his paintings integrate self-portraiture with genre scenes of Jewish life. Like Beller, Kirshenblatt recalls Jewish life in his hometown as childhood experience—he, too, emigrated as a teenager during the interwar years—from the vantage of old age. Beller did not begin to paint until he was sixty years old; Kirshenblatt made his first memory painting when he was seventy-three. And like Zalman Kaplan's photographs of life in Szczuczyn, collected decades later by his grandson, Kirshenblatt's work is part of an intergenerational project. Decades before he first turned to painting, Kirshenblatt was a regular informant for his daughter Barbara Kirshenblatt-Gimblett's research on immigrant storytelling and Jewish folklore. Struck by the strong visual component of her father's prodigious memory of his hometown of Opatów, she and other family members encouraged him to document his recollections through art. Eventually, Kirshenblatt created over two hundred paintings until his death at the age of ninety-three in 2009.

Kirshenblatt's daughter understood these paintings as integral to his process of remembering, which began with storytelling. Topics for his paintings grew out of her interviews, and paintings, in turn, inspired more discussion and then ideas for yet more canvases. Eventually, Kirshenblatt-Gimblett compiled these stories and images into an integrated documentation, *They Called Me Mayer July: Painted Memories of a Jewish Childhood in Poland Before the Holocaust*, published in 2007. This volume would not have come into existence without Kirshenblatt-Gimblett's scholarly vision or her encouragement of her father to take up this task. At the same time, *They Called Me Mayer July* reflects Kirshenblatt's remarkable capacity to remember and, moreover, his boundless, enduring curiosity about his hometown.

In Kirshenblatt's stories and paintings, everything in Opatów appears equally meaningful and is recalled with the same acuity of detail and interest. He does not avoid the seemingly trivial (e.g., saving lead seals from packages to melt down to make *dreydlekh* [spinning tops] for

Hanukkah), unflattering (men's naked bodies in the bathhouse), vulgar (Jadźka, the town prostitute, displaying "her wares" in the marketplace), or alien (the suicide of a Christian friend's father). When Kirshenblatt recalls sneaking into a Christian woman's funeral to see how the body was displayed, he simply explains, "I had to see everything."[22] His paintings are typical of self-taught memory artists in their attention to detail and composition, especially the use of a splayed perspective that enables the artist to incorporate images of complete people and objects, rather than partial, overlapping views of these elements as seen from single-point perspective. This panoptic vantage reflects Kirshenblatt's childhood desire to be a chimney sweep, so that he could view the whole town from above.

They Called Me Mayer July integrates Kirshenblatt's paintings with his storytelling, following the complementary nature of their creation. The book's organization reflects the associative flow of Kirshenblatt's recollections, shaped by the give-and-take of conversations with his daughter, rather than a strict chronology or other rubrics (such as the annual calendar or life cycle) used in similar projects. Like the work of other *shtetl* memory painters, Kirshenblatt's canvases have been exhibited—in museums in Western Europe and North America, as well as in Opatów in 2008—and have inspired other creative endeavors, including two documentary films on the artist and a 2004 toy theater piece, *The White Pajamas*, based on one of Kirshenblatt's stories about Opatów.[23]

Shtetl memory art, typically the work of "naïve" artists who sometimes take up painting or sculpture only for this purpose, is deceptive in its apparent simplicity. As mediations of lived experience, often recalled decades later, these works reflect their creators' textual and visual literacy and art training (or lack thereof) as much as their recollections. These artists' depictions of holiday celebrations, for example, sometimes suggest a familiarity with similar genre scenes or literary accounts of these occasions. In turn, these works inspire other creative projects, including films and live performances. Even as they offer distinctly personal visions of the artist's past, these works exist within a cascade of visual remediations of the *shtetl*.

Place

As is true for other places widely known for their symbolic importance, vicarious engagements with the *shtetl* stimulate desires to visit actual sites in postwar Eastern Europe. Interest in more thorough engagement with the former locus of a vibrant, ostensibly comprehensive Jewish way of life inspires wishes for a kinetic experience—"breathing the same air" or "walking in the footsteps" of former *shtetl* residents. This desire to inhabit the *shtetl* entails negotiating the disparity between past and present, the imagined and the actual. Visits to these sites can entail contending with challenging physical environments, in which absence—not simply of Jewish life but even of traces of its past—looms larger than presence. A 1962 guidebook to Jewish sites in Europe says of Poland, "Everywhere there are wrecked or neglected cemeteries, ruins of synagogues and other Jewish communal buildings, and scattered memorials to victims of the catastrophe which has left Poland a vast Jewish graveyard."[24] These sites' social environments can also prove daunting, whether or not their current inhabitants recall or are aware of the local Jewish past. Such challenges can, in turn, prompt the creation of new virtual places—on the Internet, in performance or display—that conjure the *shtetl* one desires, be it a site of intercultural accord, a trove of East European cultural riches, or a thoroughly Jewish milieu.

The outbreak of World War II had halted the wide variety of interwar travels to see Jews in provincial East European towns. The first Holocaust survivors to return to these towns—where Jews had been rounded up and deported to ghettos and camps or executed in situ—typically describe their visits as confirming the worst fears of these Jewish communities' destruction. Hostile receptions from former neighbors often compounded returnees' anguish.[25] Early postwar visits to Eastern Europe by Jewish relief agencies from the West focused on the rescue and rehabilitation of survivors, as most of this "saving remnant" relocated to urban centers in the region or to new countries. Many *shtetlekh* were abandoned as sites of a Jewish future, becoming instead sites of memorializing—or forgetting—the Jewish past.

The consolidation of communist control of Eastern Europe in the late 1940s constrained travel from abroad. During the Cold War, Jewish tourism from the West was limited and centered on officially sanctioned sites of Jewish culture (e.g., state Yiddish theaters in Warsaw and Bucharest) or Holocaust remembrance. Erecting memorials to Jewish victims of Nazi persecution, especially "pastiche" monuments made of fragments of Jewish tombstones vandalized during the war, often provided the only reason for Jews' postwar visits to small towns where their communities had once thrived.[26] Cold War ideology shaped visits from the West to Jews living behind the Iron Curtain. During the 1960s and 1970s, missions to visit Soviet Jews to provide economic support and expressions of solidarity from the West focused on Jews living in major cities and on the politics of the present rather than curiosity about the past. Indeed, these ideologically charged visits assumed that Soviet Jewish life, pre- or postwar, was untenable and devoid of cultural value. Yet within the USSR, local Jewish culture was a subject of considerable internal interest that occasionally received public attention, as when the state-sponsored Yiddish periodical *Sovetish heymland* (Soviet Homeland) printed Shmuel Gordon's accounts of visiting sites of Jewish life, past and present, in provincial towns of northwestern Ukraine in the 1960s.[27]

The resumption of hasidic pilgrimages to the graves of *rebeyim* proved a notable exception to the dearth of Jewish travel to East European provincial towns during the Cold War.[28] The most renowned of these visits is the annual pilgrimage of Bratslaver hasidim to the grave of Nahman of Bratslav in Uman, a magnate town founded in the seventeenth century. Visiting the Bratslaver rebbe's grave on Rosh Hashanah dates back to 1811, the year following his death. Disciples of Nahman of Bratslav maintained this annual rite into the twentieth century, as Uman grew to the size of a small city. The practice continued during the interwar years, though it was increasingly difficult for Jews outside the USSR to enter the country and the Bratslaver synagogue was shut in 1937. The pilgrimage resumed shortly after World War II, at first on a very limited scale, becoming more established during the 1960s. Since the fall of communism, the annual visit to Nahman of Bratslav's grave has attracted tens of thousands of Jews, including many who are not Bratslaver hasidim. As is true for other sites of East European Jewish tourism, this development has had a complex impact on the local economy and has fostered ambivalent relations between local residents and international Jewish communities.[29]

The recent expansion of hasidic travel to Eastern Europe occurred within a larger burgeoning of tourist practices to sites associated with Jewish life, past and present. East European Jewish landmarks are now the subject of multiple guidebooks and tours prepared by educators, museums, religious and political organizations, as well as travel professionals. Organized tours typically center on Jewish landmarks in major cities—exemplified by the Kazimierz district in Cracow—or on major sites of Holocaust remembrance, including the grounds of former death camps.[30] Though at first these tourist productions usually neglected smaller sites of prewar Jewish life, some have been featured in guidebooks, including promotional material produced by the state-owned Polish travel agency Orbis in the 1980s.[31] Jack Kugelmass reports that in the early 1990s, individuals on group trips would "sometimes leave the tours for half a day in order to visit their family's home village."[32]

Travelers to *shtetlekh* in the post-communist era include groups interested in touring landmarks of a bygone era of Yiddish culture, such as the "Cultural and Folkloristic Tour in Ukraine" led by Israeli folklorist Dov Noy in 1998. This week-long expedition "in the footsteps of Hassidic founders and Yiddish writers" included visits to the towns of Medziboz, Nemyriv, Pereiaslev-Khmel'nyts'kyi, Shargorod, and Vinnytsia.[33] More common are Jewish travelers seeking familial connections to particular East European locations. Shtetl Schleppers, a travel service founded in 1999, guided tourists on "their first steps into the journey of a lifetime," culminating in "four days of visits in your ancestral shtetls, customized just for you! Accompanied by an experienced guide/translator, you will walk on the same pathways in the footprints of your ancestors."[34] Other Jews travel to Eastern Europe primarily to conduct genealogical research in archives. These two missions are often interrelated. Miriam Weiner, a pioneer of contemporary East European Jewish genealogy, offers "Routes to Roots" trips that entail both "going to your ancestral town" and discovering "if you still have family in the 'old country.'"[35] These trips configure *shtetlekh* as foundational sites of family history, rooting its geographic sprawl and disjunctures—including those caused by immigration, war, and other upheavals—in a single locus of origin. In this conjoining of geography and lineage, encountering one's ancestral hometown includes the possibility of discovering unknown living relatives in situ, a double restoration of a violated, ruptured past.

Jewish tourism now figures prominently in some local economies, transforming the postwar culture of several East European towns with few or no Jewish inhabitants. As this book goes to press, plans are under way to refashion Biłgoraj into "a 19th century town," including a synagogue and a "Jewish market square."[36] A more established site of *shtetl* tourism in Poland is Tykocin, renowned for its baroque masonry synagogue, originally built in 1642 and restored in the late 1970s. The synagogue attracts tens of thousands of visitors annually, including group visits organized by March of the Living, which brings Jewish youth to Poland's landmarks of Holocaust remembrance. The popularity of Tykocin's synagogue inspired local Poles to open a Jewish museum, located in a nearby building that once housed a *besmedresh*, and a "Jewish-style" café.[37]

More remarkable is the town's annual staging of a Purim play, a practice begun at the turn of the millennium, in which local Poles enact the Book of Esther's account of ancient Persian Jewry's rescue from annihilation. Tykocin's Purim play is not a revival of a traditional Yiddish *purim-shpil* but a provocative cultural innovation, the consequence of touristic attention to the town as a former center of Jewish life that has redounded onto the local population of Catholic Poles. Their masquerade elides a complex local history, especially the mass murder of most of the town's Jewish population in August 1941. Photographer Frédéric Brenner, who documented the play in 2002, notes its trenchant irony: "Tykocin is a town without Jews, where the inhabitants . . . dress up as the Jews whom they never saw but whose memory they wish to preserve. This is

Purim—the only festival in the Jewish calendar that is as much about inversion as it is about remembrance." Noting that the Purim story prefigures the Holocaust, in which Tykocin's Poles had been either bystanders or abettors, Brenner writes: "The children and grandchildren of those Poles [now] celebrate a Purim twice-reversed. . . . There is no mention of the massacre sixty years ago, or the pillaging of Jewish homes that directly preceded it. In this parody of Purim, the villagers of Tykocin are so sincere and so well disguised, how could they be the children of the collaborators of the butchers, of those who chose to remain silent?"[38]

Tykocin's Purim play "fulfills three conflicting functions," according to performance studies scholar Brigitte Sion: "It commemorates pre-war Jewish heritage in Poland; it uses theatrical entertainment to mask Holocaust history, and it serves as a journey to self-discovery and identity formation for third-generation Poles." Given this complex of agendas, the performance "defies common accusations of abuse or commodification of memory; it would also be too simplistic and judgmental to call it anti-Semitism disguised as philo-Semitism. . . . [The play] is something else, precisely because it is a theatrical performance predicated on a story of inversion and reversal. . . . It is a form of homage, but can be interpreted as hijacking. It may ask for forgiveness, and yet it avoids mentioning the reason for forgiveness."[39] Tykocin has become a site of layers of memory practices—architectural restoration, museum exhibition, tourism, live performance—which all rely on selective remembrance and forgetting. In this town, estranged populations' diverging agendas for conjuring the *shtetl* intersect uneasily, but the discomfort their memory practices engender reveals what the various participants seek in this fraught cultural project of making claims on a vanquished local past.

Strong emotional engagement with environments that were once home to Jewish communities impel even those trips Jews make to Eastern Europe that are ostensibly centered on acquiring information, be it genealogical records in local archives, the details of local landscapes as they conform to vintage photographs or ancestors' memories, or evidence of the scope of the Holocaust. Historian Rona Sheramy notes that March of the Living structures its trips, which strive to "inspire 'memory' of the Holocaust . . . in a generation that lacked personal recollections of these critical events," not through a "scholarly approach" but through "affective learning."[40] Anthropologist Jackie Feldman likewise observes that trips bringing Israeli Jewish youth to Poland on similar missions rely on the "overwhelming sensory stimuli" of Holocaust memorial sites to "bring forth tears," which both the young people and the trips' organizers regard "as an index of the profundity and authenticity of the students' experience."[41]

A different but no less powerfully affective engagement structures many Jewish travelers' visits to ancestral hometowns. Author Ruth Ellen Gruber describes these visits' emotional force, which is imbricated with elements of the journey:

> Many Jews on such trips weep; they want to touch physical objects, to talk. Many recite the Kaddish, the prayer for the dead, bringing Jewish religious ritual to onetime Jewish population centers for the first time in decades. . . . Jews often express forceful feelings of discovery on these trips. Geographies and even types of trees or flowers evoke intense and surprising feelings of familiarity. The physical difficulties of travel in remote places—bad roads, crowded buses, difficult border crossings, wrong turns, lost luggage, horses and carts—frequently become a compelling part of the narrative, too, fostering a sense of contact with somewhere so far away and so hard to get at that it must be the past.[42]

Contemporary Jewish tourists often feel compelled to document and reflect on these travels, producing photo albums, videos, and websites. Though most such efforts remain private family documents, some are shared more widely, suggesting that a common interest in these travels affirms Jewish connections to the past on a large scale. For example, the genealogy organization JewishGen provides a platform on its website—KehilaLinks (formerly ShtetlLinks)—for members to post pictures and information about their travels to ancestral hometowns in Eastern Europe.[43]

In addition to these many amateur efforts, professional writers, photographers, and filmmakers have documented similar journeys. In his 1995 book *Konin: A Quest*, journalist and filmmaker Theo Richmond chronicles his six-year search for information about the eponymous Polish town, where his parents had lived before they immigrated to England. As the title indicates, the author's lengthy process of discovery—interviewing aging relatives and their fellow Koniners, scrutinizing photographs and archival documents, and, ultimately, visiting Konin in the early 1990s—is as much the author's subject as is the town itself. Similarly, writer Daniel Mendelsohn's *The Lost: A Search for Six of the Six Million* provides an exhaustive account of the author's efforts to learn about relatives murdered in the Holocaust, culminating in his visit to their hometown of Bolechów. Like Richmond, Mendelsohn's ignorance fuels the narrative:

> Once, I overheard my grandfather saying to my mother, *I know only they were hiding in a kessle.* Since I knew by then how to make adjustments for his accent, when I hear him say this I simply wondered, What castle?

> Bolechow, to judge from the stories he told me, was not a place for castles; it was a small place, I knew, a peaceful place, a little town with a square and a church or two and a shul and busy shops. It was only later on, long after my grandfather was dead and after I had studied more seriously the history of his town, that I learned that Bolechow, like so many other little Polish shtetls, had at one time been owned by an aristocratic Polish landowner, and when I learned this fact I naturally fitted the new information into my old memory of what I'd overheard my grandfather saying.[44]

Even as Mendelsohn's and Richmond's quests (and resulting books) stem from what Richmond terms a "parochial curiosity," they reveal the authors' anxieties about a lack of command of their East European Jewish past, especially in contrast to their professional accomplishment as writers and their security in American or British culture. The painstaking process of recounting the struggles to research their pasts is perhaps a tacit reconciliation with this deficiency, a debt paid to a neglected heritage, as well as a reckoning with the onus of not having succumbed to the Holocaust. Richmond thus recalls that, as a boy, he was intrigued by ancient Roman artifacts displayed in the local museum in his hometown of Hertfordshire: "But whether the Jewish world of Konin would have gripped me as much is questionable. None of us knew then what was happening to that world. While I, an English schoolboy in short trousers and school cap, was gazing enthralled at the remains of a vanished civilization, my Konin relatives, some of them children my own age, were being exterminated. The Jewish communities that had blossomed for so many centuries in Eastern Europe were soon to become part of a vanished world, like that of the Ancient Romans."[45]

Photography emerged as an important instrument of reconnaissance in response to the growing interest in what remains of Jewish life in postwar Eastern Europe. Books of photographs of these traces present the work of local photographers in Poland and Ukraine as well as pictures taken by visitors from the West. These albums are part of a larger corpus of photography books on contemporary Jewish subjects, which flourished in the postwar era.[46] Besides belonging to a genre of portraits of "last Jews" in communities throughout the diaspora, the books in question complement concomitant publications of prewar East European Jewish photography, discussed above.

The agendas of these volumes of postwar photographs change over time, reflecting the political dynamics of Eastern Europe and shifting external perspectives on the region. As their titles reveal—*The Last Jews of Rădăuţi; Remnants: The Last Jews of Poland; Polish Jews: The Final Chapter;*

The Last Jews of Eastern Europe—books that appeared in the mid-1970s to mid-1980s portray Jewish communities, whether local, regional, or national, at their denouement. These books are replete with images of aging, impoverished Jews, abandoned or repurposed synagogues, and neglected cemeteries.[47] (This last category is the subject of other books published at the time: *Des Pierres Racontent; Time of Stones.*)[48] In all these books, *shtetlekh* figure as dwindling, atomized, or lifeless places. The portrayals are chronotopic, construing contemporary sites and the people inhabiting them as the vestiges of a much-vaunted bygone era that still indexes these places as "Jewish." The photographs in these books evoke this vibrant past by visual litotes, showing the absence of material upkeep (e.g., overgrown tombstones), of significant numbers (the inability to convene a *minyan*), or of youth. The epitomizing image that recurs in this genre of photographs is a niche in a doorpost that once held a *mezuzah* (amulet)—the visualization of Jews' absence.[49]

More recent photo albums, produced following the fall of communism, shift from depicting the demise of East European Jewry to portraying its tenacity—especially upon discovering that the region's "last Jews" have had children, and a considerable number of people, especially in Poland, have discovered Jewish ancestors after decades of family secrecy. Thus, Yale Strom followed his 1986 "last Jews" book four years later with *A Tree Still Stands: Jewish Youth in Eastern Europe Today.*[50] Youth are also foregrounded in Edward Serotta's *Out of the Shadows: A Photographic Portrait of Jewish Life in Central Europe since the Holocaust* (1991) and Larry Mayer and Gary Gelb's *Who Will Say Kaddish? A Search for Jewish Identity in Contemporary Poland* (2002).[51] As their titles indicate, these books situate East European Jewry at the turn of the millennium within narratives of uncertain endurance, looking back as much as forward. The photographs tend to center on Jewish life in larger cities, where critical masses of Jews live and communal institutions are based. By their relative absence, *shtetlekh* are implicitly abandoned sites in these recent books—or are explicitly so in the case of Wojciech Wilczyk's *Niewinne Oko Nie Istnieje/There's No Such Thing as an Innocent Eye*, which features over 300 photographs, taken in 2007 and 2008, of former synagogue buildings in postwar Poland, most of them in small towns.[52]

Films documenting postwar return journeys to Eastern Europe by former Jewish residents or their descendants date to Harold Becker's 1967 short documentary *Sighet, Sighet*, which follows writer Elie Wiesel back to the eponymous Romanian town where he spent his childhood.[53] Like Jewish travel to Eastern Europe generally, these films became more frequent after the fall of communism and are often conceived as intergenerational projects. In *Return to My Shtetl Delatyn* (1992), Dutch documentarian

Willy Lindwer and his daughter journey with his father to the Galician town, now in northwestern Ukraine, that had been his home before World War II. American filmmaker Jeff Bieber documented Yaffa Eliach's return to Ejszyszki (now Eišiškės, Lithuania) with members of her family in *There Once Was a Town* (1999). Pearl Gluck's *Divan* (2004) chronicles her journey from her native New York to the Hungarian town of Rohod, the prewar seat of the hasidic community in which she was raised, in an attempt to purchase a couch, a prized heirloom of her father's relatives. And in *Hiding and Seeking: Faith and Tolerance after the Holocaust* (2004), Menachem Daum takes his sons to Działoszyce—where they meet members of the Polish family that had hid their maternal grandparents during the war—in an effort to challenge the attitude of these young men toward non-Jews, which has been informed by their right-wing Orthodoxy. In each film, the *shtetl* is the emblematic locus of a personal quest, whether mourning the loss of family and community, addressing crimes of the past, reconciling with one's elders, or providing one's children with moral edification.

As in other postwar works, these cinematic portrayals of encountering the *shtetl* often center on absence—of people, landmarks, remembrance—rather than presence. Unlike tourist photography, which typically focuses on destinations, these films dwell on the journey and how it enhances—or complicates—the travelers' lives back home. The journey exposes challenges that the quest entails in relation to the distances—geographic, temporal, generational, cultural—between the point of departure and the telos: the *shtetl* and what it represents. These films seldom offer complete and satisfying resolution of the quest at its destination; rather, reaching the *shtetl* variously results in melancholy, disappointment, compromise, frustration, or uncertainty. These documentaries exemplify what literature scholar Svetlana Boym distinguishes as "reflective nostalgia," which she contrasts with "restorative nostalgia." Whereas "restorative nostalgia . . . attempts a transhistorical reconstruction of the lost home, . . . reflective nostalgia dwells on the ambivalences of human longing and belonging and does not shy from the contradictions of modernity."[54]

An especially complex dynamic among people visiting a small town where a Jewish community once thrived shapes Marian Marzynski's 1996 documentary *Shtetl*. The filmmaker—a Polish Jew who, as a child, was hidden during World War II in a Catholic convent—began his career in postwar Poland until forced to leave the country, along with the majority of its Jewish population, settling in the United States in 1969. *Shtetl* brings together three protagonists, each with a different interest in the Jewish past of the town of Bransk. First, there is Nathan Kaplan, seventy-two years old when the film was made, the American-born son of a Jewish immigrant from Bransk. In retirement, Kaplan had become curious about his father's hometown and began researching its history. This project led him to correspond with Zbigniew Romaniuk, the second protagonist. A young Pole born in Bransk after World War II, Romaniuk had developed an interest in his town's Jewish past and began documenting local Jewish history and rescuing relics of prewar Jewish life. The third protagonist is Marzynski, who appears on camera and also narrates the film. He mediates between the other two men, both generationally and culturally. Marzynski approaches Bransk's history as emblematic of Jewish life and death in provincial Polish towns, which figure in his family history (though he grew up in Warsaw). Over the course of the film, the protagonists' respective quests intersect and complicate one another.

As they seek more information about Bransk's Jewish past, especially during the war, the three men find themselves confronting a history that grows morally more murky and contradictory. Marzynski both admires Romaniuk's commitment to uncovering this history, even as his efforts provoke local controversy, and challenges him as they engage suppressed memories of wartime Polish-Jewish relations among his elderly neighbors. And, like Kaplan, Marzynski confronts the loss of his father, who died during the war. Both men approach the *shtetl* as the locus of destruction of their fathers' cultural world. Bransk emerges as a site that, under the surface of quiet, small-town life, seethes with unresolved stories of betrayal, valor, helplessness, and doubt.[55]

While some people visit East European towns in pursuit of a lost Jewish past, others strive to transform the *shtetl* into a locus of transcultural contact and accord that looks forward as well as back in time. This impulse informs several projects undertaken in post-communist Eastern Europe, part of larger efforts by countries and local communities to create new models for understanding their pasts and fostering amicable relationships among different ethnic, national, and religious groups within new nations and political orders. The Virtual Shtetl, an online resource associated with Warsaw's Museum of the History of Polish Jews, was launched in 2009 to provide a portal to this past. In addition to information about Jewish history in Polish towns and cities (per Poland's interwar boundaries), the site provides capsule biographies of important historical figures, a glossary, and bibliography. Information provided in several languages accommodates researchers in Eastern Europe, North America, and Israel.

Beyond providing resources, the Virtual Shtetl aspires to serve as an interactive platform. The site informs users that it is "a community in which you, our Internet visitor, can participate. Take pictures and upload them, collect memorabilia, listen to testimonies and exchange information.

Help us to make the 'Virtual Shtetl' a comprehensive network for all those interested in understanding the complex history of Polish Jews." Project director Albert Stankowski explains, "Virtual Shtetl is primarily a social community where mutual relations are initiated and strengthened. In the contemporary era of the developing Internet network, this community forms, above all, in the virtual space."[56] Invoking venerable notions of the *shtetl* as a paradigm of Jewish communality, the website proffers an abstracted locus for virtual encounters between Jews and Christians, as well as between the past and the present, using the social media of cyberspace. The common bond of interest in Polish Jewry's past implicitly forges new relations across cultural and geographic divides for the future.

Complementing the Virtual Shtetl is the Warsaw museum's project, undertaken with Handshouse Studio, to fabricate a replica of the ceiling of the eighteenth-century wooden synagogue that once stood in Gwoździec.[57] Through instruction in traditional woodworking, an international group of students was taught that "history does not need to be only written, spoken, remembered or interpreted. History can also be *made*." As part of its larger effort to transform the presence of Polish Jews' history in the public sphere, the museum vaunts this project as providing participants with "a unique opportunity to become acquainted with history in the making."[58] Whether a virtual or hands-on construction, these two projects envision revisiting the *shtetl* as pedagogy promoting cross-cultural accord, especially among youth, through collaborative, creative acts.

The same goal is central to the Borderland (Pogranicze) Foundation, a nongovernmental organization founded in 1990, which revisits prewar East European Jewish life through other practices offered in a different configuration. The foundation is headquartered in Sejny, a town in northeastern Poland that was once home to a sizeable Jewish population (about half of its approximately 4,000 inhabitants at the turn of the twentieth century). Today Sejny's residents include both Poles and Lithuanians, and it is close to Poland's borders with Belarus, Lithuania, and Russia. The foundation is "devoted exclusively to propagating the ethos of the borderland, and to building bridges between the peoples of different religions, ethnicities, nationalities, and cultures."[59] Borderland pursues this agenda through an ongoing series of cultural projects—musical and theater performances, publications, festivals, and conferences—that engage the region's diverse communities, which also include Roma, Ukrainians, and Russian Old Believers.

Although no Jews now live in or near Sejny, its Jewish past is a subject of Borderland's ongoing interest, realized in a variety of ways. The foundation sponsors a *klezmer* band and uses restored buildings of the town's former Jewish quarter, including a synagogue and a yeshiva, as venues for performances, exhibitions, and workshops. Sejny's Jewish history is evoked in performance pieces that are central to the foundation's work (its founders are active in Poland's alternative theater). These productions include *Kroniki sejneńskie* (Sejny Chronicles), a 2008 piece created and performed by local youth, which "celebrates the history of their town in several languages, in song and ritual. Clay models of the temples, houses, and landmarks that once stood in their town were made by the young actors and occup[y] center stage during the performance, helping to make this theatrical meeting between past and present even more palpable."[60]

Borderland not only champions Eastern Europe's multiculturalism but also calls attention to intolerance among peoples in the region. In 2000, the foundation's press published the Polish-language edition of Jan Gross's *Neighbors: The Destruction of the Jewish Community in Jedwabne, Poland*, which describes how the 1941 massacre of hundreds of Jedwabne's Jews was perpetrated not by German occupying forces but by the town's Poles.[61] Gross's book provoked a "complex and often acrimonious debate" in Poland, disrupting longstanding public evasion of Jewish issues and raising questions about the nature of the country's new democracy.[62] The publication of *Neighbors* exemplifies Borderland's commitment to addressing the ongoing challenge of promoting amicable relations among different populations living in the new democratic nations of post-communist Eastern Europe, a task that entails coming to terms with past intolerance and violence.

Culture is central to realizing the ethos of Borderland, which earned praise and support from Polish poet and Nobel laureate Czesław Miłosz. Performances have special primacy in realizing the foundation's mission, serving as symbolic enactments of accord. Borderland intends culture to inspire politics and perhaps even displace its negative ties to nationalism, which the foundation views as intolerant chauvinism. By contrast, one of its advocates writes, "the borderland . . . is a life-giving buffer zone . . . protecting diversity."[63] Sejny serves the foundation as a hub for both centripetal and centrifugal movement, attracting international visitors to its programs and creating cultural works that tour internationally.

The Borderland ethos does not merely embrace difference but requires its presence. Sejny serves as a tactical as well as symbolic site for the nations it adjoins and the connections it might facilitate. Jews figure strategically in conceptualizing the town's diversity both synchronically, wherein Jews are visibly absent, and diachronically, wherein the narrative of their flourishing and destruction exemplifies intergroup accord and its breakdown. Remarkably, some locals in Sejny refer to the foundation's activists as Jews (though none actually are), thereby stigmatizing Borderland as Other. This association also reflects fears that Jews will return to reclaim property that belonged to their families before World War II, a concern frequently voiced in Poland.[64] Though actual Jews have limited involvement with the foundation's undertakings, Jews of the town's past and its imagined present play a spectral role in transforming Sejny into a paradigmatic site of multiculturalism's accord as well as its discontents.

Postwar notions of the *shtetl* as a paradigm and as a virtual Jewish locus have facilitated efforts to inhabit this bygone time and place in sites beyond Eastern Europe. Cultural festivals and museums provide especially productive opportunities for re-creating *shtetl* milieus and reenacting bygone folkways. These venues proffer visitors intensive, immersive, multisensory experiences of other places, peoples, and times. Using various strategies of display and performance, participants strive to encounter an inaccessible quotidian existence through an embodied adventure in the subjunctive mode.[65]

Cape Town's South African Jewish Museum, which opened in 2000, houses "a reconstruction of a typical Eastern European shtetl." The museum positions the *shtetl* as the point of origin for most South African Jews, who immigrated from Lithuanian provinces of the Russian Empire at the turn of the twentieth century. Walking through this installation, museum visitors tread on cobblestones past an "old well" and "glimpse . . . Sabbath candles through the window of [a] modest home."[66] The reconstruction deftly merges an enlarged photograph of a street (taken at the turn of the century in the town of Rietavas) with full-scale fabricated facades, enabling visitors to enter—and, if they wish, to be photographed in—a virtual *shtetl*, which hovers between two and three dimensions, sepia and color, the specific and the generic, Eastern Europe and South Africa, past and present. This hyper-real installation prompted Aage Myhre, editor-in-chief of the e-magazine *Vilnews*, to declare the museum "more Lithuanian than Lithuania itself."[67] Others have restaged the *shtetl* to recall the origins of East European Jewish spirituality. In 1998, Lubavitsher hasidim marked the 300th birthday of the Baal Shem Tov by setting up a "Hasidic theme park for children" in Kfar Habad, Israel. This "reimagining of an 18th century Eastern European shtetl" invited children to "draw water from the village well, pet sheep and goats, ride in a horse drawn cart, and hear stories and music from the Baal Shem Tov's time."[68]

The most elaborate effort to fabricate a *shtetl* environment is the Shtetl Museum. Initiated at the turn of the millennium and, as of this writing, unfinished, it is the latest in a series of projects undertaken by Yaffa Eliach to commemorate Ejszyszki's Jewish past. Eliach has pursued more projects, on a grander scale, to recall prewar East European Jewish life in her hometown than has any other individual.[69] Her efforts include a massive photo collection, displayed in the United States Holocaust Memorial Museum (discussed above); participation in an audio documentary for Israeli radio and a documentary film for American public television, both about Jewish life in Ejszyszki; and an 800-page book that chronicles this community from the eleventh century to World War II.[70] These efforts culminate with the Shtetl Museum, described on its promotional website as "an open-air Museum of East-European Jewish history and culture in the form of a life-size Shtetl."[71]

Though rooted in personal ties to a specific place, Eliach's memorial projects have grown increasingly paradigmatic. She conceptualizes the remembrance of Ejszyszki as meaningful for Jews generally and even for the world at large. In the rationale for her projects, Eliach asserts the importance of remembering prewar East European life as an imperative for Jewish continuity. Moreover, she positions her hometown not only as "the very paradigm of the . . . shtetl" but as "a world . . . , a veritable microcosm of Western civilization, and beyond that of the entire family of humankind," asserting that "there is hardly any major trend in the last nine hundred years of history that did not manifest itself in [Ejszyszki]."[72]

Situated on sixty-seven acres in Rishon LeZion, Israel's fourth-largest city, on land once intended for a golf course, the completed Shtetl Museum will comprise a complex of forty buildings, including synagogues, Jewish schools, and private homes. There will also be a Jewish cemetery, a public bathhouse with a *mikve*, a marketplace lined with shops, and a castle. These structures will be surrounded by a re-creation of Ejszyszki's forest and river. Some four hundred actors impersonating the town's prewar residents—rabbis, teachers, merchants, craftsmen, etc.—will inhabit the Shtetl Museum.[73]

Like other living history museums, the Shtetl Museum is most revealing at those points where the simulation reaches its limits. How, for example, will the museum deal with the geographic shift from the Israeli landscape to the re-creation of Lithuania? What language(s) will reenactors speak among themselves or with visitors? Will the town's Christian population figure in this re-creation? What are the implications of including among proposed activities for visitors stagings of trips to the cemetery or the departure of members of a Zionist youth organization for Palestine? Regardless of whether the Shtetl Museum is ever realized, these questions reveal how the desire to reanimate the prewar *shtetl* is implicated with other cultural aspirations and is challenged by the limits of the subjunctive.

Fantasy

Fiction allows the imagination freest rein to conjur *shtetl* life unconstrained by a lack of access to actual sites or documentary material, for postwar *shtetl* prose relies primarily on prewar literature on this subject. Although this more recent writing involves new readerships and often new languages, it approaches the *shtetl* as an established literary construct. Postwar *shtetl* writing is inherently intertextual, expanding on the relations among prewar literary works on this subject. Even when this postwar fiction entails radical departures from prewar works, it postulates the *shtetl* as a cultural terrain to be accessed through the literary imagination, irrespective of one's acquaintance with its actuality. Indeed, for growing numbers of writers and readers, the *shtetl* exists only as a literary phenomenon.

Reading multiple works of *shtetl* literature can provide postwar audiences with an imagined sense of at-homeness in this virtual milieu. The burgeoning of Yiddish literary translations after World War II is fundamental to this reading practice. As I have written elsewhere, translations have remade the way Yiddish literature engages a vernacular readership, not only by rendering texts into a new language but also by translating the vernacular literary experience itself.[74] English translations have brought Yiddish literature to its largest postwar readership, starting with collections of Sholem Aleichem rendered by Frances and Julius Butwin and anthologies assembled by Howe and Greenberg.[75] More recent translators have both expanded this canon and rethought its significance. Several collections, for example, have focused on Yiddish writing about immigrant life, rather than works set in Eastern Europe, or on works by women writers, who were largely absent from the first major postwar collections.[76]

Among the most innovative Yiddish translators and anthologists is Joachim Neugroschel, who produced several collections designed to reconfigure the canon as it had coalesced in English-language anthologies. In addition to creating collections focused on the role of the supernatural and mystical in Yiddish, challenging earlier anthologies that stressed works in a realist idiom, Neugroschel reworked the literary canonization of the *shtetl* with his 1979 collection *The Shtetl: A Creative Anthology of Jewish Life in Eastern Europe*. The translator introduces this volume as a corrective to the sentimentalized and homogenized image of the *shtetl* then prevalent. He stresses the imaginary nature of literary engagement with this diverse and dynamic subject—"a crazy quilt through time and space"—as comparable to "the mirrors in the fun house of an amusement park" rather than the "objective" mirroring sought in this literature by earlier anthologists and critics.

Tracking the chronological rise and fall of Yiddish letters in Eastern Europe, the volume begins with examples of vernacular religious literature: the opening chapters of the *Tsene-rene*—the seventeenth-century rendering of the Hebrew Bible and commentaries widely read by generations of Yiddish speakers, especially women—and early hasidic literature, including one of Nahman of Bratslav's enigmatic tales. Works by maskilic writers (including Yisroel Aksenfeld's *Dos shterntikhl*) follow, succeeded by authors of the late nineteenth and early to mid-twentieth century, including less well known works by major figures (e.g., Sholem Aleichem's early novel *Stempenyu*) and introducing writers largely unfamiliar to readers of Yiddish literature in translation (Fishel Bimko, Der Nister). The final selections, depicting "War, Revolution, Destruction," mark both the "end of a civilization" and its artistic apotheosis, as "the people of the shtetl took up permanent abode in the literature created about them."[77]

Isaac Bashevis Singer plays a leading role in the postwar literary imagining of the *shtetl*. Bashevis, as he is referred to by Yiddish speakers, first gained acclaim in Poland with the publication of his novel *Sotn in Gorey* (discussed in chapter 1) in 1935. That year, Bashevis followed his older brother and more established Yiddish writer, Israel Joshua Singer, to the United States. There, Bashevis wrote prolifically for the Yiddish press, publishing features as well as fiction, mostly in the *Jewish Daily Forward*, through the mid-1980s.[78]

Unlike earlier Yiddish writers who relied on readers' shared familiarity with the *shtetl*, Bashevis came to depend on a widespread lack of familiarity with this subject, as his postwar audience shifted from a small number of Yiddish readers to a much larger public encountering his work in translation. English renderings of his work have a special primacy, as this is the first language into which Bashevis's fiction was translated. He typically supervised these translations closely, creating texts that sometimes differ significantly from the Yiddish originals. Critics note that these "second originals" appear to be designed more for the sensibilities of readers unfamiliar with the Yiddish-speaking culture of prewar Eastern Europe.[79]

Bashevis's work now offers the most widely familiar literary point of entry to the *shtetl*. Literature scholars Joseph Sherman and Seth Wolitz note that Bashevis's stories about *shtetl* life "tend to be set in specific and narrowly circumscribed topographical locations," most of them towns in the Lublin province, where he spent part of his youth. Drawing on "personal observations," Bashevis took "particular care to describe some distinguishing physical characteristics" of each locale and deployed them selectively to "foreshadow . . . the events of the tale that is to unfold," linking the "physical and metaphysical dimensions" of his fiction.[80]

Though the *shtetlekh* in Bashevis's fiction have nominal significance as specific locales, their artistic value is greater as emblematic sites for exotic storytelling, generally centered less on the actualities of the East European Jewish past than on the supernatural, mystical, and (often perversely) erotic.

Bashevis's commitment to writing in Yiddish, even as his work reached a much wider readership in translation, is strategic to his stature as the "last great emissary" to *shtetl* culture.[81] Bashevis frequently characterized his use of Yiddish in deceptively playful terms. On receiving the Nobel Prize for Literature in 1978, he drolly explained that he wrote in Yiddish because "I like to write ghost stories, and nothing fits a ghost better than a dying language. . . . Ghosts love Yiddish; they all speak it."[82] For many readers of Bashevis's stories in translation, knowing that they were originally written in this spectral language roots them in a culturally authentic idiom and positions the author as the readers' guide to a lively land of ghosts, to which he had uncommon, if not exclusive, access.

Bashevis thus "revived" the *shtetl* as a site for supernatural engagement, drawing on and transforming an established trope (in works by Peretz, An-ski, and others) of the *shtetl* as haunted. In the postwar context, this trope endows Jewish Eastern Europe with an afterlife that acknowledges its demise and, at the same time, provides a means of reanimating it in the literary imaginary. Exploiting notions of the *shtetl* as alien and spectral to create a literary landscape of the sensational not only made Bashevis an enormously popular author; his strategy also has provided other writers and creative artists, younger than he and not native speakers of Yiddish, with a model for fabricating phantom *shtetlekh*, his stories serving some of these projects as an authenticating source text. Thus, a critic describes Helen Wecker's 2013 novel *The Golem and the Jinni* as beginning "in Singer territory, a shtetl in Poland," where the protagonist asks a kabbalist to make a golem.[83]

Though Bashevis looms largest in the postwar landscape of *shtetl* fiction, he is far from the only Jewish author born in prewar Eastern Europe to have addressed this subject after the Holocaust. S. Y. Agnon revisited his hometown of Buczacz, the encrypted subject of several works of his prewar Hebrew fiction, in a postwar anthology of local lore, *'Ir u-Melo'ah* (A City and Everything in It; published posthumously in 1973).[84] Something akin to a spiritual *yizker-bukh*, this volume relates tales and legends about Buczacz Jewry's religious life, especially its rabbis and other religious leaders. The title, a reference to Amos 6:8 ("I will deliver up the city and everything in it"), also evokes the Hebrew idiom *'olam u-melo'o* (the world and everything in it), intimating that Buczacz comprised a metonym of comprehensive Jewish religiosity.

The *shtetl* remained a fixture of postwar Yiddish literature, even for authors whose work largely addressed other subjects. Some writers deployed the *shtetl* as a setting for secular portraits of prewar religiosity. Chaim Grade's novels about Jewish life in prewar Lithuania occasionally deal with *shtetl* life, notably *Tsemakh Atlas* (1967–1968, translated into English as *The Yeshiva*), in which the protagonist's spiritual questing is tracked through his movement among towns around Vilna. Joseph Erlich's *Shabes* (*Sabbath*, 1970) offers an elegiac ethnography of provincial religious life, inflected by the author's Zionism (Erlich immigrated from his native Wolbrom to Palestine in 1933). Literature scholar Hana Wirth-Nesher characterizes Erlich's perspective as "nostalgia that comes of grief, with the caress born of hindsight."[85]

Other Yiddish writers, such as Yehuda Elberg (*Kalmen kalikes imperye* [*The Empire of Kalman the Cripple*], 1983) and Chava Rosenfarb (*Botshani* [*Bociany*], 1982), who each survived the Holocaust and then settled in Canada, revisit the prewar *shtetl* in novels that recall realist Yiddish fiction of the prewar era. Rosenfarb's *Bociany*, loosely based on her parents' lives, follows the intertwined fates of a boy and girl from the eponymous *shtetl*, who meet again as young adults in Łódź, where they marry. Rosenfarb situates the fictitious town both in an actual East European landscape, near the border between the Russian and Habsburg Empires, and in relation to a mythical sense of place: town residents could "discern, at a great distance, what they believed to be the Mountains of Darkness, which stood on the border of this world and the next."[86] The *shtetl* is doubly liminal, in both a historicized political geography and the cosmology of Jewish folklore. The town's name similarly locates it in an ecological as well as symbolic landscape. Bociany is the Polish word for "storks"; these birds, a prominent presence in the town, embody its ideals. Exemplary family figures, the storks are good omens for fertility, and their valued presence in the town brings Jews and Christians together.

Elberg's novel, which chronicles the transformation of its misanthropic, scheming title character into a devoted member of the Jewish community, situates his intrigues in a thriving provincial Polish town. Elberg acknowledges the *shtetl*'s destiny only in the novel's final pages. It concludes on the fateful day of 31 January 1933, as a character reads in the newspaper that "Reichs-Chancellor Hitler became the new leader of Germany."[87] Rosenfarb's novel has a similarly implicit telos. *Bociany* is conceived as the prequel to her earlier novel, *Der boym fun lebn* (*The Tree of Life*, 1972), which chronicles Jewish life in Łódź through the establishment of its ghetto under Nazi occupation during World War II. Both Elberg and Rosenfarb construe the *shtetl* as a proving ground for the traditional East European Jewish ethos—on one hand, a society challenged by modernity; on the other hand, a milieu in which daily life could be conducted and esteemed entirely according to Jewish principles. Their narratives integrate extensive ethnographic detail with characters' ethical reflections, thereby fabricating a virtual milieu in which the particulars of a bygone quotidian signify resilient, pervasive Jewish convictions. Against the implicit destruction wrought by the Holocaust, these novels sustain the literary life of the *shtetl* in its vernacular.

Postwar Soviet Jewish writing on the *shtetl* offers a different kind of belletristic continuity. Harriet Murav notes that these works "represent ongoing reality in Jewish spaces dense with particular Jewish ways of doing things, . . . show[ing] a sense of connection to the past."[88] Exemplary is the work of Grigorii Kanovich, who portrayed prewar Jewish life in Lithuanian provinces in a series of Russian-language novels, published in the 1970s and 1980s, chronicling the lives of the Dudaks, a fictional Jewish family. Kanovich's novels are landmarks in postwar Russian literature, noted for their forthright affirmation of Jews' presence in Lithuania and of a distinct Lithuanian Jewish culture. "His protagonists," notes literature scholar Christina Parnell, are "closely attached to the culture and nature of the Lithuanian-Polish-Belorussian space they understand to be their home just as much as do their Lithuanian fellow citizens."[89] At the same time, another Russian Jewish writer, Anatoli Rybakov, chronicled the integration of provincial Russian Jews into the Soviet mainstream in *Tiazhelyi pesok* (*Heavy Sand*, 1979). As it follows a Russian Jewish family from the early twentieth century through the start of World War II, Rybakov's novel repositions the *shtetl* in a narrative that valorizes Jews' Sovietization by invoking images from classic Yiddish literature as a counter-model:

> In those days, especially in a little township, a visiting foreigner was automatically taken for a millionaire. . . . At least, that's what would happen if our story took place in some impoverished *shtetl* of the sort Sholom Aleichem wrote about, where the people lived on air. You couldn't say that about our town. Our town was different from the other *shtetls* in the Pale of Jewish Settlement. . . . Although these were still Tsarist times when, as you know, the minorities—Jews in particular—were being persecuted, the people of our town were anything but beggars. They practiced trades and had status.[90]

These and other postwar works employ the *shtetl* as an organizing locus for Jewish narratives that reexamine established themes associated with this setting: tradition versus modernity, Jewish-gentile relations, intergenerational dynamics, responding to poverty and violence. The *shtetl*'s endurance as a narrative rubric differs from other fixtures of prewar literature about East European Jewry—the city, the multigenerational family, the immigrant journey, institutional life (synagogues, yeshivas, political parties, etc.)—as these all have a postwar continuity of some kind in actual life. By contrast, the *shtetl* is understood, if tacitly, as lost—indeed, it epitomizes loss and therefore engenders a different kind of retrospection.

Authors address this sense of loss in different ways, reflecting their nationality, language, and age. Literature scholar Katarzyna Wieclawska notes a telling shift in approaches to *shtetl* fiction among postwar writers, both Poles and Jews, in Polish from earlier works by those who had lived in these towns before the war to a younger generation with no direct knowledge of prewar Jewish life. Older writers "considered commemorating the Jewish world, which had tragically passed away, as their basic moral duty." By contrast, more recent work, appearing since the mid-1980s, approaches the *shtetl* as "an autonomous, private territory of their [authors'] imagination, . . . governed by its own laws which allow for the mixture of realism and fantasy."[91] These writers represent the *shtetl* using literary devices rooted in the mediating practices through which postwar generations have come to know East European Jewish culture. Piotr Szewc's novel *Zagłada* (Annihilation) provides a detailed portrait of quotidian routines on a single day in Zamość in 1934 in what Wieclawska terms "literary photography"; Bogdan Wojdowski's short story "Pascha" (Passover) presents the *shtetl* like "a play in the Jewish theatre in postwar Warsaw"; in *Nawrocenie* (Turning Back), novelist Andrzej Kusniewicz revisits the *shtetl* like "a tourist." Even as "the topography of the towns is often perfectly retained" in these works, Wieclawska argues, the *shtetl* "eludes realistic presentation" as it "moves toward the sphere of myth and legend."[92]

Despite its geographic as well as cultural remove, the *shtetl* has also fueled the imaginations of North American Jewish authors writing in English. Among earlier postwar examples is Robert Kotlowitz's 1972 debut novel, *Somewhere Else*, which critic David Stern praised for "recreating *shtetl* life . . . [as] neither the best nor the worst of all possible worlds." Stern hailed Kotlowitz's "commonplace" account of the *shtetl* as "all the more remarkable in light of other recent attempts to evoke Jewish life in Eastern Europe before the Holocaust and the near-universal failure of such attempts to come to terms with *shtetl* life in its essence." By this point, English-language readers could discriminate among a range of *shtetl* representations, evaluating their historical accuracy and affective register. Stern observes that "efforts to capture [the *shtetl*] in fiction have either tended to emphasize the grotesque and the demonic side of its religious life, as in the novels of I. B. Singer, or have succumbed to a pervasive sentimentalism marked all too often by ignorance and unimaginativeness."[93] Thus, authors of postwar American *shtetl* fiction were charged with the onus of answering to concerns for historical accuracy, on one hand, and offering alternatives to derivative modes of imaginary engagement—especially nostalgia—on the other hand.

In the face of these challenges, North American writers, many born after the Holocaust, produced a spate of fiction in English at the turn of the millennium that either is set, at least in part, in a *shtetl* or evokes the *shtetl* when scrutinizing Jews living elsewhere. Several authors have published work about American Jewish life in which the *shtetl* serves, at least nominally, as its rubric, including Alan Lupo's *The Messiah Comes Tomorrow: Tales from the American Shtetl* (2000), Robert Rand's *My Suburban Shtetl: A Novel about Life in a Twentieth-Century Jewish American Village* (2001), and Sylvia Geller Lisnoff's *Tales of an American Shtetl* (2011).[94] Whereas these writers envision America as accommodating the intimate communality of Old World Jewish life, other North American authors reimagine Jewish life in the prewar *shtetl* with an awareness, if tacit, of the disparities between it and postwar America.[95]

In *Stories of an Imaginary Childhood* (1992), Melvin Jules Bukiet envisages growing up in his father's hometown of Proszowice during the interwar years as a contemporary of his father, a Holocaust survivor, rather than as his son. Like Marzynski and Kirshenblatt-Gimblett, among others, Bukiet turns to the *shtetl* to engage his father's past. Bukiet imagines himself living in Proszowice as a child, ostensibly innocent of the challenges that an adult would understand, similar to Sholem Aleichem's use of young Motl as the hero of his last major work about Kasrilevke. Bukiet recounts a series of childhood misadventures—again, reminiscent of Motl—but, unlike Sholem Aleichem, focuses on conjuring his narrator's inner life. While imagining a Jewish boyhood in an interwar *shtetl*, Bukiet seems at times to draw on details of his own postwar American youth. For example, in "The Apprentice," he describes foodways that are more typical of American Jewish life than of prewar Poland and makes puns that are meaningful in English but not in Yiddish or Polish. These choices point up, if tacitly, the disparity between the actual prewar Proszowice and the one Bukiet projects.

In this collection's afterword, the author explains that he did not set out to write these stories but discovered the *shtetl* was "fertile territory" for his literary imagination—more so than places he actually knew living in New York. There is no larger narrative linking the collection's individual stories. Bukiet explains this strategy as a necessary avoidance of addressing the ultimate fate of Proszowice's Jews during the Holocaust, even though "its shadow hangs over the book, and any sane reader ought to know what will happen to every single person in the book ten years after the last page." Eliding the Holocaust liberates the author to envisage prewar *shtetl* life on its own terms, suspended within history, allowing the narrator's imagined father to ask, in all innocence, "What harm could possibly come to us in 1928?"[96] At the same time, Bukiet intends this question to provoke the informed reader to appreciate the ironies framing the naïveté of his fictional world.

Whereas Bukiet's fiction rests on a desire to inhabit his father's childhood, other authors of *shtetl* fiction extend these subjunctive exercises beyond personal ancestry to rethink the possibilities of prewar Jewish life more generally. Several novels with *shtetl* settings written at the turn of the millennium interrogate past Jewish mores concerning gender and sexuality. Canadian writer Lilian Nattel's *The River Midnight* (1999) offers a feminist narrative of *shtetl* life, in which a secret, female-centered folk culture thrives, replete with its own rituals and lore. At the same time, Nattel's novel conjures a lost family that hovers between fact and fantasy. In a note to readers, she explains:

> My family history was somewhat mythical to me because I never met my father's immediate family; they'd all died in the war. When I was little, I'd imagine that maybe his older sisters had survived because he hadn't actually seen them die and perhaps I'd be able to find them. So when I came to the end of the first draft of *The River Midnight*, it occurred to me that since I knew nothing about my great-grandmother, she could have been [the character] Misha. By imaginatively reinventing my lost family history, I felt that broken threads were in some way retied.[97]

In another feminist novel, *Your Mouth Is Lovely* (2002) by Canadian author Nancy Richler, the *shtetl* provides a point of entry not into alternative spirituality but into radical politics and the pursuit of justice in early-twentieth-century Russia, as a young Jewish woman recalls her hometown from the vantage of political exile in Siberia. Elana Dykewoman's 1997 novel *Beyond the Pale*, which traces the lives of Russian Jewish lesbians who immigrate to America at the turn of the twentieth century, also begins in "a poor shtetl of tormented Jews." Provincial life in Eastern Europe serves as the point of departure for the protagonists' journey and the narrative of their struggle for self-realization. In addition to established tropes of poverty and antisemitism, the *shtetl* exemplifies the oppressively patriarchal and heteronormative world from which these women flee. Extensively researched—in her acknowledgments, Dykewoman thanks librarians and archivists at several institutions, as well as friends and colleagues who assisted her—*Beyond the Pale* inflects the history and culture of East European Jewry with a lesbian feminist polemic. Even entries in the novel's extensive glossary demonstrate this agenda of fusing historical fiction with advocacy. For example, the gloss on Lilith explains that, when "the legendary first partner of Adam . . . found she couldn't achieve the equality with Adam that she demanded, she pronounced the secret name of God and chose to become a demon. . . . Feminists and lesbians have reclaimed her as a symbol of rebellion against male authority."[98]

K. David Brody's *Mourning and Celebration* (2009) similarly ponders what it would be like to be gay in a *shtetl*. Like other recent works of *shtetl* fiction, the author begins with a personal quest that centers on imagining a subjunctive family member in this fictive milieu:

> Had I been born 100 years earlier, at a time when my ancestors lived in ghettos or in *shtetls*, Jewish villages, to parents with a similar [Orthodox Jewish] worldview to that of my own parents, how would I have reacted [as a gay man]? How would they have reacted? Shtetl society was a fortress against external influences, . . . [functioning] along strict Jewish religious lines. Non-conformity was anathema. How would I have survived in that totally closed, totally conformist society? . . . I close my eyes, picturing an ancestor sitting there, someone just like I had been years ago—lonely, isolated, alienated and desperate as a result of being gay. I'm sure someone like me must have existed and I feel an overwhelming affinity with this stranger from another world, this long-lost cousin.[99]

This fiction entails a double projection; the *shtetl* is not a milieu Brody knows directly, as he does know being gay and an Orthodox Jew in the United Kingdom or Canada. Moreover, he envisions being gay, a contemporary construct, in the *shtetl* as itself a construct of the post–World War II imaginary (here, conceived as uncompromising and uniform in its religiosity). Impelling this subjunctive exercise are desires to repair these displacements—Jews from the *shtetl*, gay people from Orthodoxy—by conjoining them.

Some writers root the impulse to conjure the prewar *shtetl* in a scrutiny of present-day American life. Rebecca Goldstein reports that she began her 1995 novel *Mazel*, set in both prewar Eastern Europe and a contemporary New Jersey suburb, by exploring relationships among three generations of women in a family. Only after she had started to write, Goldstein explains, had "Jewishness snuck up on me, in the course of unraveling *Mazel*." When Sasha, one of her protagonists, winds up "in an ersatz shtetl recreated in New Jersey," Goldstein realized, "I would have to try to travel some of the distance traversed by Sasha [and] . . . try to imagine myself back in the shtetl."[100]

To do so, Goldstein turns to established tropes of *shtetl* fiction. She dubs her fictitious Galician town *Shluftchev* (i.e., "Sleeptown"), emulating classic Yiddish writers' coining emblematic, faux-Slavic names for towns in their prose. In what literature scholar Anna Ronell characterizes as "an attempt to make Shluftchev a member of the celebrated group of other literary shtetls,"[101] Goldstein provides an inventory of the town that corresponds to literary convention, as if ticking off the elements required by this subgenre:

> Shluftchev was a little place, a shtetl, or village, like many others. . . . It had fewer than a hundred families, almost all of them Jewish, although there were plenty of Gentiles living in the surrounding countryside.
> It had laborers, scholars, a ritual slaughterer, a cheder teacher.
> It had a cemetery, a study house, a prayerhouse, a post office with a telegraph.
> It had a few better-off people, many paupers. . . .
> Its buildings were wooden, largely unwhitewashed, largely dilapidated. . . .
> Shluftchev had just one road, and that one was unpaved, a river of mud in the autumn rains.[102]

Goldstein's remediation of earlier literary conjurings of the Jewish Old World is occasionally self-conscious, such as when Isaac Bashevis Singer makes a cameo appearance as a character in the section of *Mazel* set in interwar Warsaw. After disparaging "Itzkele Singer" as a reckless Lothario, another character describes him as "acquiring experiences for his future [literary] masterpieces."[103]

In contrast to Yiddish fiction about the *shtetl*, which assumes its readers have a shared cultural literacy, these recent English-language works address a more diverse readership, including those with no prior acquaintance with the subject at hand. Hence these works make frequent use of paratexts—glossaries and appendices that explain foreign terms, historical contexts, or authors' agendas. Some authors shift among different literary registers within the text itself, as they strive to engage readers having varying familiarity with the canon of *shtetl* literature, East European Jewish history, or Jewish religious life. For example, Alan Hoffman sets his 1996 novel *Small Worlds* in the fictional town of Krimsk—another pseudo-Slavic name, which plays on the Yiddish word *krum* (pronounced *krim* in some dialects), meaning "crooked"—and peppers his narrative with faux folklore (e.g., a legend that Napoleon's army crossed the river at Krimsk during his ill-fated Russian campaign). Yet Hoffman also weaves into the text explanations of Jewish practices and mores for a reader who may lack even basic cultural literacy.[104]

Instead of either relying on historical research or assuming familiarity with the *shtetl* as a literary locus, other authors create *shtetl* fictions that are forthrightly, self-consciously counterfactual. Some of these works engage the supernatural, an established device of Yiddish *shtetl* literature. Steve Stern's 2010 novel *The Frozen Rabbi* opens with the discovery of the title character—who had been cryonically preserved in a nineteenth-century Polish *shtetl*—in suburban Memphis, Tennessee, at the turn of the millennium. In his earlier fiction, Stern created narratives about Memphis Jews replete with types and tropes familiar from Yiddish literature—in his words, "dybbuks and dreidels, the odd wonder rabbi, here a golem, there an everlasting light"—feeling, at first, like "the thief of an experience that did not belong to me."[105] Literature scholar Janet Hadda observes that Stern was grappling with a core question for modern Jewish writers: "What are his responsibilities, his liberties? . . . How much is he beholden to the past, how much to the present?" Hadda regards Stern's prose as emblematic of a larger cultural challenge for people drawn to the "immense energy, power, and creative force" of the East European Jewish past: "What are we to do with it, since we are aware of its end?"[106]

This challenge is central to Joseph Skibell's 1997 novel *A Blessing on the Moon*, which addresses the destruction of *shtetl* life during the Holocaust through the idiom of magic realism. In a war-torn European landscape, the moon has disappeared and Jews are accused of stealing it. The murdered rabbi of a destroyed town is reincarnated as a sagacious crow. And, reminiscent of Peretz's play *Baynakht afn altn mark*, dead Jews rise from their graves to reanimate a phantom *shtetl*. As in Stern's novel, supernatural plot devices enable post-Holocaust imaginings of East European Jews' tenacity while also acknowledging their destruction. Notwithstanding its surreal character, *A Blessing on the Moon*, like other works discussed above, entails its author's inventive engagement with family history. In publicity for the novel, Skibell explains that he "lost at least eighteen relatives in the Holocaust" and named the novel's protagonist, Chaim Skibelski, "after his own great-grandfather."[107]

Another autobiographical motive—in this case, "an unsuccessful four-day trip to locate his grandfather's shtetl"[108]—informs Jonathan Safran Foer's 2002 novel *Everything Is Illuminated*. Like Stern's and Skibell's work, Foer's novel is forthrightly fantastic. In addition to its surreal elements, *Everything Is Illuminated* is distinguished by a postmodern interrogation of writing *shtetl* fiction from the vantage of an author born in America well after World War II. As he confronts the aesthetic challenges posed by the war's decimation of East European Jewry, Foer addresses, if often implicitly, the attendant breakdown of cultural literacy among this community's descendants. He expounds on his literary project's questionable feasibility through multiple discursive strategies: the gonzo, hypertrophic malapropisms of Alex, the Ukrainian guide hired by the novel's protagonist, Jonathan Safran Foer (who both is and is not to be identified with the actual author); the character Jonathan's manic, absurdist pseudohistory of the *shtetl* Trachimbrod, the Ukrainian town he seeks; and meta-discussions about writing, history, and memory between Alex and Jonathan.

Rather than compromising the author's undertaking, improbability and illiteracy inform the novel's aesthetic. Like Richmond's and Mendelsohn's memoirs, Foer's novel is founded on a lack of knowledge about the East European Jewish past, both familial and general. But instead of making confrontation with this unknown past the text's organizing principle, Foer posits the impossibility of fully knowing this past. Parody is central to this aesthetic strategy. Alex's English spoofs non-native speakers' struggles with fluency in a language they have yet to master, and, while Jonathan's journey is, as literature scholar Elaine Safer observes, recounted in "devices from classical epics," it is a mock-epic quest, just as Jonathan's history of Trachimbrod is an intentionally anachronistic bricolage.[109] Similar to Bukiet's stories, Foer's conjuring of *shtetl* life reflects the author's Gen-X American Jewish cultural sensibility (e.g., the strife between the Upright Congregation and the Slouchers resembles contemporary American Jewish interdenominational conflicts more so than any historical East European phenomenon).

From the start, Jonathan's chronicle of Trachimbrod is marked by uncertainties that trouble the desire for authoritative history: "It was March 19, 1791, when Trachim B's double-axle wagon either did or did not pin him against the bottom of the Brod River." Notwithstanding the unreliability of witnesses to narrate what is eventually celebrated as Trachimbrod's defining moment, the Well-Regarded Rabbi insists, "*WE MUST MAKE A SHTETL PROCLAMATION*"[110]—that is, calling into existence by fiat a Jewish settlement of dubious origin. Ultimately, the fanciful jumble that is Jonathan's narrative of Trachimbrod yields to the town's one ineluctable certainty: its destruction during the Holocaust. With this comes the revelation that the desire to know the ancestral world can never breach the gaps of time and place or of understanding. Rather, impossibility defines and even inspires the endeavor.

Harry Turtledove, a writer of fantasy and counter-history fiction, offers an extreme example of the counterfactual *shtetl* in his 2011 novel *Shtetl Days*.[111] Turtledove posits that, after having won World War II (called the War of Retribution), Nazi Germany fabricates a restaged *shtetl*, in the form of a living history museum, for the amusement of tourists.

(This plot device may have been inspired by reports of the Third Reich's plan to create a museum of the vanquished Jewish people after having won the war and successfully annihilated European Jewry.) Turtledove's *shtetl* reenactors, who are all German performers, so thoroughly immerse themselves in their roles and in the task of inhabiting the faux *shtetl* of Wawolnice that they begin to incorporate its Yiddish language, religious practices, and Jewish ethos into their own lives, doing so in quiet defiance of the totalitarian German state's aggressive scrutiny. Turtledove portrays the *shtetl* as not only possible to re-create in the absence of actual Jews (with practices that bring to mind the "virtual Jewishness" of contemporary Europe's Jewish tourist culture described by Ruth Ellen Gruber) but also worthy of doing so, its mores irresistibly compelling. As a way of life, the *shtetl* proves tenacious, reanimating itself by dint of a cultural imperative that outlives genocide.

Postwar writers of *shtetl* fiction all respond to the daunting desire to inhabit this milieu through the literary imaginary. At the same time, they grapple—sometimes tacitly, sometimes forthrightly—with what they know (or don't know) about the *shtetl* as itself posing a cultural challenge. For those authors personally familiar with prewar East European Jewish life, remembrance of the *shtetl* serves as a resource that imparts authority to their writing. At the same time, this familiarity is imbricated with the burden of knowing the *shtetl*'s demise, whether or not authors witnessed the destruction. Those writers lacking direct experience of *shtetl* life address their deficit with research, per the protocols of historical fiction, or by approaching the subject as an intertextual phenomenon and evoking tropes of earlier *shtetl* writing. Some of these writers see their distance from *shtetl* life, and even their awareness of its destruction, as opening a prospect for creating on paper a *shtetl* that suits their own sensibilities—what author Martin David terms the "shtetl in my mind" in his 2006 collection of stories[112]—while others make interrogating the possibility of writing a work of *shtetl* literature a subject in its own right.

All *shtetl* fiction by writers born after World War II entails remediating prior representations of their subject, whether literary works, histories, memoirs, theatrical performances, family lore, photographs, films, or tourist practices. As these authors assume their readership's desire to encounter the *shtetl* through literature, they rely on a shared familiarity with the *shtetl* as a subjunctive locus. The anachronisms often found in these works are therefore less a symptom of incomplete knowledge of prewar *shtetl* life than a product of the sympathetic imaginary. Indeed, they reflect what literature scholar Benjamin Harshav describes as a "panhistorical and transgeographical view of Jewish existence,"[113] which, for example, can conceive of biblical characters and events not as remote phenomena but as immanent and familiar. Envisioning oneself back in the *shtetl* is akin to this traditional sense of intimacy with ancient patriarchs.

At the same time, contemporary works of *shtetl* fiction are all somehow self-consciously counterfactual; they knowingly play with *shtetl* literature's tropes as well as with what is known of the actuality of the East European Jewish past. The counterfactual turns in these works point up their artifice and, with it, a defining ambivalence. They are the contrivances of writers who only know the *shtetl* vicariously, for whom the *shtetl* exists as a literary topos; it is meant to be—and of course can only be—experienced as a reading act. The artifice, the counter-history, therefore marks these texts as true to the *shtetl* as a literary construct.

Given authors' aspirations to conjure a bygone everyday existence, language proves a central challenge for contemporary works of *shtetl* fiction written in English. Vernacularity is fundamental to Yiddish writing about *shtetl* life, both for the "classic" authors who simulated folkloric storytelling and for more stylized modernists, who crafted Yiddish narratives that aestheticized the language's colloquialism. By contrast, these English-language works indicate the vernacularity of Yiddish obliquely, through the imagined translation of a language the authors may themselves not know. Demotic Yiddish speech is often signaled by inserting isolated Yiddish terms, employing calques of Yiddish idioms, or it is narrated as occurring, sometimes with explanations of vernacular nuance. Consider, for example, this passage in Hoffman's *Small Worlds*: "Unlike Reb Beryl, 'Mr. Weinbach' resented being called 'Reb Yitzhak' in the warm, personal Yiddish idiom with which Krimsk's Jews had bestowed honor upon one another for generations; rejecting the genteel tradition for the modern, secular world, Yitzhak preferred the cold, impersonal 'mister.'"[114]

Some authors respond to the challenge of conveying Yiddish vernacularity through non-linguistic and meta-linguistic options. In graphic novels that unfold in *shtetlekh*, dialogue in English (James Sturm's *Market Day*) or French (Joan Sfar's *Klezmer*) is framed by artwork that sets these exchanges in an East European visual idiom, indicated by details of architecture and costume.[115] The loss of vernacularity is one of many subjects addressed in *Everything Is Illuminated*, which describes Yiddish as "the most onomatopoeic of languages" in a disquisition on Jews' longstanding search "for a new way of speaking." In an exchange between Jonathan and Alex, the novel elaborates on notions of Yiddish as having become a lost indigenous idiom:

> "My grandmother and I used to scream words off her back porch at night. . . . We screamed the longest words we could think of. . . . And

> then she would scream a Yiddish word I didn't understand." . . . "What were the words that she would scream?" "I don't know. I never knew what they meant." He screamed a Yiddish word into the street. "Why did you not ask her what the words meant?" "I was afraid." "Of what were you afraid?" "I don't know." . . . "Perhaps she was shouting, Ask me! Ask me what I'm shouting!"[116]

The most elaborate stagings of imaginary *shtetlekh* are now found in feature films, which combine the inventive narratives of fiction with the simulated environments of museum installations or festivals. Prewar Yiddish films about *shtetl* life—whether made in situ (e.g., Joseph Green's *Yidl mitn fidl*) or on sets erected in the American countryside (Edgar Ulmer's *Yankl der shmid*)—relied on shared knowledge, however attenuated, of Jewish life in Eastern Europe's provincial towns, where millions of Jews still resided. After World War II, efforts to set a film in the *shtetl* face the daunting task of reenacting a destroyed quotidian. Instead of relying on recollections of actual experience, they have come to depend increasingly, if not entirely, on others' remembrances, encoded in the narratives, images, and performances of previous generations.

The *shtetl* is the setting for a small number of films made in the 1960s and 1970s in the USSR (e.g., *Komisar* [Commissar], 1966), Israel (*Shnei Kuni-Leml* [Two Men Named Kuni-Leml], 1970), and the United States (*Fiddler on the Roof*, 1971). These films, based on literary or stage works written before the war, also draw on prewar conventions of enacting *shtetl* life. *Fiddler on the Roof* and *Shnei Kuni-Leml* are indebted not only to the works of music theater from which they were adapted, but also to 1930s Yiddish films, among other sources. *Komisar*, adapted from a short story by Vasily Grossman about the Russian Civil War, recalls early Soviet films of *shtetl* life.

Though *Komisar* was filmed in the mid-1960s, Soviet officials forbade its release until 1986.[117] The Polish film *Austeria* has a similarly attenuated history. This dramatization of Julian Stryjkowski's 1966 eponymous novella was not made until 1982, also as a consequence of changing government policies regarding Jewish subjects in works of public culture. Like the politics of the film's realization, its political agenda is displaced. Though *Austeria* portrays the experience of Jews and their neighbors in provincial Galicia at the start of World War I, director Jerzy Kawalerowicz made the film in memory of Polish Jews, including those he had known during his youth, who were murdered during the Holocaust. At the same time, his approach to filming early-twentieth-century Jewish life was informed by one of its best-known representations in Poland: Michał Waszyński's 1937 film of An-ski's *Der dibek*. Literature scholar

Gabriela Safran views this aesthetic "recycling" as an effort to continue An-ski's project of documenting a moribund culture. According to Safran, *Austeria* suggests how "a common artistic vocabulary and a common teleology might break down the dichotomy between Jewish and non-Jewish art. Both describe the death of individuals or cultures, and both work to transform, overcome, or redeem it."[118]

More recent cinematic conjurings of the *shtetl* relate it to the Holocaust, which by the 1990s had become an established cinematic subject. Consider, for example, two French films portraying *shtetl* life on the cusp of genocide: *Moi Ivan, toi Abraham* (released in English as *Ivan and Abraham*), directed by Yolande Zauberman (1993), and *Train de Vie* (*Train of Life*), directed by Radu Mihaielanu (1999). Despite their common setting, the two films re-create the *shtetl* by drawing on divergent idioms of its representation. As its title intimates, *Moi Ivan, toi Abraham* offers a multicultural portrait of the *shtetl*. The film's plot centers on the friendship of its title characters: Ivan is a Russian Roma boy apprenticed to a Jewish family, whose youngest member is Abraham. Characters in the unnamed *shtetl* variously speak Polish, Romani, Russian, and Yiddish; these languages delineate ethnic divides and class tensions as well as cultural hybridity and social fluidity (Ivan, for example, speaks Yiddish with his Jewish employers).

The film's image of *shtetl* life is gritty, brooding, and earthy. Characters are repeatedly shown clinging to one another and often sitting or lying on the ground or floor, suggesting their rootedness in this environment. Filmed in black and white, *Moi Ivan, toi Abraham* recalls interwar photographs, such as the work of Alter Kacyzne or Roman Vishniac, who documented provincial East European Jewish life as outside observers, drawn to it as atavistic or precarious. An aura of decay—crumbling buildings, shabby clothes—pervades the *shtetl* of *Moi Ivan, toi Abraham*. The setting's vulnerable marginality is intimated at the start by a title locating the action "somewhere at the Polish border during the 1930s," and the film concludes with the town's destruction by antisemitic vandals.

Train de Vie, set in another unnamed town, portrays the *shtetl* even closer to genocide. The action takes place in the summer of 1941, as German troops are murdering Jewish communities across Eastern Europe. Despite this grim context, *Train de Vie* offers a light, whimsical *shtetl*. Colorful, playful, and almost exclusively Jewish in its population, this film is as indebted to *Fiddler on the Roof* as *Moi Ivan, toi Abraham* is to Isaac Babel's fiction. And like *Fiddler on the Roof*, *Train de Vie* offers postwar audiences a more accessible *shtetl*. Rather than simulating its complex multilingualism, the characters in *Train de Vie* all speak French, inflected with occasional Yiddishisms. One of a spate of "Holocaust comedies" made in the late 1990s (including Roberto Benigni's *La Vita è Bella* [*Life Is Beautiful*] and *Jakob the Liar*, the English-language film version of Jurek Becker's novel *Jakob der Lügner*), *Train de Vie* recounts a fantasy of Jewish ingenuity and pluck. To outwit their Nazi persecutors, the town's Jews flee en masse on a train they acquire, masquerading as a German convoy—a plan concocted by Shlomo, the self-proclaimed town fool. Whereas *Moi Ivan, toi Abraham* centers on its two youthfully naïve protagonists, *Train de Vie* revolves around an adult naïf. Both films thus facilitate an innocence of the imminent consequences awaiting their towns, providing audiences a point of entry into the *shtetl* as if they, too, were unaware of its fate. But whereas *Moi Ivan, toi Abraham* recalls the *shtetl* as a site of doomed Jewish indigenousness, *Train de Vie* presents the *shtetl* as a ludic, transcendent, locus of guileless Jewish resilience. At the same time, the film's framing device—the tale of a madman, who, it is revealed at the film's end, narrates from within a concentration camp—tacitly flouts the twee *shtetl* at the core of this escape farce.

Rather than eliding history, Eleanor Antin's *The Man without a World* places around its *shtetl* drama an elaborate, self-consciously historicized narrative frame. Antin, an American avant-garde filmmaker and performance and installation artist, proffers this 1991 film as a salvaged long-lost work, purportedly made in 1928 by the avant-garde Soviet director Yevgeny Antinov (one of Antin's invented alter egos). *The Man without a World* opens with a written prologue, which provides a faux account of the film's creation, disappearance, and recovery, traversing the history of twentieth-century Eastern Europe. Antinov—a "controversial" director of silent films in the USSR, known for his work's "decadent sexuality" and "questionable politics"—was allegedly approached by "affluent American entrepreneurs" to make "a film about shtetl life for the Jewish nostalgia market" in the United States. After an unsuccessful attempt to involve Isaac Babel in the project, "Antinov ended up writing the scenario himself, but his insistence on political commentary" in the film "got him into trouble." The American backers withdrew from the project, and it "seems never to have been shown in the United States." The "forgotten" film only came to light "at the end of the Cold War," when "a vintage print showed up in an obscure Odessa archive."[119]

As a late-twentieth-century avant-garde artist's conjuring of a bygone avant-garde and its discontents, *The Man without a World* both honors and flouts historicity. (The publishers of the film's screenplay argue that Antin "had to invent [Antinov] . . . . His cinematic creations were necessary to fill in the missing gaps of film history.")[120] *The Man without a World* is imagined as a companion piece to such early Soviet films as *Skvos slezy* or *Benya Krik*. Antin not only uses the framing device to re-create *shtetl* life as she imagines others imagined it. She also imagines these others engaged in a polemical clash—American nostalgia versus Soviet radicalism—that challenges contemporary sentimentality about the *shtetl*.

Antin draws on these and other representations either as negative models or as resources for her filmmaking. The film's complex of imaginings relies on a rich layering of mediations and remediations: Vishniac's photos of Polish Jewry in the 1930s (one of which Antin carefully restages), avant-garde cinematic devices that recall Soviet directors Vsevolod Pudovkin and Sergei Eisenstein, and plot elements reminiscent of Isaac Bashevis Singer's sexualized, gothic *shtetl* tales, among other sources. Through this self-conscious attention to *shtetl* representation, *The Man without a World* invites viewers to contemplate both the sources of their notions about the *shtetl* and what it means to know this milieu from such a complex cascade of mediations.

Even as Antin seeks to challenge the West's conventional view of the *shtetl* by inventing a radical film made with no foreknowledge of the Holocaust, *The Man without a World* is presented as an artifact of a destroyed culture. The pseudohistorical prologue explains that "the last known print" of Antinov's film, which "belong[ed] to a Warsaw collector, disappeared into the Holocaust with its owner." The "recovered" film concludes with an epilogue purportedly added by those who had recently "discovered" the print. After the final scene, the following text appears on the screen:

> In April, 1939, Germany invaded Poland.
> In 1941, the deportation of the Jews began.
> By 1943, the shtetl world had disappeared.[121]

The postwar *shtetl* is less seldom portrayed in feature films, and when it is (as in the 2005 film version of *Everything Is Illuminated*), the *shtetl*'s absence becomes the subject. Westerners' desires to visit ancestral hometowns in the former Soviet Union are lampooned more elaborately in Pavel Lungin's 2005 film *Bednye rodstvenniki* (Poor Relations, released with the English-language title *Roots*). As film scholar Olga Gershenson notes, this farce "satirizes both Western obsession with heritage travel and post-Communist Russian petty entrepreneurship." The film's protagonist, a hustler named Eduard, arranges to bring descendants, both Jews and non-Jews, of former residents of the Ukrainian town of Golutvin to see where their ancestors once lived. But as it turns out that Golutvin was leveled during World War II, Eduard contrives to tweak the name of the nearby town of Golotvin during the week his clients will spend visiting their ancestral "home." Moreover, Eduard hires local residents of Golotvin to impersonate his clients' long-lost relations. The film flouts the promise of the doubly authentic experience that "roots" tourism proffers—bringing immigrants' descendants into direct contact with their families' geographic origins and reconnecting with unknown relatives—by suggesting that such encounters may be of a dubious and, ultimately, arbitrary veracity.

The film's Jewish subplots provide opportunities to enact (and subvert) Old World Jewishness through speaking and singing Yiddish, listening to *klezmer* music, and visiting a Jewish cemetery—all fixtures of East European Jewish heritage tourism. The pretense with which they are enacted within the film intimates the constructed nature of actual *shtetl* tours. When Eduard's scheme unravels in an escalating series of comic complications, the truth of his scam is exposed—but so is the power of his clients' desire to experience a sense of rootedness in a place their ancestors once called home, notwithstanding its remoteness from the roots-seekers' lives or even its foundation on fabrication. For Eduard's clients, "Something elusive that they were looking for is found," Gershenson argues. "In a way, Eduard's mission succeeded, despite the deception."[122]

A faux representation of Jewish rootedness in provincial Eastern Europe also figures in Joel and Ethan Coen's *A Serious Man* (2009), which presents the *shtetl* as an emblem of charged, enigmatic Jewish storytelling in a film largely set elsewhere.[123] Though it primarily concerns the trials of a Jewish family living in Minneapolis in 1967, the film opens with a short prologue set in an unnamed *shtetl* and played entirely in Yiddish (with subtitles). In *A Serious Man* the *shtetl* exemplifies a lost locus of a thoroughly Jewish way of life, signified by the use of Yiddish. This bygone milieu is imagined as including both a traditional engagement with the supernatural in the course of daily life (within minutes, a character suspected of being a dybbuk appears on the scene) and a traditional skepticism about this engagement (whether or not this character is in fact a dybbuk is debated and left unresolved). *A Serious Man* presents this encounter with the uncanny in the idiom of a folktale by evoking established tropes of East European Jewish storytelling—the anonymous *shtetl* setting, the mysterious traveler, the dead present among the living, Yiddish as the vehicle for the tale as well as the language of daily life for the tale's characters—as the episode centers on vernacular explanations of the unknown.

The prologue to *A Serious Man* is not based on an authentic East European Jewish folktale. The Coens readily acknowledge that, not having found a traditional tale to their liking, they invented one. The scene that they scripted in English was translated into Yiddish by Allen Lewis Rickman, who elaborated the dialogue with a trove of folksy idioms, most of which are lost on the non-Yiddish-speaking audience. Rickman in effect fabricated an imagined Yiddish original, as if it were from the pen of the Coens, had they been fluent in the language, or from a literary reworking of a folktale by Y. L. Peretz or Isaac Bashevis Singer, or from a prewar ethnographer's recording of a tale told by a provincial informant—each of which would mediate an actual folk narrative.

This invention of an implied original that never actually existed is apposite to the prologue and its significance in the film as a whole. Embedded within the prologue are clues that this is not genuine Ashkenazic folklore, its enactment in Yiddish notwithstanding, but is "fakelore." Like Foer, the Coens respond to the established notion of the *shtetl* as a fountainhead of Jewish culture by interrogating the possibility of engaging it from a postwar American Jewish vantage. *A Serious Man* both suggests storytelling as a resource for doing so and contravenes the possibility. The film posits American suburbia as a postwar parallel to the *shtetl* and then ridicules the notion, even as it remains appealing. After a brief portrayal in the film's opening, the *shtetl* haunts the rest of *A Serious Man*, inspiring audiences to seek (nonexistent) diegetic ties between the prologue and the postwar American drama. The *shtetl*'s spectral presence in this film and the audience's yearning to connect the *shtetl* to a more familiar Jewish culture exemplify the power of this locus and all that it has come to connote in postwar Jewish life.

The Holocaust haunts the many postwar efforts to revisit, remember, or restore *shtetlekh*, but so do other, earlier efforts: the memorialization of Jewish communities destroyed in the Ukrainian uprisings of the seventeenth century; memoirs penned by *maskilim*; hasidic pilgrimages to the courts of *rebeyim*; provincial expeditions of ethnographers and modernist writers and artists at the turn of the twentieth century; hometown visits by immigrants from America or Palestine during the interwar years; the *shtetl* pastoral of urbanites participating in *landkentenish* expeditions. Though regarded as an exemplar of diaspora Jewish indigenousness, the *shtetl* is also a locus of repeated departure and return. And yet, however much it is anticipated, one never returns to the same place. The discovery of the disparity between one's memories or aspirations and what one observes in situ—a longstanding trope of memoirs, travelogues, fiction, and poetry—defines the value invested in the *shtetl*. Far from undermining the *shtetl*'s symbolic importance, this disparity enhances it and has become essential to the *shtetl*'s meaning in modern Jewish culture.

This instability of meaning existed well before the Holocaust. Conceptualizations of the *shtetl* as a cultural subject prior to World War II—in literature, social science, performance, visual culture, political life—offered manifold, unresolved notions of redefining or reinventing provincial East European Jewish life. These open-ended possibilities in turn set the stage for postwar scholarship and cultural creativity centered on the *shtetl* as a means of addressing the post-Holocaust void. In this context, a new relationship between the actualities of East European Jewish life, past or present, and the imagined *shtetl* took shape, as did an unprecedented scrutiny of this interrelation. Much of this scrutiny has assailed *shtetl* nostalgia as idealization or sentimental kitsch. Yet this attention has also revealed the power of the imaginary to be transcendent, selective, even counterfactual, and thereby offer insight into how the actualities of East European Jewish life are understood—and, sometimes, misunderstood.

As a key word in Jewish life and in Jewish studies, *shtetl* exemplifies a larger postvernacular turn. The history of the *shtetl* as a discursive subject reveals signal shifts in conceptualizing Jewish vernacularity as a phenomenon of modernity, which distinguishes colloquial Jewishness from its imbrication with "elite" Jewish mores by dint of a new cultural self-consciousness. *Shtetl* is also, therefore, an inherently retrospective term, referencing a place, language, habit, or ethos understood as having been left behind. The association of various values with the phenomenon of prewar Jewish life in provincial Eastern Europe—traditionalism, piety, provinciality, insularity—coalesced as they, too, were perceived as having been superseded by modern developments.

More than a referent for pre-Holocaust East European Jewish culture, the word *shtetl* and what it has come to connote as a postvernacular term have become fixtures of post-Holocaust Jewish culture. A shift in the word's semantic value marks this development, as *shtetl* acquires not only added meaning but also a kind of agency. First, postvernacular use of *shtetl* indexes the recognition of an East European social geography as Jewish, given the historical presence of a critical mass of Jews in a given location, along with the full range of implications of their presence: demographic, economic, social, political, religious, cultural, linguistic, geographic, aesthetic. Subsequently, *shtetl* in the postvernacular mode is understood not merely as defined *by* Jewishness but as defining *of* Jewishness—that is, this phenomenon and the values associated with it inform the nature of Jewish life.

This shift is manifest in the expansive use of the term as a metaphor for Jewish communality (e.g., referring to an apartment building in an urban Jewish neighborhood in North America as a "vertical *shtetl*") and in the invoking, reenacting, displaying, or imagining of the *shtetl* within new Jewish definitional practices (including those that non-Jews participate in and sometimes initiate). These practices constitute new Jewish folkways, for investing added values in the term *shtetl* is primarily a self-styled, grassroots phenomenon. As it indexes a range of associations, the term exemplifies East European Jews' vernacular energy—resistant to conformity or standardization, and unashamed of its difference, humbleness, vulgarity, inconsistencies, or hybridities. Because of its vernacular base, the *shtetl* is understood as a locus for encountering Jewish rootedness in the colloquial, however that encounter might be configured.

In Jewish studies, the *shtetl* exemplifies a dynamic relationship with vernacularity. This relationship entails not only shifts in how scholars study the lives of "ordinary" Jews but also how scholars understand scholarly activity in relation to vernacular practices, past and present. The modern self-consciousness about vernacular Jewish culture as something to be left behind—even as it is subject to intellectual scrutiny—typical of the earliest scholarly attention to provincial East European Jewish life, has been complicated by innovations in Jewish culture, especially after the Holocaust. In the absence of the *shtetl* as an exemplar of Jewish vernacularity, an array of new vernacular practices have emerged, some of which—books, museum exhibitions, films, websites, live performances, tourist attractions, courses of study—engage the *shtetl* through the rubrics of scholarship. The distance between this erstwhile quotidian and the present one, which was once defined in part by scholarship, is now often obscured or collapsed. Engagé scholarship on the *shtetl*, formerly the work of activists seeking to rescue or reform the Jews in these provincial settlements, now seeks ways to bring people (whether or not they are Jews) closer to this lost vernacular sensibility.

The *shtetl* has come to conceptualize something irresistible in Jewish life—even for *maskilim*, even for Westjuden, even for Zionists, even for Jewish communists, even for Jewish cosmopolitanites, and even for many non-Jews. This despite the fact that the term *shtetl* is slippery, the origins of the phenomenon are improvised, and it has been easily overlooked. But this volatile intellectual history, too, enhances rather than inhibits the *shtetl*'s significance. The protean, populist nature of *shtetl* as a key word is therefore both its greatest challenge to Jewish studies and, at the same time, its salient virtue—the key to desires that drive a fascination with the vernacular Jewish past.

Notes

INTRODUCTION

1. Leo Rosten, *The Joys of Yiddish* (New York: McGraw-Hill, 1968), 369.

2. Alain Guillemoles, *Sur les traces du Yiddishland: Un pays sans frontières* [On the Trail of Yiddishland: A Land without Borders] (Paris: Les petits matins, 2010), 187.

3. Raj Tamás, *100 + 1 Jiddis Szó* [100 + 1 Yiddish Words] (Budapest: Makkabi, 1999), 184–185. Translated by Anna Manchin.

4. Moni Ovadia, ed., *Così Giovane e già Ebreo: Umorismo yiddish* [So Young and Already Jewish: Yiddish Humor] (Milan: Piemme, 1998), 77.

5. Konstanty Gebert et al., *Polski Alef-Bet: Żydzi w Polsce i Ich Odrodzony Świat* [Polish Alef-bet (i.e., Jewish alphabet): Jews in Poland and Their Reborn World] (Warsaw: Carta Blanca, 2009), 237.

6. [Shtetl: Jewish town] http://ru.wikipedia.org/wiki/Штетл_(еврейское_местечко) (accessed 10 June 2012).

7. Jeffrey Shandler, *Adventures in Yiddishland: Postvernacular Language and Culture* (Berkeley: University of California Press, 2005), 22, 194.

8. According to data generated by Google Books Ngram Viewer, available at http://ngrams.googlelabs.com/, for books published between 1800 and 2000 (accessed 20 September 2011).

9. Hans Peter Althaus, *Zocker, Zoff, & Zores: Jiddische Wörter im Deutschen* [Yiddish Words in German] (Munich: C. H. Beck, 2003), 119–120.

10. "About Shtetl," http://shtetlmontreal.com/about/ (accessed 15 August 2012).

11. Egon Mayer, *From Suburb to Shtetl: The Jews of Boro Park* (Philadelphia: Temple University Press, 1979), 7.

12. Maureen Dowd, "High Anxiety in the Mile High City," *New York Times*, 26 August 2008.

13. Heszel Klepfisz, *The Inexhaustible Wellspring: Reaping the Rewards of Shtetl Life* (Jerusalem: Devorah Publishing, 2003), 21.

CHAPTER 1 — TALK OF THE TOWN

1. Todd Endelman, *The Jews of Georgian England, 1714–1830: Tradition and Change in a Liberal Society* (Philadelphia: Jewish Publication Society, 1979), 7.

2. On early Jewish settlement in Poland and Lithuania, see Bernard D. Weinryb, *The Jews of Poland: A Social and Economic History of the Jewish Community in Poland from 1100–1800* (Philadelphia: Jewish Publication Society, 1972), 17–32.

3. Ibid., 311.

4. On the Polish-Lithuanian Commonwealth, see Norman Davies, *God's Playground: A History of Poland,* vol. 1, rev. ed. (New York: Columbia University Press, 2005), 93–122; Antony Polonsky, *The Jews in Poland and Russia*, vol. 1: *1350–1881* (Oxford: Littman, 2010), 160–179.

5. On Polish magnates, see Davies, *God's Playground*, vol. 1, 156–196.

6. On Jewish relations with Polish magnates, see Murray J. Rosman, *The Lords' Jews* (Cambridge, Mass.: Harvard University Press, 1990).

7. See Edward Fram, *Ideals Face Reality: Jewish Law and Life in Poland 1550–1655* (Cincinnati: Hebrew Union College Press, 1997); Adam Teller, "Rabbis without a Function? The Polish Rabbinate and the Council of Four Lands in the Sixteenth to Eighteenth Centuries," in *Jewish Religious Leadership: Image and Reality*, vol. 1, ed. Jack Wertheimer (New York: Jewish Theological Seminary, 2004), 371–400.

8. See Adam Teller, "The Laicization of Early Modern Jewish Society: The Development of the Polish Communal Rabbinate in the 16th Century," in *Schöpferische Momente des europäischen Judentums in der frühen Neuzeit* [Creative Moments of European Jewry in the Early Modern Period], ed. Michael Graetz (Heidelberg: C. Winter, 2000), 333–349.

9. Rosman, *The Lord's Jews*, 107.

10. On rural Jewish life, see Antoni Podraza, "Jews and the Village in the Polish Commonwealth," in *The Jews in Old Poland: 1000–1795*, ed. Antony Polansky et al. (London: I. B. Tauris, 1993), 299–321; Hirsz Abramowicz, "Rural Jewish Occupations," in his *Profiles of a Lost World: Memoirs of East European Jewish Life before World War II*, trans. Eva Zeitlin Dobkin (Detroit: Wayne State University Press, 1999), 41–76.

11. Gershon David Hundert, *Jews in Poland-Lithuania in the Eighteenth Century: A Genealogy of Modernity* (Berkeley: University of California Press, 2004), 53.

12. On the *kohol*, see Isaac Levitats, *The Jewish Community in Russia, 1772–1844* (New York: Columbia University Press, 1943); Polonsky, *The Jews in Poland and Russia*, vol. 1, 48–58; Anatol Leszczyński, "The Terminology of the Bodies of Jewish Self-Government," in Polansky et al., *The Jews in Old Poland*, 132–146.

13. On the Vaad Arbe Arotses, see Polonsky, *The Jews in Poland and Russia*, vol. 1, 58–67; Samuel Ettinger, "The Council of the Four Lands," in Polansky et al., *The Jews in Old Poland*, 93–109.

14. On the demography of Jews in the Commonwealth in this period, see Hundert, *Jews in Poland-Lithuania in the Eighteenth Century*, chap. 1.

15. On the Ukrainian uprisings of 1648–1649, see Weinryb, *The Jews of Poland*, 181–205; Joel Raba, *Between Remembrance and Denial: The Fate of the Jews in the Wars of the Polish Commonwealth during the Mid-Seventeenth Century as Shown in Contemporary Writings and Historical Research* (Boulder, Colo.: East European Monographs, 1995).

16. On the impact of Shabetai Zevi in Eastern Europe, see Gershom Scholem, *Sabbatai Sevi: The Mystical Messiah* (Princeton, N.J.: Princeton University Press, 1973), 591–602; Weinryb, *The Jews of Poland*, 206–235. On Frankism, see Paweł Maciejko, *The Mixed Multitude: Jacob Frank and the Frankist Movement, 1755–1816* (Philadelphia: University of Pennsylvania Press, 2011); Weinryb, *The Jews of Poland*, 236–261.

17. See Glenn Dynner, "Hasidism and Habitat: Managing the Jewish-Christian Encounter in the Kingdom of Poland," in *Holy Dissent: Jewish and Christian Mystics in Eastern Europe*, ed. Glenn Dynner (Detroit: Wayne State University Press, 2011), 104–130; Adam Teller, "Hasidism and the Challenge of Geography: The Polish Background to the Spread of the Hasidic Movement," *AJS Review* 30, no. 1 (2006): 1–29. On the origins of hasidism, see Glenn Dynner, *Men of Silk: The Hasidic Conquest of Polish Jewish Society* (Oxford: Oxford University Press, 2006); Immanuel Etkes, *The Besht: Magician, Mystic, and Leader*, trans. Saadya Sternberg (Hanover, N.H.: University Press of New England, 2005); Hundert, *Jews in Poland-Lithuania in the Eighteenth Century*, chaps. 8 and 9; Moshe Rosman, *Founder of Hasidism: A Quest for the Historical Ba'al Shem Tov* (Berkeley: University of California Press, 1996).

18. On the partitions of Poland, see Davies, *God's Playground*, vol. 2, chaps. 2–4. On the impact of the partitions on Polish Jews, see Israel Bartal, *The Jews of Eastern Europe, 1772–1880* (Philadelphia: University of Pennsylvania Press, 2002), chap. 2; Polonsky, *The Jews in Poland and Russia*, vol. 1, chaps. 7–11. On Congress Poland, see Davies, *God's Playground*, vol. 2, chap. 13.

19. On Galicia, see Bartal, *The Jews of Eastern Europe*, chaps. 6, 11; Israel Bartal and Antony Polonsky, eds., *Polin: Studies in Polish Jewry: Focusing on Galicia: Jews, Poles, and Ukrainians, 1772–1918* (Oxford: Littman, 1999); Larry Wolff, *The Idea of Galicia: History and Fantasy in Habsburg Political Culture* (Stanford, Calif.: Stanford University Press, 2010). On Jewish life in nineteenth-century Russia, see Eli Lederhendler, *Road to Modern Jewish Politics: Political Tradition and Political Reconstruction in the Jewish Community of Tsarist Russia* (New York: Oxford University Press, 1989); Michael Stanislawski, *Tsar Nicholas I and the Jews: The Transformation of Jewish Society in Russia, 1825–1855* (Philadelphia: Jewish Publication Society, 1983).

20. On Haskalah, see Bartal, *The Jews of Eastern Europe*, chap. 8; Olga Litvak, *Haskalah: The Romantic Movement in Judaism* (New Brunswick, N.J.: Rutgers University Press, 2012); Shmuel Feiner, *The Jewish Enlightenment*, trans. Chaya Naor (Philadelphia: University of Pennsylvania Press, 2004). On *misnagdim*, see Allan Nadler, *The Faith of the Mithnagdim: Rabbinic Responses to Hasidic Rapture* (Baltimore: Johns Hopkins University Press, 1997).

21. Litvak, *Haskalah*, 102. On Haskalah and reading practices, see also Iris Parush, *Reading Jewish Women: Marginality and Modernization in Nineteenth-Century Eastern European Jewish Society*, trans. Saadya Sternberg (Hanover, N.H.: University Press of New England, 2004).

22. See, e.g., "The Impact of Industrialization in Tsarist Russia on the Socioeconomic Conditions of the Jewish Population," in Arcadius Kahan, *Essays in Jewish Social and Economic History*, ed. Roger Weiss (Chicago: University of Chicago Press, 1986), 1–69.

23. On Jewish urban population statistics in 1900, see Abraham Polonsky, *The Jews in Poland and Russia*, vol. 2: *1881–1814* (Oxford: Littman, 2010), 198–211. On Jewish urbanization in Eastern Europe, see Scott Ury, "Urban Society, Popular Culture, Participatory Politics: On the Culture of Modern Jewish Politics," in *Insiders and Outsiders: Dilemmas of East European Jewry*, ed. Richard I. Cohen, Jonathan Frankel, and Stefani Hoffman (Oxford: Littman, 2010), 151–165.

24. On East European Jewish immigration to America, see Gerald Sorin, *A Time for Building: The Third Migration, 1880–1920* (Baltimore: Johns Hopkins University Press, 1992); Annie Polland and Daniel Soyer, *Emerging Metropolis: New York Jews in the Age of Immigration, 1840–1920* (New York: New York University Press, 2012).

25. On East European Jewish political movements, see Jonathan Frankel, *Prophecy and Politics: Socialism, Nationalism, and the Russian Jews, 1862–1917* (New York: Cambridge University Press, 1981); Eli Lederhendler, *The Road to Modern Jewish Politics: Political Tradition and Political Reconstruction in the Jewish Community of Tsarist Russia* (New York: Oxford University Press, 1989); Ezra Mendelsohn, *On Modern Jewish Politics* (New York: Oxford University Press, 1993); David Vital, *The Origins of Zionism* (Oxford: Clarendon Press, 1975).

26. Statistics from Benyamin Lukin, "Berdychiv," *YIVO Encyclopedia of Jews in Eastern Europe*, ed. Gershon David Hundert (New Haven, Conn.: Yale University Press, 2008), 149–151.

27. See David E. Fishman, *Russia's First Modern Jews: The Jews of Shklov* (New York: New York University Press, 1995).

28. On Jews in Eastern Europe during World War I, see Henry Abramson, *A Prayer for the Government: Ukrainians and Jews in Revolutionary Times, 1917–1920* (Cambridge, Mass.: Harvard University Press, 1999); Salo Wittmayer Baron, *The Russian Jew under Tsars and Soviets*, 2nd ed. (New York: Macmillan, 1976); Jonathan Frankel, ed., *The Jews and the European Crises, 1914–1921* (New York: Oxford University Press, 1988).

29. On Jewish life in interwar Poland, see Joseph Marcus, *Social and Political History of the Jews in Poland, 1919–1939* (Berlin: Mouton, 1983); Ezra Mendelsohn, *The Jews of East Central Europe between the World Wars* (Bloomington: Indiana University Press, 1983). On interwar return travel, see Daniel Soyer, "Revisiting the Old World: American-Jewish Tourists in Inter-war Eastern Europe," in *Forging Modern Jewish Identities: Public Faces and Private Struggles*, ed. Michael Berkowitz, Susan L. Tananbaum, and Sam W. Bloom

(London: Vallentine Mitchell, 2003), 16–38; A. Goren, "Judah L. Magnes' Trip to Przedborz," *Studies in Contemporary Jewry*, vol. 1, ed. Jonathan Frankel (Bloomington: Indiana University Press, 1984), 163–175.

30. On Jews in the USSR, see Zvi Gitelman, *A Century of Ambivalence: The Jews of Russia and the Soviet Union, 1881 to the Present* (Bloomington: Indiana University Press, 2001); Lionel Kochan, ed., *The Jews in Soviet Russia since 1917*, 3rd ed. (Oxford: Oxford University Press, 1978).

31. On Dzierżoniów, see Jacob Egit, *Grand Illusion* (Toronto: Lugus Productions, 1991).

32. On postwar East European Jewish life, see Gitelman, *A Century of Ambivalence*; Iwona Irwin-Zarecka, *Neutralizing Memory: The Jew in Contemporary Poland* (New Brunswick, N.J.: Transaction, 1990); Michael C. Steinlauf, *Bondage to the Dead: Poland and the Memory of the Holocaust* (Syracuse, N.Y.: Syracuse University Press, 1997). On return travel, see Jack Kugelmass, "The Rites of the Tribe: The Meaning of Poland for American Jewish Tourists," *YIVO Annual* 21 (1993): 395–453.

33. Dan Miron, *The Image of the Shtetl and Other Studies of Modern Jewish Literary Imagination* (Syracuse, N.Y.: Syracuse University Press, 2000), 33.

34. See Rosman, *The Lords' Jews*, 10–22.

35. On the legal implications of defining what was (not) *a shtetl* in Russia, see John Doyle Klier, "What Exactly Was a *Shtetl?*" in *The Shtetl: Papers of the Second Mendel Friedman International Conference on Yiddish*, ed. Gennady Estraikh and Mikhail Krutikov (Oxford: Legenda, 2000), 22–35.

36. Eliezer Ben Yehuda, *Milon ha-lashon ha-'Ivrit ha-yeshanah veha-hadashah* [A Complete Dictionary of Ancient and Modern Hebrew] (Jerusalem: Ben-yehuda Hozaan La'Or Lezecher Eliezer Ben-Yehuda Ltd., [1948/49]), 9:4459.

37. Samuel Kassow, "Introduction," in *The Shtetl: New Evaluations*, ed. Steven T. Katz (New York: New York University Press, 2007), 1.

38. Antony Polonsky, "The *Shtetl*: Myth and Reality," *Polin: Studies in Polish Jewry* 17 (2004): 4.

39. Klier, "What Exactly Was a *Shtetl?*" 26–27.

40. Samuel Kassow, "The Shtetl in Interwar Poland," in Katz, *The Shtetl: New Evaluations*, 125.

41. Benedict Anderson, *Imagined Communities: Reflections on the Origin and Spread of Nationalism*, rev. ed. (London: Verso, 1991), 6.

42. Ben-Cion Pinchuk, "The East European Shtetl and Its Place in Jewish History," *Revue des Études Juives* 164, nos. 1–2 (January–June 2005): 187.

43. Arnold Band, "Agnon's Synthetic Shtetl," in Katz, *The Shtetl: New Evaluations*, 234.

44. Barbara Kirshenblatt-Gimblett, "Introduction," in Mark Zborowski and Elizabeth Herzog, *Life Is with People: The Culture of the Shtetl* (New York: Schocken, 1995 [1952]), xviii–xix.

45. Haya Bar-Itzhak, *Jewish Poland: Legends of Origin* (Detroit: Wayne State University Press, 2001), 29–31.

46. See ibid., 31–44.

47. Nokhem Stutshkov, *Der oytser fun der yidisher shprakh* [Thesaurus of the Yiddish Language] (New York: YIVO, 1950), 78.

48. See Nancy Sinkoff, *Out of the Shtetl: Making Jews Modern in the Polish Borderlands* (Providence, R.I.: Brown Judaic Studies, 2004), chap. 2.

49. David G. Roskies, *The Jewish Search for a Usable Past* (Bloomington: Indiana University Press, 1999), 41.

50. Yisroel Aksenfeld, *Dos shtern-tikhl un der ershter yidisher rekrut* [The Headband and The First Jewish Recruit] (Buenos Aires: YIVO, 1971), 21. For a translation of the novel, see *The Shtetl: A Creative Anthology of Jewish Life in Eastern Europe,* ed. and trans. Joachim Neugroschel (New York: Overlook Press, 1989), 49–172.

51. On Dik, see David G. Roskies, *A Bridge of Longing: The Lost Art of Yiddish Storytelling* (Cambridge, Mass.: Harvard University Press, 1995), chap. 3. On Abramovitsh, see Dan Miron, *A Traveler Disguised: A Study in the Rise of Modern Yiddish Fiction in the Nineteenth Century* (New York: Schocken, 1973).

52. See Olga Litvak, *Conscription and the Search for Modern Russian Jewry* (Bloomington: Indiana University Press, 2006), 63–66.

53. Steven E. Aschheim, *Brothers and Strangers: The East European Jews in German and German Jewish Consciousness, 1800–1923* (Madison: University of Wisconsin Press, 1982), 28.

54. On Dvora Baron, see Naomi Seidman, *A Marriage Made in Heaven: The Sexual Politics of Hebrew and Yiddish* (Berkeley: University of California Press, 1997), chap. 3.

55. On Yiddishism, see Emanuel S. Goldsmith, *Architects of Yiddishism at the Beginning of the Twentieth Century: A Study in Jewish Cultural History* (Rutherford, N.J.: Fairleigh Dickinson University Press, 1976); Barry Trachtenberg, *The Revolutionary Roots of Modern Yiddish, 1903–1917* (Syracuse, N.Y.: Syracuse University Press, 2008).

56. See Gennady Estraikh, "Yiddish in Imperial Russia's Civil Society," in *Jews in the East European Borderlands: Essays in Honor of John D. Klier*, ed. Eugene M. Avrutin and Harriet Murav (Boston: Academic Studies Press, 2012), 50–66; Sarah Abrevaya Stein, *Making Jews Modern: The Yiddish and Ladino Press in the Russian and Ottoman Empires* (Bloomington: Indiana University Press, 2004); Jeffrey Veidlinger, *Jewish Public Culture in the Late Russian Empire* (Bloomington: Indiana University Press, 2009).

57. On Sholem Aleichem and the *shtetl*, see Miron, *The Image of the Shtetl*, chaps. 1, 5, 6, 7.

58. See Roskies, *The Jewish Search for a Usable Past*, 49–52.

59. A translation of Asch's novella appears in Sholem Asch, *Tales of My People*, trans. Meyer Levin (New York: G. P. Putnam's Sons, 1948), 3–143; a translation of Weissenberg's novella appears in Ruth R. Wisse, ed., *A Shtetl and Other Yiddish Novellas* (New York: Behrman House, 1973), 29–78.

60. Dan Miron, "Folklore and Antifolklore in the Yiddish Fiction of the Haskala," in *Studies in Jewish Folklore: Proceedings of a Regional Conference of the Association for Jewish Studies Held at the Spertus College of Judaica, Chicago, May 1–3, 1977*, ed. Frank Talmage (Cambridge, Mass.: Association for Jewish Studies, 1980), 229, 237.

61. The first collection of these stories appeared in 1867; earlier collections published in Yiddish, dating back to the turn of the seventeenth century, attribute these stories to the inhabitants of Schildburg, the archetypal town of fools in German folklore. On the reworking of these stories after the Holocaust, see Or Rogovin, "Chelm as Shtetl: Y. Y. Trunk's 'Khelemer Khakhomim,'" *Prooftexts* 29, no. 2 (2009): 242–272.

62. On the image of the Jew in Polish literature, see Aleksander Hertz, *The Jews in Polish Culture* (Evanston, Ill.: Northwestern University Press, 1988), 223–247.

63. Polonsky, *The Jews in Poland and Russia*, vol. 2, 167.

64. Ursula Phillips, "The 'Jewish Question' in the Novels and Short Stories of Eliza Orzeszkowa," *East European Jewish Affairs* 25, no. 2 (1995): 69–90.

65. See Leopold von Sacher-Masoch, *A Light for Others and Other Jewish Tales from Galicia*, trans. Michael T. O'Pecko (Riverside, Calif.: Ariadne Press, 1994). See also Samuel Spinner, "Anecdotal Evidence: Local Color and Ethnography in the 'Shtetl' Stories of Leopold von Sacher-Masoch," *Studia Rosenthaliana* 41 (2009): 65–79.

66. On philosemitism in the work of Russian writers, see, e.g., D. Rayfield, "What Did Jews Mean to Chekhov?" *European Judaism* 8 (1973–1974): 30–36; Harold K. Schefski, "Tolstoi and the Jews," *Russian Review* 41, no. 1 (1982): 1–10.

67. See, e.g., Zachary M. Baker, "The Painter as Ethnographer: Maurycy Minkowski and the European Yiddish Intelligentsia before World War I," in *Czernowitz at 100: The First Yiddish Language Conference in Historical Perspective*, ed. Kalman Weiser and Joshua A. Fogel (Lanham, Md.: Lexington Books, 2010), 125–135; Larry Silver, "Jewish Identity in Art and History: Maurycy Gottlieb as Early Jewish Artist," in *Jewish Identity in Modern Art History*, ed. Catherine M. Soussloff (Berkeley: University of California Press, 1999), 87–113.

68. Grace Cohen Grossman, *Judaica at the Smithsonian: Cultural Politics as Cultural Model* (Washington, D.C.: Smithsonian Institution Press, 1997), 5.

69. On postcards of East European Jewish life, see, e.g., Gérard Silvain and Henri Minczeles, *Yiddishland* (Corte Madera, Calif.: Ginko Press, 1999).

70. On Bersohn, see Jacob Shatzky, *Geshikhte fun yidn in Varshe* [History of Jews in Warsaw], vol. 3 (New York: YIVO, 1953), 328–332.

71. On graphic arts, see Natalie Hazan-Brunet and Ada Ackerman, eds., *Futur Antérieur: L'avant-garde et le livre Yiddish (1914–1939)* (Paris: Skira Flammarion, 2009); on theater design, see Susan Tumarkin Goodman, ed., *Chagall and the Artists of the Russian Jewish Theater* (New Haven, Conn.: Yale University Press, 2008).

72. See David G. Roskies, ed., *The Literature of Destruction: Jewish Responses to Catastrophe* (Philadelphia: Jewish Publication Society, 1989), chaps. 11–14.

73. On Motl, see Dan Miron, "Bouncing Back: Destruction and Recovery in Sholem Aleichem's *Motl Peyse dem khazns*," in his *The Image of the Shtetl*, 179–255. On "A naklit," see Moyshe-Leyb Halpern, *In New York: A Selection*, ed. and trans. Kathryn Hellerstein (Philadelphia: Jewish Publication Society, 1982), which contains a partial translation of the poem. On "Di kupe," see Roy Greenwald, "Pogrom and Avant-garde: Peretz Markish's 'Di kupe,'" *Jewish Social Studies* 16, no. 3 (2010): 65–84; Seth L. Wolitz, "A Yiddish Modernist Dirge: 'Di Kupe' of Peretz Markish," *Modern Jewish Studies Annual* 6 (1987): 56–72.

74. For a translation of *Baynakht afn altn mark*, see I. L. Peretz, *The I. L. Peretz Reader*, ed. Ruth R. Wisse (New Haven, Conn.: Yale University Press, 2002), 359–432. For a translation of *Der dibek*, see S. An-Ski, *The Dybbuk and Other Writings*, ed. David G. Roskies (New Haven, Conn.: Yale University Press, 1992), 1–49.

75. On the second memorial book, *Felshtin zamlbukh* [Felshtin Anthology], published in 1937, see Roskies, *The Jewish Search for a Usable Past*, 57–63.

76. On agricultural colonies, see Uri D. Herscher, *Jewish Agricultural Utopias in America, 1880–1910* (Detroit: Wayne State University Press, 1981); Jonathan L. Dekel-Chen, *Farming the Red Land: Jewish Agricultural Colonization and Local Soviet Power, 1924–1941* (New Haven, Conn.: Yale University Press, 2005).

77. On Soviet Jewish avant-garde art, see Ruth Apter-Gabriel, ed., *Tradition and Revolution: The Jewish Renaissance in Russian Avant-Garde Art, 1912–1928* (Jerusalem: Israel Museum, 1987).

78. On Soviet Yiddish theater, see Jeffrey Veidlinger, *The Moscow State Yiddish Theater: Jewish Culture on the Soviet Stage* (Bloomington: Indiana University Press, 2000). On *The Dybbuk*, see An-Ski, *The Dybbuk and Other Writings*.

79. "Di ratn zaynen an instrument ibertsuboyen dos shtetl . . ." [poster], YIVO Archives, RG 28, P/496.

80. Harriet Murav, *Music from a Speeding Train: Jewish Literature in Post-Revolution Russia* (Stanford, Calif.: Stanford University Press, 2011), 97, 69.

81. On *landsmanshaftn*, see Daniel Soyer, *Jewish Immigrant Associations and American Identity in New York, 1880–1939* (Cambridge, Mass.: Harvard University Press, 1997).

82. E.g., on immigrant associations in Paris, see Jonathan Boyarin, *Polish Jews in Paris: The Ethnography of Memory* (Bloomington: Indiana University Press, 1991).

83. Rebecca Kobrin discusses a similar phenomenon among Jewish immigrants from the city of Bialystok in *Jewish Bialystok and Its Diaspora* (Bloomington: Indiana University Press, 2010). While this study concerns immigrant ties to a city with a much larger Jewish population than that in a provincial town, the immigrants' conceptualization of being in exile from their European hometown applies to immigrants from these smaller locations.

84. Mary Antin, *The Promised Land* (Princeton, N.J.: Princeton University Press, 1985); Anzia Yezierska, *Bread Givers: A Novel* (New York: Persea, 2003).

85. Abraham Cahan, *Yekl and The Imported Bridegroom and Other Stories of the New York Ghetto* (New York: Dover, 1970).

86. Moyshe Leyb Halpern, "Zlotshev, mayn heym," in *Di goldene pave* [The Golden Peacock] (Cleveland: Farlag grupe yidish, 1924), 16–18. For a complete translation, see Benjamin and Barbara Harshav, *American Yiddish Poetry: A Bilingual Anthology* (Berkeley: University of California Press, 1986), 409–411.

87. Jacob Jacobs and Alexander Olshanetsky, "Mayn shtetele Belz" [sheet music] (New York: J. & J. Kammen Music Co., 1932); Chaim Tauber and Manny Fleischman, "Mein shtetele Moliff" [sheet music] (New York: J. & J. Kammen Music Co., 1947).

88. See Mikhail Bakhtin, "Forms of Time and of the Chronotope in the Novel," in *The Dialogic Imagination* (Austin: University of Texas Press, 1981), 84–258.

89. Joseph Roth, "The Jewish Shtetl," in *The Wandering Jews*, trans. Michael Hofmann (New York: W. W. Norton, 2001), 25–53.

90. See Jack Kugelmass and Jeffrey Shandler, *Going Home: How American Jews Invent the Old World* [exhibition brochure] (New York: YIVO, 1989); Jack Kugelmass, "Going Home: Preface," *YIVO Annual* 21 (1993): vii–xv.

91. Khone Gotesfeld, *Mayn rayze iber Galitsye* [My Travels through Galicia] (New York: United Galician Jews in America, 1937). Excerpts are translated in Chone Gottesfeld, *Tales of the Old World and the New* (New York: Thomas Yoseloff, 1964), 244–278.

92. See, e.g., Khayim Semyatitsky, "From American Universities to the Polish Yeshivas," in *From a Ruined Garden: The Memorial Books of Polish Jewry*, ed. Jack Kugelmass and Jonathan Boyarin (Bloomington: Indiana University Press, 1998), 110–111.

93. See Molly Picon and Jean Bergantini Grillo, *Molly! An Autobiography* (New York: Simon and Schuster, 1980).

94. J. Hoberman, *Bridge of Light: Yiddish Film between Two Worlds* (New York: Schocken, 1991), 9.

95. See Jeffrey Shandler, "*Ost und West*, Old World and New: Nostalgia and Antinostalgia on the Silver Screen," *YIVO Annual* 21 (1992): 153–188.

96. See Patricia Erens, *The Jew in American Cinema* (Bloomington: Indiana University Press, 1984), 57–63.

97. See Hoberman, *Bridge of Light*, chap. 10.

98. Ibid., 304.

99. Ruth R. Wisse, "Introduction," in Isaac Bashevis Singer, *Satan in Goray*, trans. Jacob Sloan (New York: Noonday, 1996), xl–xli.

100. See David G. Roskies, *Against the Apocalypse: Responses to Catastrophe in Modern Jewish Culture* (Cambridge, Mass.: Harvard University Press, 1984), 128–132.

101. Yiddish lyrics, English translation, and melody are found in Eleanor Gordon Mlotek, ed., *Mir trogn a gezang: The New Book of Yiddish Songs*, 2nd ed. (New York: Workmen's Circle, 1977), 231–232.

102. Eugene Kinkead, "The Tiny Landscape—II," *New Yorker*, 9 July 1955, 40. See Jeffrey Shandler, "'The Time of Vishniac': Photographs of Prewar East European Jewry in Postwar Contexts," *Polin: Studies in Polish Jewry* 16 (2003): 313–333.

103. Marianne Hirsch, *Family Frames: Photography, Narrative, and Postmemory* (Cambridge, Mass.: Harvard University Press, 1997), 22.

104. Jürgen Habermas, *The Structural Transformation of the Public Sphere: An Inquiry into a Category of Bourgeois Society*, trans. Thomas Burger (London: Polity, 1989 [1962]); Walter Benjamin, *The Arcades Project*, trans. Howard Eiland and Kevin McLaughlin (Cambridge, Mass.: Belknap Press, Harvard University Press, 1999); Louis Wirth, *The Ghetto* (Chicago: University of Chicago Press, 1928).

105. Antony Polonsky, "Introduction: The *Shtetl*, Myth and Reality," *Polin: Studies in Polish Jewry* 17 (2004): 5. See also Roskies, *The Jewish Search for a Usable Past*, 45.

106. Dynner, "Hasidism and Habitat," in *Holy Dissent: Jewish and Christian Mystics in Eastern Europe*, ed. Glenn Dynner (Detroit: Wayne State University Press, 2011), 104.

107. G[ershon] D. Hundert, "Paradisus Judaeorum: Exploring Some Fundamental Distortions of the Jewish Experience in the Polish Commonwealth of the 16th through the 18th Century," *Journal of Jewish Studies* 48, no. 2 (Autumn 1997): 335–348.

108. Sholem-Aleykhem, "Di groyse behole fun di kleyne mentshelekh" [The Great Terror of the Little People], *Ale verk fun Sholem-Aleykhem* [Complete Works of Sholem Aleichem], vol. 7 (New York: Forward, 1944), 159–160.

109. Jeffrey Shandler, *Adventures in Yiddishland: Postvernacular Language and Culture* (Berkeley: University of California Press, 2005), 193, 199.

CHAPTER 2 — *FORSHT AYER SHTETL!*

1. For folklore on *pinkeysim*, see Abraham Rechtman, "What Is a Pinkas?" in *Tracing An-sky: Jewish Collections from the State Ethnographic Museum in St. Petersburg*, ed. Mariella Beukers and Renée Waale (Zwolle: Waanders Uitgevers, 1992), 101–104; "What Is a *Pinkes?*" in *From a Ruined Garden: The Memorial Books of Polish Jewry*, ed. Jack Kugelmass and Jonathan Boyarin (New York: Schocken, 1983), 23–25.

2. See also Edward Fram, "Creating a Tale of Martyrdom in Tulczyn, 1648," in *Jewish History and Jewish Memory: Essays in Honor of Yosef Hayim Yerushalmi*, ed. Elisheva Carlebach, John M. Efron, and David N. Myers (Hanover, N.H.: University Press of New England; Brandeis University Press, 1998), 89–112.

3. See Adam Teller, "Jewish Literary Responses to the Events of 1648–1649 and the Creation of a Polish-Jewish Consciousness," in *Culture Front: Representing Jews in Eastern Europe*, ed. Benjamin Nathans and Gabriella Safran (Philadelphia: University of Pennsylvania Press, 2007), 17–45.

4. Dan Miron, "Folklore and Antifolklore in the Yiddish Fiction of the Haskala," in *Studies in Jewish Folklore: Proceedings of a Regional Conference of the Association for Jewish*

Studies Held at the Spertus College of Judaica, Chicago, May 1–3, 1977, ed. Frank Talmage (Cambridge, Mass.: Association for Jewish Studies, 1980), 219–249.

5. Gershon David Hundert, "Bandits in Bolechów: Eighteenth-Century Jewish Memoirs in Context," *Jewish History* 22 (2008): 373.

6. *The Memoirs of Ber of Bolechow (1723–1805)*, trans. M[ark] Vishnitser (London: Oxford University Press, 1922; reprint, North Stratford, N.H.: Ayer Co., 2000), 72.

7. Michael Shapiro, "Introduction," in *Solomon Maimon: An Autobiography*, trans. J. Clark Murray (Urbana: University of Illinois Press, 2001), x.

8. See Alan Mintz, "Guenzburg, Lilienblum, and the Shape of Haskalah Autobiography," *Association for Jewish Studies Review* 4 (1979): 71–110.

9. On the beginnings of East European Jewish historiography, see Shmuel Feiner, *Haskalah and History: The Emergence of a Modern Jewish Historical Consciousness*, trans. Chaya Naor and Sondra Silverton (Oxford: Littman, 2002); Benjamin Nathans, "On Russian Jewish Historiography," in *Historiography of Imperial Russia: The Profession and Writing of History in a Multi-National State*, ed. Thomas Sanders (Armonk, N.Y.: M. E. Sharpe, 1999), 397–432.

10. See Simcha Berkowitz, "Ephraim Deinard (1846–1930): A Transitional Figure" (master's thesis, Columbia University, 1964). Deinard recounted his travels in Eastern Europe in Ephraim Deinard, *Masa b'Eropa* [Travel in Europe] (Pressburg: D. Lavi, 1884/85).

11. Dubnow's major work on this topic is *History of the Jews in Russia and Poland: From the Earliest Times to the Present Day*, trans. Israel Friedlaender, 3 vols. (Philadelphia: Jewish Publication Society, 1916–1920). On Dubnow, see Sophie Dubnov-Erlich, *The Life and Work of S. M. Dubnov: Diaspora Nationalism and Jewish History*, trans. Judith Vowles (Bloomington: Indiana University Press, 1991); Robert M. Seltzer, "Coming Home: The Personal Basis of Simon Dubnow's Ideology," *Association for Jewish Studies Review* 1 (1976): 283–301.

12. On Orthodox Jewish historiography, see Israel Bartal, "'True Knowledge and Wisdom': On Orthodox Historiography," *Studies in Contemporary Jewry* 10 (1994): 178–192. This trend continues to the present; see Yoel Finkelman, *Strictly Kosher Reading: Popular Literature and the Condition of Contemporary Orthodoxy* (Brighton, Mass.: Academic Studies Press, 2011), chap. 4.

13. Leo Wiener, *The History of Yiddish Literature in the Nineteenth Century*, 2nd ed. (New York: Herman Press, 1972 [1899]), 131.

14. Avraham Ya'akov Paperna, "Iz Nikolaevskoi epokhi: Vospominaniia" [From the Nicholaen Era: Memoirs] *Perezhitoe* 2 (1910): 1–53; "Vospominaniia: Detstvo i iunost'" [Memoirs: Childhood and Youth] *Perezhitoe* 3 (1911): 264–364. A Yiddish translation was issued in 1923.

15. Yekhezkel Kotik, *Journey to a Nineteenth-Century Shtetl: The Memoirs of Yekhezkel Kotik*, ed. David Assaf, trans. Margaret Birnstein (Detroit: Wayne State University Press, 2002), 16–17.

16. Yekhezkel Kotik, *Mayne zikhroynes: ershter teyl* [My Memoirs: Part One] (Berlin: Klal-farlag, 1922), 7.

17. Jan Schwarz, *Imagining Lives: Autobiographical Fiction of Yiddish Writers* (Madison: University of Wisconsin Press, 2005), 27.

18. For a translation of *Bilder fun a provints-rayze*, see *The I. L. Peretz Reader*, ed. Ruth R. Wisse (New Haven, Conn.: Yale University Press, 2002), 17–84; "The Dead Town," 162–171.

19. [Jacob Lestschinsky], "Statistikah shel 'ayarah ahat" [Statistics of One Town], *Ha-Shiloah* 12 (July–December 1903): 87.

20. On Lestschinsky, see Gennady Estraikh, "Jacob Lestschinsky: A Yiddishist Dreamer and Social Scientist," *Science in Context* 20, no. 2 (2007): 215-237; Alexander Manor, "Jacob Lestschinsky: On His Eighty-fifth Birthday," *Jewish Journal of Sociology* 4, no. 1 (June 1962): 101–106.

21. Kalman Weiser, *Jewish People, Yiddish Nation: Noah Prylucki and the Folkists in Poland* (Toronto: University of Toronto Press, 2011), 97.

22. See James Loeffler, *The Most Musical Nation: Jews and Culture in the Late Russian Empire* (New Haven, Conn.: Yale University Press, 2010), chap. 3.

23. See, e.g., the following entries in L. I. Katsenel'son et al., eds., *Evreiskaia entsiklopediia* [Jewish Encyclopedia] (St. Petersburg: Izdanie Obshchestva dlia nauchnykh evreiskikh izdanii i Izdatel'stva Brokhaus-Efron, 1906–1913): S. An-skii, "Pogovorka" [Sayings], vol. 12, 598; S. An-skii, "Poslovitsa" [Proverbs], vol. 12, 769–771; I. Kaplan, "Pesni narodnyia" [Folksong], vol. 13, 144–152; M. Syrkin and R. Bernshtein, "Iskusskvo u evreev" [Jewish Art], vol. 8, 330–338.

24. Itzik Nakhmen Gottesman, *Defining the Yiddish Nation: The Jewish Folklorists of Poland* (Detroit: Wayne State University Press, 2003), 19, 172. See also Weiser, *Jewish People, Yiddish Nation*, 95–105.

25. Bal-makhshoves, "Dray shtetlekh" [Three Towns], in *Shriftn* [Writings], vol. 1 (Vilna: B. A. Kletskin, [1911]), 5–8.

26. On the An-ski expedition, see Gabriella Safran, *Wandering Soul: The Dybbuk's Creator, S. An-Sky* (Cambridge, Mass.: Harvard University Press, 2010), esp. chap. 8; Eugene M. Avrutin et al., eds., *Photographing the Jewish Nation: Pictures from S. An-sky's Ethnographic Expeditions* (Waltham, Mass.: Brandeis University Press, 2009); Beukers and Waale, *Tracing An-sky*; Semyon An-sky, *The Jewish Artistic Heritage: An Album* (Moscow: "RA," 1994); Gabriella Safran and Steven J. Zipperstein, eds., *The Worlds of S. An-sky: A Russian Jewish Intellectual at the Turn of the Century* (Stanford, Calif.: Stanford University Press, 2006); Nathaniel Deutsch, *The Jewish Dark Continent: Life and Death in the Russian Pale of Settlement* (Cambridge, Mass.: Harvard University Press, 2011).

27. S. Ansky, *The Enemy at His Pleasure: A Journey through the Jewish Pale of Settlement during World War I*, trans. Joachim Neugroschel (New York: Metropolitan / Owl, 2002), 251.

28. On Prylucki, see Weiser, *Jewish People, Yiddish Nation*; on Ringelblum, see Samuel D. Kassow, *Who Will Write Our History? Emanuel Ringelblum, the Warsaw Ghetto,*

and the Oyneg Shabes Archive (Bloomington: Indiana University Press, 2007); on YIVO, see Lucy S. Dawidowicz, *From That Place and Time: A Memoir, 1938–1947* (New Brunswick, N.J.: Rutgers University Press, 2008).

29. On Bałaban, see Israel M. Biderman, *Mayer Balaban, Historian of Polish Jewry: His Influence on the Younger Generation of Jewish Historians* (New York: I. M. Biderman Book Committee, 1976).

30. Reports on other towns in this section include Nowogródek (A. Gumener), Zdzieciol (A. Ivenitski), Olkeniki (Khaykl Lunski), and Rakov (A. Starobin). All are dated between 1926 and 1929.

31. Hirsz Abramowicz, "A Lithuanian *Shtetl*," in his *Profiles of a Lost World: Memoirs of East European Jewish Life before World War II*, trans. Eva Zeitlin Dobkin (Detroit: Wayne State University Press, 1999), 77.

32. Hirsh Abramovitsh, "A litvish shtetl (in tsifern un lebn)" [A Lithuanian Town (in Numbers and Life)] in *Af di khurves fun milkhomes un mehumes: pinkes* [On the Ruins of Wars and Upheavals: A Chronicle], ed. Moyshe Shalit (Vilna: EKOPO, 1931), 384. When Abramowicz reissued the essay in his postwar collection *Farshvundene geshtaltn: zikhroynes un siluetn* [Vanished Images: Memories and Silhouettes] (Buenos Aires: Tsentral-farband fun Poylishe Yidn in Argentine, 1959), he changed the tense of these last sentences to the past. Cf. Abramowicz, *Profiles of a Lost World*, 98.

33. G. Urinski, M. Volanski, and N. Tsukerman, *Pinkes fun der shtot Pruzshene* [Chronicle of the Town of Pružany] (Pružany: Wydawnictwo "Pinkos," 1930).

34. Maria and Kazimierz Piechotka, *Wooden Synagogues* (Warsaw: Arkady, 1959), 7–8.

35. Samuel Kassow, "Travel and Local History as a National Mission: Polish Jews and the Landkentenish Movement in the 1920s and 1930s," in *Jewish Topographies: Visions of Space, Traditions of Place*, ed. Julia Brauch et al. (Hampshire, UK: Ashgate, 2008), 248.

36. Michal Bursztyn, "A New Factor in Jewish Life" [Yiddish], *Landkentenish* 1 (1933): 11, as cited in Kassow, "Travel and Local History as a National Mission," 255.

37. Yeshaye Trunk, *Di geshikhte fun Yidn in Plotsk, 1237–1567* [The History of the Jews in Płock, 1237–1567] (Warsaw: YIVO, Historishe sektsye, Komisye far Poyln, 1939), v.

38. See Max Weinreich, "Der Yivo in a yor fun umkum" [YIVO during a Year of Mass Murder], *YIVO-bleter* 21 (1943): 88.

39. See Barbara Kirshenblatt-Gimblett, "Coming of Age in the Thirties: Max Weinreich, Edward Sapir, and Jewish Social Science," *YIVO Annual* 23 (1996): 1–103; Dan Miron, "Between Science and Faith: Sixty Years of the YIVO Institute," *YIVO Annual* 19 (1990): 1–15.

40. Khayim Khayes and Naftuli Vaynig, *Vos is azoyns yidishe ethnografye? hantbikhl farn zamler* [Just What Is Jewish Ethnography? Handbook for Fieldworkers] (Vilna: YIVO, 1929). Excerpts (translated by Jeffrey Shandler) in Paul Mendes-Flohr and Jehuda Reinharz, eds., *The Jew in the Modern World: A Documentary History*, 3rd ed. (New York: Oxford University Press, 2010), 270–272.

41. Mordkhe Veynger, *Yidishe dialektologye* [Yiddish Dialectology] (Minsk: Vaysrusisher melukhe-farlag, 1929); L. Vilenkin, *Yidisher shprakhatlas fun Sovetn-farband* [Language Atlas of Yiddish in the Soviet Union] (Minsk: Vaysrusishe visnshaft-akademye, 1931); on Viner, see Mikhail Krutikov, "Between Mysticism and Marxism: Meir Wiener as Writer, Critic, and Literary Historian," *Jews in Eastern Europe* (Jerusalem) 25 (1994): 34–40; Moshe Beregovski, *Old Jewish Folk Music: The Collections and Writings of Moshe Beregovski*, ed. and trans. Mark Slobin (Syracuse, N.Y.: Syracuse University Press, 2000).

42. A. Pulner and D. Bentsionov, *Baveglekhe un sportive masn-shpil in shtetl* [Calisthenics and Team Sports in the (Jewish) Town] (Moscow: Farlag shul un bukh, 1925).

43. Deborah Yalen, "'On the Social-Economic Front': The Polemics of Shtetl Research during the Stalin Revolution," *Science in Context* 20, no. 2 (2007): 255.

44. H[illel] Aleksandrov, *Forsht ayer shtetl!* [Research Your Town!] (Minsk: Institut far vaysrusisher kultur, 1926), 8, 9.

45. Yalen, "'On the Social-Economic Front,'" 239.

46. Anna Shternshis: *Soviet and Kosher: Jewish Popular Culture in the Soviet Union, 1923–1939* (Bloomington: Indiana University Press, 2006), 36, 40.

47. See Steven E. Aschheim, *Brothers and Strangers: The East European Jew in German and German Jewish Consciousness, 1800–1923* (Madison: University of Wisconsin Press, 1982), especially chap. 8.

48. Arnold Zweig, *The Face of East European Jewry*, ed. and trans. Noah Isenberg (Berkeley: University of California Press, 2004), 20, 22, 27–28.

49. Alfred Döblin, *Journey to Poland*, trans. Joachim Neugroschel, ed. Heinz Graber (New York: Paragon House, 1991), 75.

50. Zweig, *The Face of East European Jewry*, 6–7.

51. On the term *ghetto*, see Salo Baron, "Ghetto and Emancipation," *Menorah Journal* 14, no. 6 (June 1928): 515–527; Max Weinreich, "The Reality of Jewishness versus the Ghetto Myth: The Sociolinguistic Roots of Yiddish," in *To Honor Roman Jakobson: Essays on the Occasion of His Seventieth Birthday* (The Hague: Mouton, 1967), 2199–2211; Louis Wirth, *The Ghetto* (Chicago: University of Chicago Press, 1928).

52. On this visit, see Daniel Soyer, "Soviet Travel and the Making of an American Jewish Communist: Moissaye Olgin's Trip to Russia in 1920–1921," *American Communist History* 4, no. 1 (2005): 1–20.

53. M[oyshe] Olgin, *Mayn shtetl in Ukraine* [My Town in Ukraine] (New York: M. Gurevitsh, 1921).

54. Yitskhok Blum, *A shtetele in Poyln* [A Small Town in Poland] (New York: Farlag Blum, 1939), 9.

55. On Y. L. Cahan, see Gottesman, *Defining the Yiddish Nation*, especially chap. 6.

56. Yehuda Bauer, *My Brother's Keeper: A History of the American Jewish Joint Distribution Committee, 1929–1939* (Philadelphia: Jewish Publication Society, 1974), 188–189.

57. Bauer, *My Brother's Keeper*, 189, citing a 1937 report by CENTOS (Centrala Opieki nad Sierotami), an agency caring for orphans.

58. Bauer, *My Brother's Keeper*, 33.

59. Kassow, *Who Will Write Our History?*, 270, 272. See also "Appendix C: Guidelines for a Study of the Jewish Shtetl," 396–399.

60. See Barbara Kirshenblatt-Gimblett, "Problems in the Historiography of Jewish Folkloristics" (Paper delivered to Folklore and Social Transformation: A Dialogue of American and German Folkloristics, Bloomington, Indiana, 1–3 November 1988), 44–47.

61. See Jeffrey Shandler, *Adventures in Yiddishland: Postvernacular Language and Culture* (Berkeley: University of California Press, 2005), 15–19.

62. For example, Benjamin Harshav, *Marc Chagall and the Lost Jewish World: The Nature of Chagall's Art and Iconography* (New York: Rizzoli, 2006); Alvydas Nikžentaitis et al., eds., *The Vanished World of Lithuanian Jews* (Amsterdam/New York: Rodopi, 2004); Roman Vishniac, *A Vanished World* (New York: Farrar, Straus, and Giroux, 1983).

63. Kugelmass and Boyarin, *From a Ruined Garden*, 5, 6, 8, 11.

64. Ibid., 2.

65. Shabtai Unger, ed., *Kalush: hayeha ve-hurbanah shel ha-kehilah* [Kałusz: The Life and Destruction of a Jewish Community] (Jerusalem, 1980); Shimon Kents, ed., *Yizker-bukh tsum fareybikn dem ondenk fun der khorev-gevorener yidisher kehile Voyslavits* [Memorial Book for Preserving the Memory of the Destroyed Jewish Community of Wojsławice] (Tel Aviv, 1970).

66. Mordechai Zalkin, "From the Armchair to the Archives: Transformations in the Image of the 'Shtetl' during Fifty Years of Collective Memory in the State of Israel," *Studia Judaica* 8 (1999): 260.

67. See, e.g., Naomi Seidman, "Elie Wiesel and the Scandal of Jewish Rage," *Jewish Social Studies* 3, no. 1 (Fall 1996): 4.

68. See Barbara Kirshenblatt-Gimblett, "The Popular Arts of American Jewish Ethnography," in *Divergent Jewish Cultures: Israel and America*, ed. Deborah Dash Moore and Ilan Troen (New Haven, Conn.: Yale University Press, 2001), 155–191.

69. Abraham Joshua Heschel, *The Earth Is the Lord's: The Inner World of the Jew in Eastern Europe* (New York: Farrar Straus Giroux, 1978 [1950]), 15, 89. For more on this book, see Jeffrey Shandler, "Heschel and Yiddish: A Struggle with Signification," *Journal of Jewish Thought and Philosophy* 2 (1993): 245–299.

70. Barbara Kirshenblatt-Gimblett, "Introduction," in Mark Zborowski and Elizabeth Herzog, *Life Is with People: The Culture of the Shtetl* (New York: Schocken, 1995), xxviii, xxxi, xxxiii. Originally published as *Life Is with People: The Jewish Little-Town of Eastern Europe* (New York: International Universities Press, 1952).

71. Ibid., xxxii.

72. Ruth Benedict, *Patterns of Culture* (Boston/New York: Houghton Mifflin, 1934).

73. Bernard Richards, "The Small Town That Was a World," *New York Times*, 3 August 1952.

74. See Seth L. Wolitz, "The Americanization of Tevye or Boarding the Jewish Mayflower," *American Quarterly* 40, no. 4 (1988): 514–536; Alisa Solomon, *Wonder of Wonders: A Cultural History of "Fiddler on the Roof"* (New York: Metropolitan Books, 2013).

75. Mark Zborowski and Elizabeth Herzog, *Life Is with People: The Culture of the Shtetl* (New York: Schocken, 1974), front cover.

76. David Grupper and David G. Klein, *The Paper Shtetl: A Complete Model of an East European Jewish Town* (New York: Schocken, 1984). *Life Is with People* is cited on the book's back cover.

77. Barbara Myerhoff, *Number Our Days* (New York: E. P. Dutton, 1978); see her discussion of *Life Is with People* and of the term *shtetl*, 273–274.

78. M[ark] Zb[orowksi], "Shtetl," *Encyclopedia Judaica* (Jerusalem: Keter, 1971), vol. 14, cols. 1466–1473. The second edition of the *Encyclopedia Judaica* (2007) reproduces Zborowski's entry with addenda by Chae-Ran Freeze; vol. 18, 524–527. The entry on *mestechki* in Katsenel'son et al., eds., *Evreiskaia entsiklopediia* (vol. 11, 438–439), focuses primarily on Russian legislation regarding the status of these settlements from the early 1880s through the early 1900s.

79. Irving Howe and Eliezer Greenberg, eds., *A Treasury of Yiddish Stories* (New York: Viking, 1954).

80. Ibid., 2, 3.

81. See my discussion of the anthology in "Anthologizing the Vernacular: Collections of Yiddish Literature in English Translation," in *The Anthology in Jewish Literature*, ed. David Stern (New York: Oxford University Press, 2004), 304–323.

82. David Roskies, "The Treasures of Howe and Greenberg," *Prooftexts* 3 (1983): 111.

83. Howe and Greenberg, *A Treasury of Yiddish Stories*, 28.

84. See Marvin Herzog et al., *The Language and Culture Atlas of Ashkenazic Jewry*, vol. 1: *Historical and Theoretical Foundations,* vol. 2: *Research Tools*, vol. 3: *The Eastern Yiddish-Western Yiddish Continuum* (Tübingen: Max Niemeyer, 1992, 1995, 2000).

85. Uriel Weinreich, "Mapping a Culture," *Columbia University Forum* 6, no. 3 (1963): 19.

86. Abraham Ain, "Swislocz: Portrait of a Shtetl," *YIVO Annual of Jewish Social Science* 4 (1949): 86–114; Yekhiel Shtern, *Kheyder un besmedresh* (New York: YIVO, 1950).

87. On the Yiddish chair, see Yael Chaver, *What Must Be Forgotten: The Survival of Yiddish in Zionist Palestine* (Syracuse, N.Y.: Syracuse University Press, 2004), 113–120.

88. Roni Stauber, "Confronting the Jewish Response during the Holocaust: Yad Vashem—A Commemorative and a Research Institute in the 1950s," *Modern Judaism* 20, no. 3 (October 2000): 277.

89. *Pinkas ha-kehilot: entsiklopedyah shel ha-yishuvim ha-Yehudim le-min hivasdam ve-'ad le-ahar Sho'at Milhemet ha-'Olam ha-Sheniyah: Polin* [Record of Jewish

Communities: Encyclopedia of Jewish Settlements from Their Founding to Their Destruction during World War II: Poland], vol. 1 (Jerusalem: Yad Vashem, 1976), vii, viii, xi. Translation by Efraim Zuroff.

90. Dan Miron, "Introduction," *The Image of the Shtetl and Other Studies of Modern Jewish Literary Imagination* (Syracuse, N.Y.: Syracuse University Press, 2000), xii.

91. Steven J. Zipperstein, *Imagining Russian Jewry: Memory, History, Identity* (Seattle: University of Washington Press, 1999), 29.

92. Kirshenblatt-Gimblett, "Introduction," in *Life Is with People*, xxiv.

93. Lucy S. Dawidowicz, ed., *The Golden Tradition: Jewish Life and Thought in Eastern Europe* (New York: Schocken, 1984 [1967]), 5, 88–89.

94. Ruth R. Wisse, ed., *A Shtetl and Other Yiddish Novellas* (New York: Behrman House, 1973), x, 14–15, 16, 20.

95. Diane K. Roskies and David G. Roskies, *The Shtetl Book*, 2nd ed. (New York: Ktav, 1979 [1975]), vii–viii.

96. Lucjan Dobroszycki and Barbara Kirshenblatt-Gimblett, *Image Before My Eyes: A Photographic History of Jewish Life in Poland, 1864–1939* (New York: Schocken, 1977). See also the eponymous 1980 documentary film, directed by Josh Waletzky.

97. Robert Perlman, *From Shtetl to Milltown: Litvaks, Hungarians, and Galizianers in Western Pennsylvania* (Pittsburgh: Historical Society of Western Pennsylvania, 2002); Ilex Beller, *De mon shtetl à Paris* [From My Shtetl to Paris] (Paris: Editions du Scribe, 1991); Philip N. Mendes, "From the Shtetl to the Monash Soviet: An Overview of the Historiography of Jewish Radicalism in Australia," *Australian Journal of Jewish Studies* 14 (2000): 54–77; Sol Gittleman, *From Shtetl to Suburbia: The Family in Jewish Literary Imagination* (Boston: Beacon Press, 1978); Eliyho Matzozky, comp., *From Shtetl to Destruction: The Jewish Experience in Eastern Europe*, ed. Joel M. Halpern (Monticello, Ill.: Council of Planning Librarians, 1977); Antony Polonsky, ed., *From Shtetl to Socialism: Studies from 'Polin'* (London: Littman, 1993).

98. D. Wachsstock, "Jewish Antwerp, A Shtetl in Transition," *In the Dispersion* 5–6 (1966): 68–76; Abraham Nahum Stencl, *Vaytshepl shtetl d'Britn* [Whitechapel, Shtetl of Britain] (London: Loshn un lebn, 1961); Abraham Blinderman, "1449 Minford Place: In the 1920s, East Bronx Was a Shtetl," *National Jewish Monthly* 94, no. 9 (1980): 36–39; Terry Barr, "A Shtetl Grew in Bessemer: Temple Beth-El and Jewish Life in Small-Town Alabama," *Southern Jewish History* 3 (2000): 1–44; Herbert M. Engel, *Shtetl in the Adirondacks: The Story of Gloversville and Its Jews* (Fleischmanns, N.Y.: Purple Mountain Press, 1991); W. M. Finkelstein, "Moises Ville: A Yiddish Shtetl in Argentina," *Judaica Philatelic Journal* 10 (1974): 1307–1308.

99. See journals published in Tel Aviv (*Gal-Ed: On the History and Culture of Polish Jewry*, formerly *Gal-Ed: On the History of the Jews in Poland*, in Hebrew since 1973, bilingual format [English and Hebrew] since 1987), Jerusalem (*Jews in Russia and Eastern Europe*,

formerly *Jews in Eastern Europe*, since 1985), Oxford (*Polin: Studies in Polish Jewry*, since 1986), and Cracow (*Studia Judaica*, since 1998).

100. Gershon David Hundert, ed., *The YIVO Encyclopedia of Jews in Eastern Europe* (New Haven, Conn.: Yale University Press, 2008).

101. Accessed from proquest.umi.com on 6 September 2012. A smaller number of dissertations and theses include *shtetl* in their abstracts, but these also reflect the same trend: none before 1980; five in 1980–1989; seven in 1990–1999; thirteen in 2000–2009; two in 2010–2011.

102. Gershon David Hundert, *The Jews in a Polish Private Town: The Case of Opatów in the Eighteenth Century* (Baltimore: Johns Hopkins University Press, 1992), xiii–xv. For other recent studies of individual towns, see, e.g., Yohanan Petrovsky-Stern, "The Marketplace in Balta," *East European Jewish Affairs* 37, no. 3 (2007): 277–298; Immanuel Etkes, "A Shtetl with a Yeshiva: The Case of Volozhin," in *The Shtetl: New Evaluations*, ed. Steven T. Katz (New York: New York University Press, 2007), 29–38; Viacheslav Selemenev, "Kolyshki: A 'Shtetl' in the Late 1930s," *Jews in Eastern Europe* 2, no. 45 (2001): 48–72.

103. Antony Polonsky, "The Shtetl: Myth and Reality," *Polin: Studies in Polish Jewry* 17 (2004): 23.

104. David G. Roskies, *The Jewish Search for a Usable Past* (Bloomington: Indiana University Press, 1999), 41.

105. Samuel Kassow, "Introduction," in *The Shtetl: New Evaluations*, 1.

106. Gennady Estraikh and Mikhail Krutikov, eds., *The Shtetl: Image and Reality* (Oxford: Legenda, 2000), 3.

107. See Beukers and Waale, *Tracing An-sky*. The catalog for this exhibition, when presented at the Israel Museum in Jerusalem, was titled *Ba-hazarah la-'ayarah* (Return to the Shtetl).

108. Omer Bartov, *Erased: Vanishing Traces of Jewish Galicia in Present-day Ukraine* (Princeton, N.J.: Princeton University Press, 2007); Shimon Redlich, *Together and Apart in Brzezany: Poles, Jews, and Ukrainians, 1919–1945* (Bloomington: Indiana University Press, 2002).

109. See, e.g., Olga Vladislavovna Belova, "The Jews as Seen by the Country Folk of Polesie and Podolia," *Jews and Slavs* 13 (2004): 110–126; Alla Sokolova, "House-building Tradition of the Shtetl in Memorials and Memories (Based on Materials of Field Studies in Podolia)," *East European Jewish Affairs* 41, no. 3 (2011): 111–135.

110. See, e.g., *Spell Your Name* [documentary film], dir. Sergey Bukovsky, 2006, produced by the USC Shoah Foundation Institute.

111. "About AHEYM," http://www.indiana.edu/~aheym/aheym-project.html (accessed 23 August 2011). See also Jeffrey Veidlinger, *In the Shadow of the Shtetl: Small-Town Jewish Life in Soviet Ukraine* (Bloomington: Indiana University Press, 2013).

112. V. A. Dymshits, A. L. L'vov and A. V. Sokolova, eds., *Shtetl XXI vek: polevye issledovaniia* [The Shtetl of the 21st Century: Field Research] (St. Petersburg: European University in St. Petersburg, 2008).

113. Deborah Yalen, review of *Shtetl XXI vek: polevye issledovaniia*, *East European Jewish Affairs* 40, no. 2 (2010): 177, 178.

114. See, e.g., Deborah Yalen, "On the Social-Economic Front" and "Documenting the New Red Kasrilevke: Shtetl Ethnography as Revolutionary Narrative," *East European Jewish Affairs* 37, no. 3 (December 2007): 353–375; Anna Shternshis, *Soviet and Kosher* and "White Concert Piano from the Real Shtetl: Material Culture and Ethnic Identity in the Post-Soviet Jewish Urban Community," *Jewish Social Studies* 16, no. 2 (Winter 2010): 111–126; Harriet Murav, *Music from a Speeding Train: Jewish Literature in Post-Revolution Russia* (Stanford, Calif.: Stanford University Press, 2011).

115. Olga Litvak, *Haskalah: The Romantic Movement in Judaism* (New Brunswick, N.J.: Rutgers University Press, 2012); Marc Caplan, *How Strange the Change: Language, Temporality, and Narrative Form in Peripheral Modernisms* (Stanford, Calif.: Stanford University Press, 2011).

116. Jan T. Gross, *Neighbors: The Destruction of the Jewish Community in Jedwabne, Poland* (Princeton, N.J.: Princeton University Press, 2001). Originally published in Polish as *Sąsiedzi: historia zagłady żydowskiego miasteczka* in 2000.

117. Yehuda Bauer, *The Death of the Shtetl* (New Haven, Conn.: Yale University Press, 2009).

118. Zipperstein, *Imagining Russian Jewry*, 3; see also Steven Zipperstein, "Shtetls There and Here: Imagining Russia in America," in his *Imagining Russian Jewry*, 15–39; Mikhail Krutikov, "Imagining the Image: Interpretations of the Shtetl in Yiddish Literary Criticism," *Polin: Studies in Polish Jewry* 17 (2004): 243–258; Kirshenblatt-Gimblett, "Introduction," in *Life Is with People*, ix–xlviii; Frank Fox, "Mark Zborowski, the Spy Who Came Out of the 'Shtetl,'" *East European Jewish Affairs* 29, nos. 1–2 (1999): 119–128.

CHAPTER 3 — *SHTETL* FABULOUS

1. Raphael Abramovitsh, *Di farshvundene velt/The Vanished World* (New York: Forward Association, 1947), 8–9.

2. Ibid., 11.

3. *And I Still See Their Faces: Images of Polish Jews/I ciągle widzę ich twarze: Fotografia Żydów polskich* (Warsaw: Fundacja Shalom, 1996).

4. Kersten Brandt et al., eds., *Before They Perished . . . : Photographs Found in Auschwitz* (Munich: Kehayoff / Oswiecim: Auschwitz-Birkenau Museum, 2001), and Ann Weiss, *The Last Album: Eyes from the Ashes of Auschwitz-Birkenau* (New York: W. W. Norton, 2001).

5. Brandt et al., *Before They Perished*, 15, 5.

6. See Louis D. Levine, ed., *Lives Remembered: A Shtetl through a Photographer's Eye* (New York: Museum of Jewish Heritage, 2002). Kaplan's photographs can be viewed online at http://www.szczuczyn.com/kaplan.htm (accessed 3 May 2013).

7. Michael Berenbaum, *The World Must Know: The History of the Holocaust as Told in the United States Holocaust Memorial Museum* (Boston: Little, Brown, 1993), x.

8. Marianne Hirsch, *Family Frames: Photography, Narrative, and Postmemory* (Cambridge, Mass.: Harvard University Press, 1997), 252–254. See also Marianne Hirsch, *The Generation of Postmemory: Writing and Visual Culture after the Holocaust* (New York: Columbia University Press, 2012).

9. Z[inovi] Tolkatshov, *Dos shtetl* [The Town] (Warsaw/Lodz: Dos naye lebn, 1946), [7–8].

10. Cecil Roth, "Introduction," in Lionel Reiss, *My Models Were Jews: A Painter's Pilgrimage to Many Lands* (New York: Gordon Press, 1938), 71.

11. Lionel Reiss, *New Lights and Old Shadows: New Lights of an Israel Reborn, Old Shadows of a Vanished World* (New York: Reconstructionist Press, 1954), 89–90.

12. Lionel S. Reiss, *A World at Twilight: A Portrait of the Jewish Communities of Eastern Europe before the Holocaust* (New York: Macmillan, 1971), 154.

13. The full series of lithographs, including this prefatory text, can be viewed at "The Shtetl," http://library.syr.edu/digital/exhibits/g/Gropper/scrc.htm (accessed 25 September 2012).

14. Marc Chagall, *My Life* (New York: Orion Press, 1960); Bella Chagall, *Burning Lights* (New York: Schocken, 1946); Irving Howe and Eliezer Greenberg, eds., *A Treasury of Yiddish Stories* (New York: Viking, 1954).

15. Maria and Kazimierz Piechotka, *Wooden Synagogues* (Warsaw: Arkady, 1959), 6, 5.

16. Mark Godfrey, *Abstraction and the Holocaust* (New Haven, Conn.: Yale University Press, 2007), 98.

17. Moshe Verbin, "*Wooden Synagogues of Poland in the 17th* and *18th Century/Batey kneset me-ets be-Polin be meot y''z y''h*, 2nd ed. ([Herzliya]: Herzliya Museum, 1992), [English section, p. 4].

18. Mary Hufford et al., *The Grand Generation: Memory, Mastery, Legacy* (Washington, D.C.: Smithsonian Institution / Seattle: University of Washington Press, 1987), 59–60.

19. See, e.g., Baruch Mairantz, *My Jewish Shtetl: Recreated in Rafia and Wood* (Tel Aviv: Amir, 1972); Barel Satt, *A Jewish Town in Wood Sculpture*, 2nd ed. (Los Angeles: Satt Album Committee, 1958).

20. Alfred Werner, "The Artist Samuel Rothbort" [exhibition brochure] (New York: Theodor Herzl Institute, 1962), unpaginated. Reproduced online at http://www.samuelrothbort.com/links.htm.

21. Ilex Beller, *Life in the Shtetl: Scenes and Recollections*, trans. Alastair Douglas Pannell (New York: Holmes & Meier, 1986), 7.

22. Meyer Kirshenblatt and Barbara Kirshenblatt-Gimblett, *They Called Me Mayer July: Painted Memories of a Jewish Childhood in Poland before the Holocaust* (Berkeley: University of California Press, 2007), 123, 198.

23. See *Shtetl* [documentary film] 1995, dir. Jack Kuper; *Paint What You Remember* [documentary film] 2009, dir. Sławomir Grünberg. *The White Pajamas*, a toy theater piece created by Jenny Romaine with Mayer Kirshenblatt, was commissioned in 2004 by the French Ministry of Culture and the Festival International de Papierthéâtre, Mourmelon, France.

24. Bernard Postal and Samuel H. Abramson, *The Landmarks of a People: A Guide to Jewish Sites in Europe* (New York: Hill and Wang, 1962), 191.

25. See, e.g., Jack Kugelmass and Jonathan Boyarin, eds., *From a Ruined Garden: The Memorial Books of Polish Jewry* (Bloomington: Indiana University Press, 1998), 215–221.

26. See James E. Young, *The Texture of Memory: Holocaust Memorials and Meaning* (New Haven, Conn.: Yale University Press, 1993), chap. 7.

27. Gordon's essays were published in book form as *Friling* [Spring] (Moscow: Sovetskii Pisatel', 1970). See Harriet Murav, *Music from a Speeding Train: Jewish Literature in Post-Revolution Russia* (Stanford, Calif.: Stanford University Press, 2011), 268–274.

28. See Zalman Alpert, "Selected Bibliography of Books Dealing with Hasidic Pilgrimages to Eastern Europe," *Jewish Folklore and Ethnology Review* 17, nos. 1–2 (1995): 14–15.

29. See Mitsuharu Akao, "A New Phase in Jewish-Ukrainian Relations? Problems and Perspectives in the Ethno-politics over the Hasidic Pilgrimage to Uman," *East European Jewish Affairs* 37, no. 2 (2007): 137–155; Mitsuharu Akao, "Hasidic Pilgrimage to Uman, Past and Present: The Ambiguous Centrality of a Jewish Sacred Place in Ukraine," in *Jews and Slavs*, 11: *Jewish-Polish and Jewish-Russian Contacts*, ed. Wolf Moskovich and Irena Fijałkowska-Janiak (Jerusalem: Hebrew University / Gdańsk: Gdańsk University, 2003), 121–151.

30. See Ruth Ellen Gruber, *Virtually Jewish: Reinventing Jewish Culture in Europe* (Berkeley: University of California Press, 2002); Erica T. Lehrer, *Jewish Poland Revisited: Heritage Tourism in Unquiet Places* (Bloomington: Indiana University Press, 2013).

31. E.g., "Judaics [*sic*] Poland" [brochure] (Warsaw: Orbis, 1987?), which includes a page of "Synagogues as Cultural Centres," featuring historic buildings in Zamość, Tykocin, Łańcut, Lesko, Rzeszów, Szydłów, Kazimiesz nad Wisłą, and Chmielniki.

32. Jack Kugelmass, "The Rites of the Tribe: The Meaning of Poland for American Jewish Tourists," *YIVO Annual* 21 (1993): 443n21.

33. "Cultural and Folkloristic Tour in Ukraine" [flyer], World Council for Yiddish Culture, [1998].

34. "Shtetl Schleppers," http://www.jewishgen.org/shtetlschleppers/; this service ceased operations in 2008.

35. "Routes to Roots: Customized Tours," http://www.routestoroots.com/serv2.html (accessed 14 October 2011).

36. "Biłgoraj Will Turn into a 19th Century Town," http://www.sztetl.org.pl/en/cms/news/3056,bilgoraj-will-turn-into-a-19th-century-town/ (accessed 23 January 2013).

37. Gruber, *Virtually Jewish*, 162.

38. Frédéric Brenner, *Diaspora: Homelands in Exile* (New York. HarperCollins, 2003), xiv–xv.

39. Brigitte Sion, "From Purimspiel to Polish Masquerade: Performing Jewish Memory in Tykocin," in *Jewish and Theater in an International Context*, ed. Edna Nahshon (Leiden/Boston: Brill, 2012), 324, 329.

40. Rona Sheramy, "From Auschwitz to Jerusalem: Re-enacting Jewish History on the March of the Living," *Polin: Studies in Polish Jewry* 19 (2006): 310.

41. Jackie Feldman, "'Roots in Destruction': The Jewish Past as Portrayed in Israeli Youth Voyages to Poland," in *The Life of Judaism*, ed. Harvey E. Goldberg (Berkeley: University of California Press, 2001), 166.

42. Gruber, *Virtually Jewish*, 152.

43. "JewishGen KehilaLinks," http://kehilalinks.jewishgen.org/ (accessed 28 August 2012).

44. Daniel Mendelsohn, *The Lost: A Search for Six of the Six Million* (New York: HarperCollins, 2006), 19.

45. Theo Richmond, *Konin: A Quest* (New York: Pantheon Books, 1995), xx, 8.

46. See Aviva Weintraub, "The Photoethnography of Jewish Communities: Related Books, Articles, and Museum Catalogues," *Jewish Folklore and Ethnology Review* 10, no. 1 (1988): 3–10.

47. Brian Blue and Yale Strom, *The Last Jews of Eastern Europe* (New York: Philosophical Library, 1986); Ayşe Gürsan-Salzmann and Laurence Salzmann, *The Last Jews of Rădăuţi* (Garden City, N.Y.: Doubleday, 1983); Malgorzata Niezabitowska and Tomasz Tomaszewski, *Remnants: The Last Jews of Poland* (New York: Friendly Press, 1986); Earl Vinecour and Chuck Fishman, *Polish Jews: The Final Chapter* (New York: New York University Press, 1977).

48. Zalman Gostynski, *Des Pierres Racontent* (Paris: Union des Juifs d'Origine de l'Europe de l'Est, 1973); Monika Krajewska, *Time of Stones* (Warsaw: Interpress, 1983).

49. E.g., Niezabitowska and Tomaszewski, *Remnants*, 175; Konstanty Gebert et al., *Polski Alef-Bet: Żydzi w Polsce i Ich Odrodzony Świat* [Polish Alef-bet (i.e., Jewish alphabet): Jews in Poland and Their Reborn World] (Warsaw: Carta Blanca, 2009), 165.

50. Yale Strom, *A Tree Still Stands: Jewish Youth in Eastern Europe Today* (New York: Philomel Books, 1990).

51. Edward Serotta, *Out of the Shadows: A Photographic Portrait of Jewish Life in Central Europe since the Holocaust* (New York: Carol Publishing Group, 1991); Larry N. Mayer and Gary Gelb, *Who Will Say Kaddish? A Search for Jewish Identity in Contemporary Poland* (Syracuse, N.Y.: Syracuse University Press, 2002).

52. Wojciech Wilczyk, *Niewinne Oko Nie Istnieje/There's No Such Thing as an Innocent Eye* (Łodz: Atlas Sztuki, 2009).

53. See also *Song of Rădăuţi* [documentary film], dir. Laurence Salzmann, 1979; *The Last Journey: Lost Jews of Russia* [documentary film], dir. Philip Gittelman, 1981.

54. Svetlana Boym, *The Future of Nostalgia* (New York: Basic Books, 2001), xviii.

55. On Bransk, see also Eva Hoffman, *Shtetl: The Life and Death of a Small Town and the World of Polish Jews* (Boston: Houghton Mifflin, 1997).

56. "Virtual Shtetl: The Project," http://www.sztetl.org.pl/en/cms/the-project/ (accessed 29 August 2012).

57. "Gwozdziec Synagogue," http://www.handshouse.org/gwozdziec.html (accessed 27 February 2013).

58. "Gwoździec Reconstruction," http://www.jewishmuseum.org.pl/en/cms/gwozdziec-re-construction/view/ (accessed 18 May 2012). On the synagogue, see Thomas C. Hubka, *Resplendent Synagogue: Architecture and Worship in an Eighteenth-Century Polish Community* (Hanover, N.H.: University Press of New England, 2003).

59. "Pogranicze: Foundation," http://www.pogranicze.sejny.pl/foundation,129.html (accessed 29 August 2012).

60. Magdalena J. Zaborowska, "The Borderland Foundation in Sejny, Poland," *Journal of the International Institute* (Ann Arbor, Mich.) 16, no. 2 (Spring 2009): 4.

61. Jan T. Gross, *Neighbors: The Destruction of the Jewish Community in Jedwabne, Poland* (Princeton, N.J.: Princeton University Press, 2001).

62. Antony Polonsky and Joanna B. Michlic, eds., *The Neighbors Respond: The Controversy over the Jedwabne Massacre in Poland* (Princeton, N.J.: Princeton University Press, 2004), 1.

63. Zaborowska, "The Borderland Foundation in Sejny," 3.

64. Ibid., 5; see also Ian Fisher, "Using a Peaceful Tie to Reclaim a Painful Past," *New York Times*, 5 October 2002.

65. See Barbara Kirshenblatt-Gimblett, *Destination Culture: Tourism, Museums, and Heritage* (Berkeley: University of California Press, 1998), 57–61.

66. "The Shtetl," http://www.sajewishmuseum.co.za/immigrant_jewish_life/origins.asp (accessed 29 August 2012).

67. Aage Myhre, "Lithuanian Foortsteps in South Africa," *Vilnews*, 29 January 2011, http://vilnews.com/?p=1703 (accessed 15 October 2011).

68. David Holzel, "Shtetl Chic," *Moment* 23, no. 6 (December 1998): 37.

69. Another creator of multiple works of remembrance for a native *shtetl* is Aaron Ziegelman, who underwrote several projects commemorating the town of Luboml, including a translated *yizker bukh:* B[erl] Kagan, ed., *Luboml: The Memorial Book of a Vanished Shtetl* (Hoboken: Ktav, 1997); an exhibition: see Elly Dlin, ed., *Luboml: A Small Jewish World* [exhibition catalogue] (Jerusalem: Yad Vashem, 1997); a documentary film: *Luboml: My Heart Remembers*, dir. Ron Steinman, 2004; and a website: http://www.luboml.org/index.htm (accessed 29 August 2012).

70. Jeff Bieber, dir., *There Once Was a Town* [documentary film], 2000; Deganit Paikowsky, "Grandpa's Stories" [Hebrew] (audio documentary for Galey Zahal, the Israeli Defense Force radio station), 1998; Yaffa Eliach, *There Once Was a World: A 900-Year Chronicle of the Shtetl Eishyshok* (Boston: Little, Brown, 1998).

71. "The Shtetl Museum," http://www.shtetlfoundation.org/shtetl (accessed 30 July 2002).

72. Eliach, *There Once Was a World*, 6.

73. For further discussion of the Shtetl Museum, see Jeffrey Shandler, "The Shtetl Subjunctive: Yaffa Eliach's Living History Museum," in *Culture Front: Representing Jews in Eastern Europe*, ed. Benjamin Nathans and Gabriella Safran (Philadelphia: University of Pennsylvania Press, 2007), 288–306.

74. See Jeffrey Shandler, "Anthologizing the Vernacular: Collections of Yiddish Literature in English Translation," in *The Anthology in Jewish Literature*, ed. David Stern (New York: Oxford University Press, 2004), 304–323.

75. E.g., Sholom Aleichem, *The Old Country*, trans. Julius and Frances Butwin (New York: Crown, 1946); Howe and Greenberg, eds., *A Treasury of Yiddish Stories*.

76. E.g., *Yiddish Literature in America 1970–2000*, trans. Barnett Zumoff (Jersey City, N.J.: Ktav, 2009); Frieda Forman et al., eds., *Found Treasures: Stories by Yiddish Women Writers* (Toronto: Second Story Press, 1994).

77. "Introduction," Joachim Neugroschel, ed. and trans., *The Shtetl: A Creative Anthology of Jewish Life in Eastern Europe* (New York: Richard Marek, 1979), n.p.

78. See Roberta Saltzman, *Isaac Bashevis Singer: A Bibliography of His Works in Yiddish and English, 1960–1991* (Lanham, Md.: Scarecrow Press, 2002).

79. On Bashevis in translation, see Anita Norich, "Isaac Bashevis Singer in America: The Translation Problem," *Judaism* 44, no. 2 (1995): 208–218; Naomi Seidman, *Faithful Renderings: Jewish-Christian Difference and the Politics of Translation* (Chicago: University of Chicago Press, 2006), chap. 6.

80. Seth L. Wolitz and Joseph Sherman, "Bashevis Singer as a Regionalist of Lublin Province," in *The Hidden Isaac Bashevis Singer*, ed. Seth L. Wolitz (Austin: University of Texas Press, 2001), 219, 223–224.

81. Dan Miron, *The Image of the Shtetl and Other Studies of Modern Jewish Literary Imagination* (Syracuse, N.Y.: Syracuse University Press, 2000), 336.

82. As cited in Paul Kresh, *Isaac Bashevis Singer: The Magician of West 86th Street* (New York: Dial Press, 1979), 418.

83. Patricia Cohen, "Amid the Tenements of New York, Two Immigrants from Very Strange Lands," *New York Times*, 7 May 2013.

84. S. Y. Agnon, *'Ir u-Melo'ah* [A City and Everything in It] (Tel Aviv: Schocken, 1973).

85. Hana Wirth-Nesher, "Introduction," in Joseph Erlich, *Sabbath* (Syracuse, N.Y.: Syracuse University Press, 1999), xxiv.

86. Chava Rosenfarb, *Bociany* (Syracuse, N.Y.: Syracuse University Press, 2000), 11.

87. Yehuda Elberg, *The Empire of Kalman the Cripple* (Syracuse, N.Y.: Syracuse University Press, 1983), 326.

88. Murav, *Music from a Speeding Train*, 249.

89. Christina Parnell, "Images of Jewish Identities in Lithuanian Literature of the Twentieth Century: Grigorii Kanovich and Markas Zingeris," *East European Jewish Affairs* 38, no. 2 (August 2008): 170.

90. Anatoli Rybakov, *Heavy Sand*, trans. Harold Shukman (New York: Viking, 1981), 13.

91. Katarzyna Wieclawska, "The Image of the Shtetl in Contemporary Polish Fiction," in *The Shtetl: New Evaluations*, ed. Steven T. Katz (New York: New York University Press, 2007), 244, 245.

92. Ibid., 245, 247, 249, 251.

93. David Stern, "Odyssey of a Jew," *Commentary*, January 1973, 102–103.

94. Alan Lupo, *The Messiah Comes Tomorrow: Tales from the American Shtetl* (Amherst: University of Massachusetts Press, 2000); Robert Rand, *My Suburban Shtetl: A Novel about Life in a Twentieth-Century Jewish American Village* (Syracuse, N.Y.: Syracuse University Press, 2001); Sylvia Geller Lisnoff, *Tales of an American Shtetl* (Seattle: CreateSpace, 2011).

95. Here, too, there is a precedent work from earlier in the postwar period: Elkanah Schwartz, *American Life, Shtetl Style* (New York: J. David, 1967).

96. Melvin Jules Bukiet, *Stories of an Imaginary Childhood* (Madison: University of Wisconsin Press, 2002), 199, 201, 197.

97. Lilian Nattel, *The River Midnight* (New York: Scribner Paperback Fiction, 1999), [417–418].

98. Elana Dykewoman, *Beyond the Pale* (Vancouver: Press Gang Publishers, 1997), 13, 400.

99. K. David Brody, *Mourning and Celebration: Jewish, Orthodox, and Gay, Past & Present* (n.p.: Transcréation, 2009) 5, 8.

100. Rebecca Goldstein, *Mazel* (Madison: University of Wisconsin Press, 2002 [1995]), 364, 366–367.

101. Anna P. Ronell, "Three American Jewish Writers Imagine Eastern Europe," *Polin: Studies in Polish Jewry* 19 (2007): 383.

102. Goldstein, *Mazel*, 66–67.

103. Ibid., 207.

104. Alan Hoffman, *Small Worlds* (New York: Abbeville Press, 1996).

105. Steve Stern, "A Brief Account of a Long Way Home," *YIVO Annual* 19 (1990): 85–86.

106. Janet Hadda, "Ashkenaz on the Mississippi," *YIVO Annual* 19 (1990): 95, 102.

107. Andrew W. M. Beierle, "Making Sense of the World," *Emory Magazine* 75, no. 3 (Autumn 1999), http://www.emory.edu/EMORY_MAGAZINE/fall99/skibell.html.

108. Jeremy Shere, "Imagined Diaspora: The *Shtetl* in Allen Hoffman's *Small Worlds* and Jonathan Safran Foer's *Everything Is Illuminated*," *Polin: Studies in Polish Jewry* 22 (2010): 456.

109. Elaine Safer, "Illuminating the Ineffable: Jonathan Safran Foer's Novels," *Studies in American Jewish Literature* 25 (2006): 114. Compare Foer's account with the history of Trochenbrod—a settlement in Ukraine originally founded as a Jewish agricultural colony in the nineteenth century, and the town that inspired Foer's novel—as recounted in Avrom Bendavid-Val, *The Heavens Are Empty: Discovering the Lost Town of Trochenbrod* (New York: Pegasus, 2010).

110. Jonathan Safran Foer, *Everything Is Illuminated* (Boston: Houghton Mifflin, 2002), 8, 12.

111. Harry Turtledove, *Shtetl Days* (New York: Macmillan, 2011), ebook.

112. Martin A. David, *Shtetl in My Mind: Stories* ([Bradenton, Fla.]: Booklocker.com, 2006).

113. Benjamin Harshav, "The Only Yesterday of *Only Yesterday*," introduction to S. Y. Agnon, *Only Yesterday*, trans. Barbara Harshav (Princeton, N.J.: Princeton University Press, 2000), xxiv.

114. Hoffman, *Small Worlds*, 25.

115. James Sturm, *Market Day* (Montreal: Drawn & Quarterly, 2010); Joan Sfar, *Klezmer*, trans. Alexis Siegel (New York: First Second, 2006).

116. Foer, *Everything Is Illuminated*, 159.

117. See Olga Gershenson, *The Phantom Holocaust: Soviet Cinema and Jewish Catastrophe* (New Brunswick, N.J.: Rutgers University Press, 2013), chap. 13.

118. Gabriela Safran, "Dancing with Death and Salvaging Jewish Culture in *Austeria* and *The Dybbuk*," *Slavic Review* 59, no. 4 (Winter 2000): 781.

119. Yevgeny Antinov/Eleanor Antin, *The Man without a World: A Screenplay* (Los Angeles: Green Integer, 2002), 7, 8.

120. Ibid., back cover.

121. Ibid., 8, 86.

122. Olga Gershenson, "Roots Lost and Found," 2010, *New Vilna Review*, http://www.newvilnareview.com/homepage/roots-lost-and-found.html (accessed 14 January 2012)

123. For further discussion of the film, see the collection of essays in *AJS Review* 35, no. 2 (2011): 349–391.

Index

Note: Illustrations are indexed by number, e.g., *fig. 1*.

About the Author

JEFFREY SHANDLER is the author of *While America Watches: Televising the Holocaust*, *Adventures in Yiddishland: Postvernacular Language and Culture*, and *Jews, God, and Videotape: Religion and Media in America*. His edited books include *Profiles of a Lost World: Memoirs of East European Jewish Life before World War II*, *Awakening Lives: Autobiographies of Jewish Youth in Poland before the Holocaust*, *Entertaining America: Jews, Movies, and Broadcasting*, and *Anne Frank Unbound: Media, Imagination, Memory*. Shandler is a professor of Jewish Studies at Rutgers University and lives in New York City.